Psychology
and the
Economic Mind

Cognitive Processes
& Conceptualization

Robert L. Leahy

Robert L. Leahy, PhD, is President-elect of the International Association of Cognitive Psychotherapy, the Founder and Director of the American Institute for Cognitive Therapy in New York City (www.CognitiveTherapyNYC.com) and Clinical Associate Professor of Psychology in Psychiatry at Weill-Cornell University Medical School. He is Editor of *Journal of Cognitive Psychotherapy* and he serves on the Executive Committee of the International Association of Cognitive Psychotherapy and with the Executive Board of the Academy of Cognitive Therapy. Dr. Leahy's recent books include *Cognitive Therapy: Basic Principles and Applications, Practicing Cognitive Therapy, Treatment Plans and Interventions for Depression and Anxiety Disorders* (with Holland), *Overcoming Resistance in Cognitive Therapy, Bipolar Disorder: A Cognitive Therapy Approach* (with Newman, Beck, Reilly-Harrington, & Gyulai) and *Clinical Advances in Cognitive Psychotherapy* (ed. with Dowd).

Psychology
and the
Economic Mind

Cognitive Processes
& Conceptualization

Robert L. Leahy, PhD

 *Springer Publishing Company*

Springer Publishing Company, Inc.
536 Broadway
New York, NY 10012-3955

Acquisitions Editor: Sheri W. Sussman
Production Editor: Sara Yoo
Cover design by Joanne Honigman

01 02 03 04 05 / 5 4 3 2 1

Library of Congress Cataloging-in-Publication-Data

Leahy, Robert L.
 Psychology and the economic mind : cognitive processes and conceptualization / Robert L. Leahy.
  p. cm.
 Includes bibliographical references and index.
 ISBN 0-8261-5042-X
 1. Risk-taking (Psychology)—Economic aspects. 2. Decision making.
 3. Cognitive therapy. 4. Economics—Psychological aspects.
 5. Cognition. I. Title.

 RC480.5L369 2003
 658.4'03'019—dc21

                 2002075751

Printed in the United States of America by Maple-Vail Book Manufacturing Group.

for Helen

Contents

Part IV Development of Conceptions of Inequality

Acknowledgments

I would like to thank Randye Semple, my editorial assistant, for her tireless work in getting this book in shape. Lisa Wu, Jessica Hirsch and Tony Papa worked diligently to collect data. Also, I would like to thank my colleagues at the American Institute for Cognitive Therapy in New York City for their thoughts and feedback. Thanks go to Stephen Holland, Christiane Humke, Lynn Marcinko, Laura Oliff, and Elizabeth Winkelman. Philip Tata and Paul Gilbert have been supportive voices over the years—many thanks to you. All mistakes are mine to take credit from and to learn from.

Introduction

I have been interested in economics for many years, primarily because of my attraction to models that appear logical and my fascination with the fact that few people in the real world follow a logical model. The current volume brings together some previously published work and some new works on the interface between cognitive psychology and economic conceptualization. There is no single theory that informs these chapters.

Part I includes several articles on a model of decision-making that I have advanced. Fifty years ago, Markowitz (1952) published his classic article on "portfolio theory." According to this model, individuals differ as to their assumptions and strategies in investment decisions. For example, a man in his 50s, anticipating little in the way of future earnings but anticipating living another 30 years, might be more cautious about spending or taking financial risks. His reasoning is likely to be that he cannot afford big losses because he does not have a long time to recover from them. Moreover, if he is not diversified in his investments, he might view himself as being at greater risk. I have expanded a multidimensional model of decision-making that applies to how individuals make "mundane decisions"—that is, decisions about pursuing relationships, exercise, work, or anything in which they might have to "invest" time or behavioral effort.

This portfolio theory model of decision-making applies economic concepts to everyday life and may help us understand why individuals differ in their willingness to take risks. In these chapters, I outline a model of decision-making for depression and mania that is based on the idiosyncratic portfolio theories of these groups. I present data from a study on a clinical sample of adult psychiatric patients that offers considerable support to this model. The model is then expanded to examine how personality disorders or personality styles may be partially understood in terms of their portfolio theories. Since the goals of the therapist are to help individuals make changes, the portfolio model may be utilized to understand how depressed and manic individuals can be, respectively, risk-averse and risk-loving.

Part II is based on self-limitation and pessimism. The chapters delineate how some individuals can manage their everyday risk by utilizing hedging, straddling, information demands, and pessimism as self-protective "investment styles" for making mundane decisions. Furthermore, the investment concept of *sunk-costs* is proposed as a model of how individuals get locked into "riding a loser" in order to redeem their losses, avoid the finality of loss and waste, and buy an option on hope. Suggestions on how to reverse the sunk-cost effect are also offered.

Part III focuses on the issue of insatiability. Classic studies of functional autonomy or brain stimulation demonstrated that some behaviors continue beyond the point at which, to all appearances, they serve any purpose. Other studies of resistance to extinction—a form of insatiability—indicated that animals would avoid shock even when they no longer were being shocked. The issue of insatiability appeared to me to be particularly relevant to an economic conception of human behavior. How do humans decide that they have had enough? What accounts for dissatisfaction among individuals who may have more possessions than 99% of people who have ever lived?

Having originated from rather modest means myself, I was struck by how many wealthy individuals I saw in my practice who appeared to be insatiable in their desires. No matter how much they had, it was never enough. This insatiability manifested as an inability to be satisfied with money, success, partners, fame, or power. Indeed, the issue of insatiability seemed to violate both established models of drive and motivation, and to fly in the face of common sense. I have developed a multidimensional model of insatiability that, I hope, will be useful in conceptualizing this problem and in reversing its effects.

In Part IV, I have attempted to utilize cognitive-developmental theory to understand how children and adolescents "construct" the economic system—that is, how they make sense of economic inequality. Thinking that this approach would be rather simple or tautological, I avoided a simple social learning model which postulates that increasing age is associated with increasing knowledge. Indeed, how could it be otherwise? The approach I have taken here suggests that children conceptualize or construct the economic system as a reflection of structural aspects of their thinking. These structural aspects of thinking include children's awareness of the "inner world" of others (e.g., thoughts, traits, perspectives, and values) and their ability to understand social structure that supersedes individuals. In a sense, one could view this as a cognitive-developmental approach to class consciousness.

Having said this, however, Marxists will be disappointed to see that many of the findings on class conceptions are more consistent with cognitive-developmental and functionalist models than with a strict conflict model. My approach to this was politically neutral, since I believe that the data speak for themselves and are more important than the interests of the academic scholar. However, these data suggest that increasing age is associated with increased justification and fatalistic thinking about economic inequality—a finding that lends some "stability" to a society marked by unequal distribution of income and wealth. As children and adolescents get older, they view the rich and the poor as different kinds of people, with different degrees of ability and effort. They also view unequal distribution as both justified and, to some extent, inevitable.

PART I

Portfolio Theory and Decision-Making

CHAPTER 1

An Investment Model of Depressive Resistance

Cognitive models of depression have focused on information processing biases (Beck, Rush, Shaw, & Emery, 1979), negative explanatory style (Abramson, Seligman, & Teasdale, 1978), the perception of noncontingency (Seligman, 1975), deficits in self-regulation and self-control (Rehm, 1990), and excessive self-focus (Carver & Scheier, 1990; Nolen-Hoeksema, 1987). Although these cognitive models have proven to be useful in developing therapeutic interventions and programmatic research, these models do not directly address a central issue of depression—specifically, the process of decision-making and the motivation to change.

Characteristic of depression is the apparent low motivation, low energy, indecisiveness, and self-criticism that constitute a core of resistance to change. Beck's (1987) schematic model is useful in identifying the negative triad as a resistant barrier to change—namely, the depressed individual's negative view of self, experience, and the future undermines his motivation to modify his behavior. The proposed model extends the schematic processing model. I propose that the schematic processing model does not sufficiently explain active resistance to change as seen in chronic and refractory depressions. The theoretical model proposed here adapts the schematic model as the foundation for a decision-making model based on individual differences in the perception of utility.

The model proposed here is an investment model of decision-making drawn from modern portfolio theory. According to this model, individuals make decisions about how to allocate their resources based on their estimate of present and future resources available, tolerance for risk, and probability and value of gains and losses. In the present chapter, I shall argue that depressed individuals resist change, and hesitate in making decisions, because of their specific portfolio theories. I shall elaborate this model by examining the *depressive paradox,* information search biases in decision-making, depressive evaluations of losses, ambivalence about gains, and protection against risk.

Depressive Paradoxes

A commonplace observation in both animal and human literature is that organisms are motivated to pursue rewards and avoid punishments. The opportunity to achieve an increase in rewards should increase the probability of a behavior occurring. Yet, a cursory observation of depressed patients suggest that they often reject opportunities to engage in positive behavior and may commit their time to apparently self-punitive behaviors such as self-criticism or depressive rumination. Should we conclude from this that depressed individuals are an exception to the law of effect—that is, unlike pigeons, rats, and nondepressed humans, they do not pursue rewarding behavior, but rather pursue masochistic goals? Indeed, a similar observation led Freud (1917) to conclude that depression was anger turned inward—or, simply, a form of psychological masochism resulting from an overly repressive superego. Another observation that appears at first glance to defy general learning theory principles is that depressed people who are in a higher state of deprivation are in fact less motivated than nondepressed people to engage in positive activities. Students of operant conditioning know that it is useful to deprive the organism (usually, of food) to increase the strength and frequency of responding. Yet depressed individuals appear to defy this rule of deprivation—their response level is lower than that of nondepressed people.

I shall argue that a solution to these apparent paradoxes is that response decisions are based on expectancies of future outcomes. Past reinforcement (or extinction) histories may be important, but the cognitive mediation of depression determines how the historical information will be used in making future predictions about outcomes. I shall argue that persons with depression develop loss-avoidant strategies that hinder them from taking the risk necessary to effect self-change. Consequently, depression may be viewed as a risk-management strategy.

Maximization and Minimization Strategies

The depressive paradox can be clarified if we consider the assumptions guiding optimistic and pessimistic decision-makers. Take, for example,

Mr. Jones—who is considering an investment and who believes that he has substantial assets and substantial future earning potential. He is presented with the option of investing $8,000 with a moderate probability of making a 50% return on his investment. He also believes that, even if he does not make 50%, he has a good probability of making some profit and very low probability of losing his entire investment. Jones enjoys the things that he buys with his wealth and he enjoys playing the game of investments. Given the offer of this investment, he reasons that he has substantial resources to absorb the unlikely losses that might occur. He takes the investment.

In contrast to our optimistic risk-taking Mr. Jones, the unfortunate Mr. Smith believes he is down to his last $100. He is offered an investment of $80, with a possibility of gaining $40 (a 50% return on his investment). Smith believes that he has little likelihood of gaining employment and that he has bills coming due next week. Moreover, he attributes his dire financial straits to foolish investments that recently headed south. Jones is a nervous Nellie and passes on this opportunity to invest.

Both investors, optimistic Jones and pessimistic Mr. Smith, operate from what they believe are rational considerations given the information they possess and the goals they pursue. Optimists pursue a maximization strategy—that is, a growth strategy, because they are willing to take risks. Pessimists, like our depressed Mr. Smith, believe that their minimization strategy is rational, since their goal is to avoid further losses. The depressive paradox describes the pessimistic, but apparently rational Mr. Smith. Perhaps Mr. Smith is incorrect (or correct) about his evaluation of his current and future resources, perhaps he is unduly negative of his chances of gaining, but there is an internal logic that tells him that he cannot absorb any further losses. His self-protective strategy instructs him to avoid change unless there is a near certainty of gain.

In the pages that follow, I shall outline the elements of a depressive style of decision-making. I refer to this as an *investment model*, since decision-makers are often in the position of determining how they will allocate resources for the purpose of achieving gains or protecting against loss. Modern portfolio theories in finance theory are useful in providing us with the concepts necessary to describe the strategy of investment of optimistic and pessimistic players.

First, I will indicate how negative schemas are formed and maintained at a structurally primitive level. Second, I describe how these schemas inform decision-making in depression by constraining information search and retrieval. Third, and most important for the investment model, I indicate how depression is not simply a distortion or bias in thinking, but rather a strategy of adaptation.

Schematic Biases and Developmental Regression

Beck and his colleagues (Beck, 1976; Beck et al., 1979; Leahy & Beck, 1988) have proposed that depression is characterized by negative sche- mas about self and others that, while an individual is depressed, are activated and become predominant in the processing of information. These schemas are often formed during early childhood and may be character- ized by qualities associated with preoperational thinking, such as egocen- trism, centration, magical thinking, moral realism, rigidity and dichotomization (Leahy, 1995, 1996, in press). Because of the primitive structural qualities of early maladaptive schemas, many with depression (especially, chronically depressed individuals) have difficulty treating their thinking as objects of thought. The ability to identify and test negative thoughts, especially deeply embedded assumptions and schemas, requires *metacognition.* For example, the ability to decenter from the self and treat one's thoughts and feelings as objects of thoughts or potential rather than as realities. Developmental social-cognitive research indicates that very young children are not able to engage in this metacognitive process (Leahy, 1985; Selman, 1980). Indeed, similar to the preoperational child, individuals who are depressed tend to experience their negative thoughts as reality and their emotions as if they are the only way one might feel. For these structurally regressed schemas, there appears to be no alterna- tive and no escape from the present construction of reality.

Given the predominance of early maladaptive schemas, many with depression are over-inclusive of negatives and under-inclusive of posi- tives. Schemata are self-sustaining information systems that reconfirm themselves through selective attention, recall, and recognition of infor- mation consistent with the schema. Because these schemata are often formed at a preoperational level of intelligence, the individual has diffi- culty decentering or distancing himself from his perspective and has difficulty recognizing how his actions and choices have confirmed the schema. Of course, the task of cognitive therapy is to suggest alternative realities, but individuals with depression are often captured by their own constructions of reality.

Schema theory suggests four reasons why negative schemata are main- tained. First, these schemas are structurally limited, lacking the ability to decenter—that is, lacking metacognitive self-reflection. Second, schemas are selective information processing systems which are self-fulfilling or self-verifying. Third, schemas are not directly challenged because of compensations and avoidance. Finally, schemas are reconfirmed by neg- ative life events. Although these structural and strategic factors are important in maintaining negativity, they do not sufficiently explain active efforts of resistance to change. For example, how would schema theory explain why patients would actively defend a negative schema, often responding with anger and rigidity when negativity is challenged? The proposed model of resistance extends schema theory to include what I refer to as *motivated negative cognition*—that is, cognitive (and behavioral) tactics and strategies that are used to maintain and defend a negative schema. I shall attempt to demonstrate that depressed individuals often believe that abandoning a negative schema makes them vulnerable to experiencing further loss.

Because of a long history of reconfirming negative schema, recurrent depressive episodes and dysthymia are often characterized by resistance to change. The therapist often finds that the patient generates, apparently ad hoc, seemingly irrational reasons not to change, which justify his procrastination and refusal to take risks. Although one can recognize the power of the schema for information processing, it is not altogether obvious from schema theory why the patient should resist modification of negative thinking. Guidano and Liotti (1983) have suggested that these early maladaptive schemas are guarded by a *protective belt* of defensive maneuvers, although it is not clear why one would want to guard a negative belief. I propose that this protective belt can be understood as an attempt to guard against further loss (a view consistent with Guidano and Liotti) and that the patient adapts a strategy of investment and pessimism that he believes protects him from total devastation. To advance this position, I have drawn on neoclassical microeconomic models of investment strategies.

Strategic Pessimism

The argument advanced in this chapter is that depressed individuals often resist change because they believe that they cannot absorb the costs of further losses. Their pessimism is a consequence of the experience of recent negative life events and underlying negative schemata, which direct their attention to negatives rather than positives. The proposed model is consistent with Beck's (1976) cognitive model (i.e., negative schemata are assumed), Abramson, Seligman, and Teasdale's (1978) attribution model (i.e., explanatory styles result in low self-esteem), and life-event and social skills models, such as Lewinsohn and Gotlib's (1995) (i.e., life events constitute losses and low skills reflect estimation of personal resources). Many depressed individuals have some motivation for thinking negatively, but their negative schemata and negative explanatory style further exacerbate this negativity.

Evolutionary psychiatry suggests that what appear to be maladaptive modes of response have, indeed, had evolutionary value (Wenegrat, 1990). For example, innate fears of heights, strangers, the dark, or animals may confer a self-protective function against real danger in primitive environments (Bowlby, 1968; Marks, 1987). Similarly, one can argue that depression and pessimism are sometimes adaptive (perhaps in small doses). For example, it might be useful to give up in the face of certain failure, to question your ability when events turn out badly so that you can correct yourself, or even to adapt a submissive posture in a group (Gardner, 1982; Sloman & Price, 1987). Indeed, excessive optimism, as evidenced in mania, can be exceptionally destructive (Leahy & Beck, 1988). Depressive pessimism is not always a distortion in thinking, but rather a bias: Sometimes the worst actually happens and it is wise to be prepared for it.

The investment model takes these cognitive-behavioral models a step further. I argue that many depressed people assess their current and future resources as negative and view the world as a poor source of rewards, most of which are viewed as uncontrollable and unpredictable. Given this negative triad of self, experience, and future, depressed individuals attempt to protect themselves against further losses. They adapt pessimism as a strategy which, they believe, will help them conserve their meager resources and will protect them against losses which are believed to be devastating. Consequently, they take an ambivalent position regarding hope, since hope may lead to foolhardy exposure to even greater losses. Those with depression guard against hope in order to protect themselves from loss. Contrary to the psychodynamic model that suggests that depression is anger turned inward or a form of masochism, the investment model proposes that depressed persons are so undermined by negatives that they direct most decision-making to avoid further negatives. They are exquisitely risk-averse, as a strategy to avoid losses that they believe will devastate them.

PORTFOLIO THEORIES

The application of microeconomic concepts to mundane decision-making has been advanced by Nobel-prize laureate Gary Becker and his colleagues. Decision-makers calculate costs and benefits, utilizing rational models, in making marital choices, criminal behavior, discrimination, and religious preference (Becker, 1976; Tommasi & Ierulli, 1995). Similarly, operant conditioning models have been compared to neoclassical models of economic decision (Schwartz, 1978). The investment model proposed here argues that individuals maintain strategies as to how they should invest their resources. A portfolio represents a variety of investment tools in finance theory (e.g., stocks, bonds, or cash) and, as applied here, a portfolio represents a variety of *behaviors*—similar to a behavioral repertoire or hierarchy of responses (Markowitz, 1952).

Individual portfolio theories represent investors' understanding of their current and future resources, their perceptions of market variation or volatility, their investment goals (growth, conservative self-protection, or income generation), the perceived functional utility of gains ("how much will this gain be valued?"), beliefs in the opportunity to replicate investments ('Is this a single opportunity or will I be able to 'play many hands'?"), the expected duration of investing, and the tolerance of risk (Bodie, Kane, & Marcus, 1996). For reasons that will become clearer in the subsequent sections of this chapter, depressed and nondepressed individuals hold different portfolio theories (Markowitz, 1952). These are depicted in Table 1.1 below.

Table 1.1 illustrates the phenomenological differences between pessimists and optimists. From Beck's schema theory of depression and from the model of the negative triad (Beck et al., 1979), we can see that depressed individuals may underestimate their current and future positives. Negative filters, overgeneralization, negative prediction, and discounting the positives all result in their beliefs that they have few assets available and bleak futures. Because depressed individuals tend to be anhedonic, deriving little pleasure from rewards, and because they discount their positives, they expect low functional utility of gains. They believe they have much to lose and little to gain.

Table 1.1 Portfolio Theories of Depressed and Nondepressed Individuals

Portfolio Concern	Depressed	Nondepressed
Assets available	Few	Some/Many
Future earning potential	Low	Moderate/high
Market variation	Volatile	Low/predictable
Investment goal	Minimize risk	Maximize gain
Risk-orientation	Risk averse	Risk neutral/risk lover
Functional utility of gain	Low	Moderate/high
Replications of investment	None/few	Many
Duration of investment	Short-term	Long-term
Portfolio diversification	Low	High

For those with depression, loses have added negative utility because they are overgeneralized, exaggerated, and personally internalized (Abramson et al., 1978; Beck et al., 1979). When these individuals lose, to this loss is added the high cost of self-criticism. Compared to the nondepressed individual who attempts to absorb the cost of loss as part of playing the game, the depressed individual magnifies the loss through self-recrimination. Because of this overvaluation of loss, the depressive's strategy is to minimize loss at all costs. We shall now examine how depressives process information about loss and gain and the decision rules that guide their mundane investments.

Limited Search

Depressive schematic processing does not allow the individual to engage in an exhaustive search of alternatives, information, or current resources. Ideal rational decision-making suggests that one consider all alternatives, weigh the costs and benefits, consider all the information about the current situation, and choose the best alternative (Baron, 1994; Janis & Mann, 1977). However, almost all decision-makers are imperfect, since exhaustive searches of alternatives would be so time consuming that no decisions would be possible. Search rules are employed. For example, when you go to a restaurant for a quick lunch, it is unlikely that you compare the costs and benefits of every entree. Rather, you have a selective search question—for example, it might be, "Do they have a chicken salad sandwich?" Once the search question is answered affirmatively, the search is discontinued.

Depressive searches are similarly limited and they are guided by the "default question"—namely, "How can I lose?" Cost is the default. Once this is answered affirmatively, future questions about gains overshadowing losses are avoided. The search is myopic in that the focus is on the up-front costs—that is, the effort or risk that one incurs to achieve a gain. Thus, much of depressive avoidance appears to conflict with purposive behavior of seeking rewards. Because losses are overvalued, the depressive searches for reasons not to change. "Is it possible that I could lose?" "Do I need more information?" or "Could I regret this action?" all enter into the inquiry, inevitably leading to affirmative conclusions and further avoidance.

Waiting is often viewed as a positive alternative, since waiting provides the depressive with the perceived opportunity of gaining more information, reducing risk, and acquiring the motivation or desire to act. To the nondepressed individual, waiting can be viewed as a cost, since opportunities to invest or act are foregone. This is why investors demand interest on their investments—they have opportunity costs of delaying the enjoyment of their capital. As the depressive waits, searching for reasons not to change and demanding certainty in an uncertain world, opportunities are missed. Although his immediate goal in waiting was to protect against risk, his procrastination then becomes a further focus of his self-criticism.

The limited search, or biased search, of the depressive also leads him to undervalue current and future resources. Rather than directing his search to "How much do I have already?" "How much do I have to absorb costs?" or "How much can I gain in the future?" the depressive investor myopically searches for losses that will draw down his perceived limited resources. Consequently, the costs have high negative utility, and are to be avoided at all cost.

Because the schema is focused on the negative, the depressive search seeks to find reasons not to act. An example of "searching for reasons not to change" was a woman who feared doing poorly at work and, therefore, generated ad hoc reasons not to look for a job. Another example was a commodity trader who feared making mistakes and who continually sought reasons why he should not take particular trades. In his case, the consequences of his trading were decreased by having him do "paper" trades (rather than actual monetary trades), giving him the opportunity to immunize himself against loss. By practicing losing and gaining on paper trades, he was able to recognize that the pay-off in trading came with replications and duration.

Loss Orientation

Many of the cognitive distortions of depression emphasize the severity, personal implication, and generality of losses. For example, the depressive attributes loss to a personal deficit of his that is stable, losses are catastrophized, and losses are generalized to other areas of his life. The depressive is focused on negative delta (negative change)—either actual or anticipated. The loss orientation is magnified because the depressive has a low threshold for defining loss, he is driven by scarcity assumptions, he views loss as depleting, he has a high stop-loss criterion, and he has a short-term focus. Examples of the loss orientation are depicted in Table 1.2.

Let us examine each of the loss issues. Examples of the low threshold for defining loss include patients who view small rejections and minor inconveniences as significant personal failures of major proportions. Be-

Table 1.2. Loss Orientation in Depression

Loss Orientation	Example
Low threshold	The slightest decrease is viewed as a loss of significant proportion.
High stop-loss criteria	A small loss leads to termination of behavior. Consequently, the depressive gets stopped out early.
Scarcity assumptions	The world is viewed as having few opportunities for success. This is generalized to a zero–sum model of rewards for self and other.
Depletion assumptions	Losses are not simple inconveniences or temporary setbacks. They are viewed as permanently drawing down resources.
Cost-cascades	Losses are viewed as linked to an accelerating linear trend of further losses.
Temporal focus	The depressives take a short–term focus, viewing their investments only in terms of how they will pay off or lose in the short term.
Reversibility and revocability	Losses are viewed by depressives as irreversible and not compensated or offset by gains. Negative investments are irrevocable– they cannot see themselves as able to pull out easily.
Regret orientation	Losses are followed by regret that one should have known better. Hindsight bias of depressives is focused on the assumption that they should have been able to make perfect decisions with limited information.

cause the depressive views any loss as polarized to the negative extreme, he attempts to avoid further losses by *stopping-out* or quitting, early. An example of the search for loss and a low threshold for defining loss is a woman who assumed that she would be rejected by men and who was hypervigilant for any signs of rejection. Immediately on seeing any sign of disinterest in the man, she would excuse herself and walk away. The therapist encouraged her not to stop-out early and to stay in the situation longer. This dramatically improved her social interactions. Seligman's descriptions of helplessness are consistent with the low threshold for defining failure and the stop-loss orientation.

Depressives are often driven by scarcity and depletion assumptions. Because they view the world as an unlikely source of future rewards and because losses are considered depleting, the depressive attempts to avoid any failure by waiting until he is certain of success. For example, a salesman avoided making calls because he believed that there were few opportunities for success and that the economy was in the middle of a depression (which it was not). He viewed rejections as personally depleting and evidence of his incompetence. The longer he waited to make sales, the more evidence he thought he had that sales were impossible to make. He believed that he could only make sales when he was sure of a positive outcome and when he felt motivated and comfortable. His therapist assisted him in recognizing that his self-fulfilling scarcity and failure assumptions, coupled with his energy depletion idea, confirmed his negative view. Alternative views presented to him—, "The world is a natural reinforcer for positive behavior," and "You don't need energy to act" helped him overcome an inertia that had plagued him for several years.

Losses are viewed as the beginning of a linear trend of increasingly accelerating losses. I refer to these as *cost-cascades,* a concept borrowed from Becker's microeconomic model. The depressive often fears that he will step on a trap door of loss, dropping him into a neverending chasm of failure. Because he fears these cost-cascades, he will stop out quickly. Linked to this cost-cascade theory is the depressive view that negative consequences are irreversible—they are not compensated by future (or past) gains. Furthermore, actions are viewed as irrevocable—that is, he fears that, once committed, he will be unable to pull out. This catalyzes him to stop-out soon "while I have the chance." For example, a single man feared getting involved with a woman he liked because he believed that, once involved, he would be trapped and would be unable to be assertive and pull out if the relationship did not work out. He believed that he would be better off not dating her further lest he enter into an irreversible, irrevocable relationship. Examining his rights to be assertive—and the value to the woman if he was assertive—was helpful in assisting him in pursuing the woman. Revoking decisions helped him make decisions.

Depressive loss orientation is not only focused on long-term losses or hopelessness, but it is also overly focused on short-term costs or investments. Prudent and proactive individuals will view investments as *purposive*—that is, "I exercise to get into shape." For optimists, the costs are *up front,* that is, they view costs as a means to an end, while pessimists view costs as an end in themselves. Effort and risk serve the purpose of producing positive outcomes. In contrast to purposive optimists, the depressives view losses as the entire field of experience. Their temporal focus is short-term on the depletion of loss: "It's too much effort" and "I feel uncomfortable and tired" are examples of this short-term focus. The therapist may assist patients in transcending the short time frame by imagining how they will feel after they have exercised (or engaged in productive behavior). Losses may be reconstrued as costs with a purpose.

Finally, depressives respond to loss with regret and self-recrimination. Ironically, they believes that they should have been able to avoid past mistakes but that they will be unable to control future mistakes. Regret and self-criticism are added costs to loss and failure, further motivating depressives to avoid any loss by stopping-out (quitting) early. In short, depressives assume loss as a default function and search for reasons not to act in order to avoid further costs.

Gain Orientation

Similar to the negative orientation toward loss, the depressive takes an ambivalent attitude toward gains. Since his negative schemata predict that reality is negative, gains are viewed with skepticism. This ambivalence toward gains is reflected in the fact that the depressive has a high threshold for defining gains, gains are undervalued and viewed as having low probability, there is a demand for immediate gains, small reductions in frustration are preferred to longer term investments ("contingency traps"), gains are viewed as out of the control of the depressive and gains are viewed as self-correcting toward the negative norm ("gains have gravity"). These issues are illustrated in Table 1.3.

Let us keep in mind that the depressive strategy is viewed as an attempt to guard against further losses. If the depressive finds himself becoming overly optimistic, he runs the risk, he believes, of added exposure. I shall describe, later, how depressives manages expectations to handle their loss and gain orientation, but here we shall examine the ambivalence toward gain so characteristic of resistant depressives. Some of this resistance appears to be primarily a consequence of negative schemata, while other aspects of the resistance are cognitive strategies to avoid greater exposure.

Because the schema is negative, there is selective focus on the negative and either lack of processing of or discounting of the positives. Depressives have a high threshold for defining positives—often a positive must be close to perfection to be counted as a positive, whereas the negative category is overly inclusive. This underinclusion of positives

Table 1.3. Gain Orientation in Depression

Gain Orientation	Example
High threshold for definition	A major change is required to be considered a gain.
Low valuation	Gains are viewed as having little hedonic or personal value. They are often discounted.
Low probability	Future gains are viewed as unlikely and unpredictable.
Immediate demand	There is little ability to delay gratification. The depressive is "myopic", getting caught in the immediate consequences of an action.
Contingency traps	Focusing on short-term frustration, the depressive will continue to avoid or engage in pointless behavior simply because it provides short-term reduction of anxiety.
Lack of control	Gains are viewed as noncontingent—out of the control of depressives. Although they believe that they can produce losses, they do not believe that they have control over producing gains.
Gravity of gains	Since the norm is negative, gains are viewed as self-correcting toward the negative—that is, they have gravity.

results in the difficulty in recognizing gains from reinforcement, since they are not viewed as reinforcing in the first place. Further, because of the anhedonia of depression, positives have low pleasure or mastery value—that is, they have low positive utility. This further undermines the reinforcing value of positives. Similarly, positives are expected to be improbable, further enhancing the low *expectancy* of further reinforcements. A string of positives is not generalized to a trend of future positives, since positives are not noticed, discounted, undervalued, compartmentalized, or are viewed as nonpredictive. Given the discounting of gains, reinforcements provide little incentive.

Depressives, however, do experience positives, but often positives are defined as the reduction of a negative—namely, the reduction of frustration or anxiety. This negative reactive orientation is a result of the demand for immediate gratification. Like the starving man, the depressive seeks relief from his discomfort as quickly as possible—he acts as if he cannot afford delay of gratification. The "myopia" that is so common with drug and alcohol addiction (which are often comorbid with anxious depression) is the result of the shortsighted demand for discomfort reduction without consideration of long-term costs. Short-term gains are traded against longer-term costs—often because the depressive believes that he needs the gain desperately. This results in contingency traps—that is, the repetition of an ultimately self-defeating behavior simply because it produces short-term reinforcement. Examples of contingency traps are substance abuse, avoidance, and escape, without consideration of the advantage of alternatives that might ultimately enhance the depressive's condition. The depressive, trapped in a contingency, follows a rigid rule— "When frustrated, do X," where X refers to substance abuse, escape, or avoidance. The depressive becomes trapped in the contingent payoff, without considering or testing alternatives.

Risk Management

Individuals who believe that they have few resources and few opportunities of future earnings are wise to take a low-risk approach to their investments. Prudent investors, often with substantial capital reserves, are able to protect against risk by taking the long-duration approach to investment and diversifying across a variety of investments. In contrast, the depressive, driven by his sense of deprivation and desperation, takes a short-term view, seeking to reduce frustration immediately. Moreover, he perceives himself as having few resources to provide himself with diversification, further adding to his exposure for his single investment ("If I lose this, I lose everything"). Unlike the optimist who believes that he has many "hands" to play, the depressive views himself as having few replications. Thus, this hand must be a winner.

Risk can be managed by demanding more information before investments are made—that is, the depressive can require that he wait it out before he is certain that he will show a gain. Waiting, as we have noted above, has opportunity costs, but these costs are discounted in depression because any alternative is viewed as having a low payoff anyway. He does not view himself as sacrificing attractive opportunities and he offsets this by focusing on how he can minimize devastating losses by waiting.

Another strategy for the depressive in risk management is to reject hope whenever hope arises. This is because the pleasure that one might derive from hope is often offset by the anxiety it arouses about further exposure—especially in a market that is viewed as volatile, negative, and uncontrollable. Hope carries risk of rising expectations that will lead to

disappointment. For many depressives it is disappointment, loss, or negative delta that is feared more than the absence of rewards. Losing something is far more aversive than never having it in the first place.

Because hope is viewed as carrying the risk of unrealistic positive
expectations, the depressive often argues that there are good reasons not
to hope. For example, a research assistant for a company became angry
with the therapist when the therapist argued that she (the patient) might
have the ability to take on more challenging work. Although the patient
had been criticizing herself for her lack of progress in the company, the
idea of raising her expectations precipitated considerable anxiety: "What
if I get my confidence up and then fail? Everyone will notice. I'll be far
more visible." In her case, hopelessness was a strategy to avoid further
risk— that is, more public exposure.

The rejection of hope underlies depressive attempts to aggressively
lower expectations in self and other. By lowering expectations of his
performance, the depressive guards against disappointment. An alternative is to raise standards so excessively that almost no one would achieve
the standard, thereby providing a face-saving attribution strategy: "Well,
no one would achieve A+, so it means little about me. And at least I have
the highest standards."

Common strategies for reducing risk involve straddling and hedging.
For example, the depressive, fearing that his efforts will not work out,
may bet against himself by minimizing his effort (minimizing his investment) and pulling out at the first sign of failure (straddling). This appears
to be what happens in the case of helplessness—attempts at success,
followed by a single failure, lead to early stopping-out. The depressives
who straddle will sit on the fence, put in minimal effort, and then give
up. Their rationale is that this protects against further loss. For example,
a husband in marital therapy, pessimistic about his marriage, put minimal
effort into homework, demanding complete compliance from his wife.
When he received less than perfect positive feedback from his wife, he
discontinued his efforts at improving the relationship.

Hedging involves covering a potential loss in one investment with a
possible insurance policy with another investment. Infidelity is an example of hedging in that the individual protects against the loss of one
partner by having another readily available. For example, a woman who
feared rejection by men, began pursuing an extramarital affair as soon as
she got married. This was coupled with her hypervigilance that no man
could be trusted. Ironically, her hypervigilance focused on her concern
that her husband would find other women more appealing while she
herself was pursuing other men. Her rationale was that she could protect

herself against abandonment by proving to herself that she was still attractive to other men.

Another self-handicapping strategy that protects against deflation in self-esteem is to manufacture excuses or reasons why productive behavior cannot be pursued. For example, the salesman referred to earlier, would get up late during the day, focus his attention on trivial office details in his apartment, and carry out errands. He would complain about aches and pains that would become excuses for not making sales calls. He would tell the therapist that he was not yet ready to pursue sales calls, each week inventing new reasons why the calls could not be made. In fact, examining his fear of rejection revealed that he had very few rejections because he was making few calls. Indeed, the problem was not so much that he was failing when he made calls (which was his greatest fear), but rather that he almost never made calls. In fact, his goal was to avoid making calls at all costs. Thus, he would generate as many reasons as possible *not* to make calls. Some depressives use "not trying" as an options play: "If I don't try now, I keep open the option of trying in the future." Self-handicapping is like a smoke screen that prevents self and others from evaluating true ability. It protects against the risk of failure because it prevents any direct evaluation of capability. These risk management strategies are identified in Table 1.4.

Accounting Principles in Depression

An assumption in cognitive therapy is that the individual will examine the evidence and weigh the evidence or advantages of specific thoughts. Thaler (1985) has suggested that individuals may enter evidence into two unrelated accounts—as if their accounting principle leads them to consider these two accounts as part of separate systems. Typically, most individuals will have a superordinate account of positives and negatives, such that negatives are offset by positives. Consider how you calculate your net income: You subtract your expenses from your income, yielding your final net income.

Depressed individuals appear to keep separate unrelated accounts, a loss account and a gain account. The loss account is not offset by the gain account, because the depressive does not consider them similar and because his schema directs him toward losses. For example, nondepressed people have a self-esteem account, which includes all the positives and negatives related to their performance or qualities. One might argue that nondepressed individuals fudge their returns by exaggerating their gains and minimizing their losses (Taylor, 1989). Depressed individuals appear

Table 1.4. Risk Management Strategies in Depression

Risk Management Concerns	Example
Diversification	Low diversification: Depressives believe that they have only a single investment—the one at hand—and, therefore, are highly exposed to loss.
Duration	Short-term: Because they believe that they are in the game for the short term, they are highly exposed to volatility.
Replication	Low or none: They believe that they will not have additional chances to succeed in this situation. Therefore, they must be sure that their first attempt will work.
Waiting	They believes that they need to wait for a more opportune moment to act and forgoe opportunity costs because no alternative seems attractive.
Information demands	High: They require close to certainty before they decide.
Disappointment aversion	High: They are less concerned with the ongoing lack of reinforcement than they are with the possibility of a negative change. They avoid negative delta at all costs.
Manipulation of expectations	They attempt to either lower expectations that they will succeed or raise expectations excessively to avoid disappointment and to avoid direct assessment of their "true" ability.
Rejection of hope	High: They view hope ambivalently, believing that getting their hopes up leaves them open to greater exposure and disappointment.
Straddling	They exert a minimal effort as a probe to determine if their behavior can have some effect. Holding themselves back, they pull out at the first sign of a negative.
Hedging	They bet against themselves by keeping other options open that, ironically, may undermine their current choice.
Hiding	They attempt to maintain a low profile in order to avoid being exposed to evaluation.
Obscuring self-evaluation	They create conditions that prevent a direct assessment of their competence under optimal conditions. This provides them with the face-saving option of disattributing their failure to lack of effort, illness, poor attendance, and lack of preparation rather than to a fixed trait.

to have a low self-esteem account (which accumulates losses with interest) and another account, which I would label *irrelevant behavior* (which includes positive behavior which is not considered relevant to an account of self-esteem). Furthermore, depressed individuals act as if they are closing out their positive accounts, such that positives are not carried forward into the future.

CONCLUSION

In this chapter, I have proposed that depressive resistance is an attempt to avoid further loss. Given the negative schemata of the depressed patient, selective information processing has served to reconfirm the negative schema. Because these negative schemata are formed at a preoperational level of intelligence, metacognitive self-reflection is often absent. This limits the ability of the patient to gain distance or perspective from his negativity.

Information search is directed toward a default question—"How can I lose?"—which, when answered affirmatively, terminates further inquiry. Optimism is rejected since the depressive views his goal as prevention of loss rather than obtaining gain. Depressives have high stop-loss criteria for negatives and high criteria for defining gains.

The microeconomic utility model advanced here is applicable to other areas or psychopathology—for example, anxiety, anger, paranoia, and marital conflict. This model assists both therapist and patient in understanding resistance in a nonpejorative manner that has direct implications for interventions. The intervention strategies depend on, first, understanding the patient's portfolio theory, and, second, proposing a different portfolio theory based on an optimistic view of current and future resources, duration and replication of investment, expanding the criteria for gains, modifying the overinclusion of losses and identifying stop-loss, hedging, straddling and other self-defeating strategies. The proposed model helps us extend other cognitive models, such as Beck's, Seligman's, and Abramson's, to the area of resistance and decision-making.

CHAPTER 2

Decision-Making and Mania

In recent years, there has been an increasing interest in psychosocial factors in the activation and maintenance of mania (Alloy, Reilly-Harrington, Fresco, Whitehouse, & Zechmeister, 1999; Basco and Shaw, 1996; Leahy and Beck 1988; Miklowitz & Goldstein, 1997; Johnson & Roberts, 1995). The likelihood of manic episodes is increased due to stressful life events, increased expressed emotion in families, circadian rhythms, and other factors, such as stimulants. The emphasis has been on diathesis-stress models of mania, stressing biological diathesis, and environmental stress. In addition, cognitive theorists have proposed a *cognitive-diathesis* model, such that pessimistic and optimistic cognitive styles are viewed as cognitive-vulnerabilities for depressive and manic episodes, respectively (Alloy et al., 1999; see also Ingram, Miranda, & Segal, 1998). (Newman, Leahy, Beck, Reilly-Harrington, & Gyulai, 2001)

Despite the increased interest in psychosocial treatments, in conjunction with medication treatment for mania, there has been little emphasis on the cognitive processes that constitute mania. An exception to this is a recent study by Alloy et al. (1999), in which they found that attributional style and dysfunctional attitudes, as assessed by the Attributional Styles Questionnaire and the Dysfunctional Attitude Scales, respectively, were predictive of subsequent depressive and manic episodes in subjects with a bipolar clinical profile. The Alloy et al. (1999) study focused on explanatory style and dysfunctional attitudes, suggesting that cognitive style constitutes a latent vulnerability to affective disorder.

There are several reasons why manic decision-making processes are important: First, it is essential for the evaluation and understanding of manic phenomenology to be able to assess the specific cognitive modality of manic cognition. Similar to Beck's (1970, 1976; Beck et al., 1979) work on depressive cognitive schemata, it would be valuable to be able to assess the manic's cognitive schemata. Decision-making is an essential component of cognitive schemata. Second, in order to modify the cognitive components of mania, it would be of value to be able to specify what these components entail. Just as Beck's cognitive model specifies the components of depressive assumptions and schemata as a focus of treatment, there is a corresponding need to specify the manic individual's cognitive vulnerability if this is to be a target of treatment. Third, because the risk of mania is in the potential for over-extending oneself in harmful behavior, it would be valuable to determine the "decision-rules" guiding manic decision-making. By determining what these rules are, it may be possible to assist the manic individual in exercising control over risky decision-making.

In an earlier article, Leahy and Beck (1988) have suggested that mania may be characterized by the "mirror" of depressive schemata. The depressed individual maintains the negative mood state through a bias toward automatic thoughts focused on negative *implication*. These include mind-reading ("She thinks I'm a loser"), personalizing ("It's all my fault"), all-or-nothing thinking ("I'm a total loser"), and fortune-telling ("I'll fail"). In contrast, the manic individual has positively-valenced automatic thoughts: mind reading ("She thinks I'm terrific"), positive personalizing ("I saved the day. It's all because of me. I'm a hero"), all-or-nothing thinking ("I'm a complete success"), and fortune-telling ("I'm absolutely sure it will work out"). Furthermore, depressive assumptions ("shoulds" and "if-then" contingency statements), are turned upside down. "If I succeed at this, I must be a genius," "If I want it, I can get it," "If I like someone, then they'll love me," and "It doesn't matter at all how bad I fail at anything." To expand on these observations of the difference between manic and depressive cognition, I would suggest that in the manic state the individual's personal schemas are polarized to the opposite extreme. For example, if the individual feels unattractive when depressed, he feels extraordinarily irresistible when manic. Or, if she feels undeserving of any rewards when depressed, she feels entitled to spend enormous amounts of money she does not have when manic.

DECISION-MAKING AND MANIA

There are several reasons why decision-making is an important component of mania. First, risk behavior always entails a decision. As indicated earlier, to be able to specify how decisions are made during mania may be helpful in reducing the risks entailed. Second, decision-making is an excellent window to a variety of other cognitive elements. For example, in making a decision, we often assess the degree to which we believe that we are able to control outcomes, our risk tolerance, our regret orientation, our range and quality of resources, and our ability to absorb losses (Baron, 1994; Leahy, 1996 1997a, 1997b, 1998). Third, decision-making may link the elements of explanatory style and negative (or positive) triad with the actual behavioral investments that individuals make. There is now considerable empirical evidence supporting both Beck's (1979) cognitive model of depression, in terms of assumptions, schemata, and automatic thoughts, as well as the attributional model, which stresses explanatory styles (Abramson, Seligman, & Teasdale, 1978). However, an important extension of these models is in determining how cognitive schemata are related to the willingness to take a risk.

PORTFOLIO THEORY AND DECISION-MAKING

When individuals make decisions, they consider a number of factors. Seldom does an individual consider all the information that might be available or relevant to making a decision (Baron, 1994). Individuals use heuristics, or rules of thumb, to guide them through the process of simplifying decision making (Kahneman & Tversky, 1979), often emphasizing recent, salient, concrete, and personally relevant information, rather than assessing baselines, probabilities, and abstract information (Kahneman & Tversky, 1979; Tversky & Kahneman, 1974). Furthermore, decision-making is determined by information searches, which seldom consider all permutations but rather are guided by limited and biased search, usually directed toward satisfying an answer to a specific question. Simon (1979) has suggested that individuals utilize "satisficing" rules—that is, they search for information until they obtain data that satisfies a criterion. Thus, when individuals examine a menu, they may only search the menu until they come across an item that satisfies their criterion for an entrée—let's say, *salad nicoise*. Having satisfied their criterion, they discontinue their search. This search is "satisficing" for entrees, to use Simon's terminology.

I have proposed (Leahy 1997a, 1997b, 1998) that depressed individuals have a similar pattern of satisficing, which I would label as *dissatisficing*. Thus, the depressed individual will have a negatively biased information search that examines the possibilities for loss, mistake, or regret. Once this is found, the information search is discontinued. A prediction derived from this is that depressed individuals are likely to be risk-averse and therefore will require considerable information before making a decision to change.

To examine the decision-rules underlying risk taking, I have proposed that mundane decision-making may be based on many of the same considerations that individuals (theoretically) utilize in investing their assets in finance (Leahy, 1997a, 1997b, 1998). The model that has been proposed is not specifically a model of financial investment, but rather a general model of decision-making and risk. According to modern portfolio theory in finance, individuals consider their future prospects in terms of rewards or losses by coordinating numerous assumptions and goals. Individuals differ in their portfolio theories, since some individuals seek to maximize gains and believe that they have sufficient resources, now and in the future, to absorb potential losses (Markowitz, 1952). These optimistic individuals are inclined to be more tolerant of risk. In contrast, regret-oriented individuals who believe that they have little diversification in current resources and that they will have small future earnings will probably be less likely to tolerate risk.

Leahy (1997a; 1998) has proposed that depressed individuals utilize a negatively biased *portfolio theory* in considering their options. A portfolio theory is the individual's perception of their resources, diversification, maximization/minimization, potential for regret, hedonic utility for gains and losses, and risk tolerance. Consistent with other cognitive models, the portfolio theory model stresses the negative cognitive bias of depressive schemata. Portfolio theory of depression, based on investment models of decision-making, proposes that individual variation in risk tolerance is related to the depressed individual's assumptions of scarcity and depletion, regret-orientation, criteria for defining losses and gains, rules for quitting, and information demands prior to making decisions. This model proposes that depressed individuals are risk-averse and tend to place less emphasis on maximizing gains and more emphasis on minimizing losses.

In a recent study (Leahy, 1999), several hypotheses derived from the portfolio model of depression were tested. Seventy-five clinic patients were administered the Beck Depression Inventory and a six-point 25–item questionnaire that assessed a variety of dimensions of decision-making derived from the portfolio-theory model. Correlations were calculated among all items and for depression scores. The depressive portfolio theory, which is risk-averse, was largely supported. More depressed patients utilized a negative portfolio theory, which was based on assumptions that current and future resources are scarce, outcomes are unpredictable and uncontrollable, there is a low utility for gains, and a high disutility for losses. Depressed individuals were more inclined to blame themselves for failures and less likely to internalize success. They generalized negatives, stopped-out early, had a high criterion for defining gains and a marginal criterion for defining losses, and had a greater demand for consensus building before taking action. Depression was negatively associated with the goal of maximizing gains but was unrelated to the goal of minimizing losses. Independent of depression, there was strong confirmation for the portfolio model of risk, which largely paralleled the findings for depression and portfolio concerns indicated above. Risk-aversion was associated with almost all of the decision dimensions correlated with depression and with greater demands for information and with utilizing waiting as a strategy.

Depressed individuals are risk-averse and view themselves as having scarce resources, high regret, low control of positives, and low utility of gains. Let us consider three individuals—the first was normal, or euthymic; the second was potentially manic; and the third, was despondent and depressed. Our normal friend, named Prudent Peter, believes that he has moderate resources, some small diversification of resources in his life, a moderate future time frame for further positives, and some enjoyment of things that he achieves. He is confronted with an option to engage in a behavior that has a 1% chance of succeeding and a 50% chance of failing with heavy losses that will be publicly exposed. He values his reputation, he is not addicted to risk taking, and he does not believe that the high chance of failure and loss is worth the risk. He passes up the opportunity to gamble his assets for the small chance of a success.

The second friend, Manic Mike, is quite excited and seems to enjoy everything that he does. He takes credit for almost any positive, he believes that he has unlimited current resources and future potential earnings, and he believes that he can predict the future. If something does not work out, he does not regret it, because he tends to blame other people and he tends to think that he has so many other projects that it is not essential that this project succeed. He is offered the same opportunity as Prudent Peter—a 1% chance of success and a 50% chance of failure—but he sees this gamble as different from Prudent Paul's perception. Manic Mike believes that the odds have been misstated—he believes that these baseline estimates do not apply to him, since he is a unique individual with the ability to predict and control outcomes. Furthermore, in the perceived unlikely event that the outcome is negative, he believes that he can absorb the loss, since he sees himself as having unlimited current and future resources and an unlimited timeframe for making more to make up for any losses that could occur. Moreover, Manic Mike is a connoisseur of pleasure and greatly enjoys his gains, both for their general hedonic value and for the fact that he can take credit for them. The fact that the decision will be viewed by everyone only adds to its enticement, since he believes that the success of this decision will only add to his already growing reputation for brilliance. He immediately decides to take this decision, refusing to believe it is a gamble, since he is assured it is a "sure thing." Manic Mike is a risk lover.

The third friend, Nervous Nellie, has been feeling particularly blue for a while. This may be due to her recent losses in work and in her personal relationships, for both of which—as is typical of Nellie—she blames herself. To make matters worse, from Nellie's point of view, she has few resources in her life, she fears she will lose her job, and she is even less certain of the support she needs, but believes she will not get, from her friends. Nellie is quick to spot a failure on the horizon—if for no other reason, she believes, than that if she spots it early, she can quit early and avoid further—inevitable, to her way of thinking—losses. When Nervous Nellie hears of the 1% chance of success and 50% chance of failure, it only reminds her of all the poor decisions that she now feels responsible to ruminate over. She turns a deaf ear to the offer.

Our three friends each approach the potential offer with certain as-sumptions. To the prudent individual, baseline probabilities (1% vs. 50%) are important. But beyond these simple calculations, Prudent Paul con-siders moderation as a goal—that is, the moderation of modest current and future resources and the limit of utility derived from something working out. He is more risk-neutral than risk-averse. He is certainly not a risk lover. The manic individual exaggerates his ability to make things work. He overestimates current and future resources and believes that he can predict and control outcomes. Moreover, he is energized by being a risk lover. And, finally, the despondent depressed friend believes she has few resources and has suffered recent losses, and she perceives herself as being depleted in the future. Thus, three individuals, given the same odds, may have different perceptions of risk and desirability.

In Table 2.1, I have indicated the portfolio considerations of depressed, nondepressed, and manic individuals. The entries for the columns repre-senting the depressed and nondepressed in this table and all subsequent tables are adapted from Leahy (1997a and 1997b), with slight modifica-tions for the nondepressed entries. Each of these dimensions is hypothe-sized to be predictive of the individual's willingness to take a risk—or, indeed, to even perceive that a risk exists.

According to the *mood-decision model,* depressed and manic individ-uals are largely mirror images of each other, with the nondepressed fall-

Table 2.1 Portfolio Concerns of Depressed, Nondepressed and Manic Individuals

Portfolio Concern	Depressed	Nondepressed	Manic
Assets available	Few	Some/Many	Unlimited
Future earning potential	Low	Moderate	Unlimited
Market variation	Volatile	Low/predictable	Certain predictability
Investment goal	Minimize loss	Minimal loss with maximum gain	Maximize gain, indifferent to loss
Risk-orientation	Risk-averse	Risk neutral	Risk lover
Functional utility of gain	Low	Moderate	Very high
Replications of investment	None/few	Many	Unlimited
Duration of investment	Short term	Long term	Short term
Portfolio diversification	Low	Moderate	Very high

ing between these polarities. If we focus on the portfolio concerns of manic individuals, we can see that they view their assets and future earnings potential as unlimited. The consequence of viewing oneself as having unlimited resources is a greater willingness to take a risk: one can recover more easily from a loss if there are resources to draw on. Manic individuals are also viewed as believing that they can predict, with close to certainty, future outcomes. Clinical observations of manic individuals demonstrates that many of these people hold steady to the belief that they will be able to realize substantial gains from their decisions, regardless of how much others view them as uncertain or risky.

I have introduced the idea of *minimax* strategy to differentiate the depressed-manic attitude toward an investment goal. A minimax strategy implies that one attempts to simultaneously balance the limitation on loss with the potential of maximizing gain. Nondepressed individuals are viewed as employing the minimax strategy. Depressed individuals are viewed as stressing the "minimize loss" to the "maximize gain" strategy—that is, they are viewed as suffering their losses more than enjoying their gains. At the other extreme, manic individuals may err toward over-emphasizing the goal of maximizing gains, regardless of the potential loss: they enjoy their gains far more than they suffer their losses. In fact, while episodic, the manic individual shows indifference toward losses.

The indifference toward losses, during mania, may be the result of other perceptions of the manic portfolio. Specifically, manics strongly enjoy their gains—in fact, gains are associated with euphoria. For example, a manic individual was euphoric over the purchase of a pair of blue jeans, which, to the euthymic therapist, appeared to represent rather pedestrian taste. Thus, to euphoric manics, what appear to others as small gains are highly valued and, therefore, worth whatever costs may be incurred. In microeconomic jargon, one can say that they have high functional utility of gains, while discounting the costs incurred.

Costs matter little to manics because they believes that they have unlimited current and future resources, many replications of behavior where they can succeed, and a wide range or variety of potential rewards (high diversification). For example, a manic patient believed that he could pay the cost of his extensive shopping spree by borrowing on his credit card while applying for other credit cards (high current and future "resources"), sell his baseball card collection for a large sum, and experience success in a variety of ventures he was planning (starting a record company, selling illegal drugs, and starting a band). Thus, if one venture failed, there were many other potential sources of rewards.

An interesting aspect of manic's perception of money is that the manic often confuses the ability to engage in a transaction with the ability to pay the debt created. For example, manics believes that if they are able to use a credit card or write a check (which ostensibly completes a transaction), then they have fulfilled their part of the deal. they fail to realize that the transaction vehicle (e.g., a credit card) does not make them richer, but only creates greater debt. [Indeed, manic individuals are simply part of the continuum of the American consumer, whose spending now exceeds income (*New York Times*, 1998)].

Loss Orientation

One of the most important aspects of the manic episode is the apparent indifference to loss and, therefore, the risk that one observes. The manic individual may gamble enormous sums, drive his car at excessive speeds, engage in high-risk drug and sexual behavior, and commit large amounts of debt to apparently frivolous and unrealistic goals. Inspection of Table 2.2 indicates how manic individuals perceive loss. First, they have a very high threshold for defining loss: that is, it takes an enormous loss to be viewed as a loss. In fact, some manic individuals are so delusional in this regard that they cannot see any potential loss or danger, even when their lives are at considerable risk. Second, the manic individual has a very low stop loss rule—if he has any stop loss rule at all. He will not quit unless the loss is overwhelming or unsurpassable. Consequently, he does

Table 2.2 Loss Orientation in Mania

Loss Orientation	Example
High threshold	Only an enormous loss is counted as a loss.
Low stop-loss criteria	Only a significant and continuous loss leads to quitting.
Abundance assumptions	The world is viewed as having infinite opportunities for success. This is generalized to a multiplication of positives—one positive implies many other positives are available
Energizing assumptions	Losses are simply inconveniences or temporary setbacks. They are viewed as not affecting or decreasing current resources.
Compartmentalized costs	Losses are viewed as unrelated to other potential losses. Losses are contained.
Time urgency	Losses (or gains) are viewed in terms of immediate gratification.
Reversibility and revocability	Losses are viewed as reversible and revocable. Negative investments are revocable—manics see themselves as able to pull out easily.
Indifference to regret orientation	Losses are not followed by regret that one should have known better. Rather than hindsight bias (that is, the assumption that he should have been able to make perfect decisions with limited information), the manic individual are tolerant or indifferent about past mistakes. They focus on future utility rather than on past disutility.

not pull out when he still has a chance. It may be possible that the manic simply assumes that events are naturally volatile and to pull out (or stop out) too early would result in quitting at the low, thereby sacrificing the opportunity to do well in a volatile market or environment. *Stop-loss* is a technique to control the downside of risk, but it may expose one to the alternative risk of always quitting in volatility—that is, it may actually add to the risk of losing repetitively in an unstable environment.

Third, manic individuals lack scarcity assumptions. They operate in the opposite direction of a pessimistic Malthusian and, in fact, view the market as having unlimited potential resources—there only for the taking. Similarly, their boundless energy is reflective of their rejection of depletion—the more they do, the more energized and encouraged they are to do more.

Contrary to the depressed individual who sees one loss as the beginning of a slippery slope of other losses, the manic views a loss as a trivial aberration from his unlimited optimism. If something does not work out, he discounts it as a compartmentalized and brief detour on the way to unlimited gains. While I have used the microeconomic term *cost-cascades*, to describe the depressed individual's belief that costs result in a chain-reaction, I will label the manic's view of cost as a *cost-compartment*, reflecting the view that costs are seen as nonpredictive aberrations. Depressives view losses as correlated with other losses and as carrying a momentum aimed toward disaster. Thus, for depressives, losses are not independent events. In contrast, the manic views losses as orthogonal to other losses: they are "noise."

The temporal focus of both depressed and manic individuals is short term, or myopic. Whereas the depressed individual attempts to feel better by reducing discomfort over the short term, the manic attempts to feel better by increasing excitement and rewards immediately. The contrast between these groups may be captured by viewing depressed individuals as avoidant and manic individuals as consummatory and appetitive. The depressed individual behaves as if he is trying to reduce stimulation, while the manic focuses on appetitive behavior—that is, seeking rewards and enjoying their consumption. A consequence of this excessive focus on appetitiveness is that manics become frustrated frequently when they are temporarily blocked from their goal. However, unlike the depressed individual who views a short-term frustration as implying inability or impossible task difficulty, the manic individual increases their effort. The response to frustration for the manic is to *increase energy to increase efficacy*. In contrast, the depressed individual *decreases energy to avoid depletion*.

Depressed and manic individuals are polarized on the dimension of reversibility and revocability. The depressed individual believes that a decision involves a *sunk cost* to be avoided unless there is absolute certainty of a positive outcome. To the depressed individual, decisions may lead to a point of no return. For example, the depressed individual may believe that he cannot pursue a goal for too long because he will be committed to having to pursue it indefinitely. I have referred to the excessive cognitive dissonance that individuals experience after they have sunk inordinate resources into a failing venture as the Vietnam Syndrome (Leahy, 1992). The depressed individual attempts to avoid the consequent regrets of the Vietnam Syndrome by a form of isolationism. The manic individual, on the other hand, is not predisposed toward regret and believes that, "If it doesn't work out, I'll try something else." One may view this "flexibility" as "empowering"—after all, the manic individual perceives his options as limitless, since he can always change them at the whim of the moment. He acts as if he can ignore the trap of sunk costs. The problem with this strategy is that sunk costs are real costs and, in some cases, they can sink the manic. In contrast to the depressed individual, the manic individual not only believes that he can bail out at any time, but he believes his parachute is golden. Unfortunately, the parachute does not always open.

Finally, depressed and manic individuals are polarized on the dimension of regret. The depressive believes that he should have known better and that he should criticize himself for his failed behavior. In contrast, the manic believes that his mistakes—if they are viewed as such—are simply due to bad luck or the impediments created by others. If anyone is to be criticized, he reasons, it is the person who got in the way. For example, a manic patient believed that the therapist, his parents, and eventually the staff at the hospital where he was committed, were to blame for his financial debt, since they prevented him from carrying out his plans for full-proof international drug smuggling.

Gain Orientation

The word mania confers a sense of enthusiasm about life. Indeed, the manic's apparently unlimited optimism and enjoyment of rewards and boundless self-reinforcement are often intoxicatingly appealing to others. In the hypomanic state, the individual may simply appear to be one who enjoys life the way we nonmanics wish we could enjoy it. Much of cognitive therapy has appeared to focus on the downside of pessimism, yet there may be even greater risks in overly optimistic behavior. It is when one is optimistic that dangerous behavior may seem plausible and pleasurable. Consequently, we may want to consider the manic's gain orientation as part of the risk profile.

Manics have a low threshold for defining and valuing gains. Everything has the potential of reward. In fact, almost every potential gain can be counted, rather than discounted, as the depressive is likely to do. Future gains are viewed as likely and predictable—the individual knows for sure that his schemes will bear fruit and that the fruit will be ripe for the eating. Similar to the myopic depressive, however, the manic is also short on delay of gratification: He must have it now, resulting in contin-

Table 2.3 Gain Orientation in Depression and Mania

Depression	Mania
High threshold for definition	Low threshold for definition.
Low valuation	High valuation
Low probability	High probability.
Immediate demand	Immediate demand, but can persist if desired
Contingency traps	Inability to recognize contingency
Lack of control	Overemphasis of control
Gravity of gains	Propulsion and chain reaction of gains

ual sense of urgency, impulsivity, frustration when impeded, and affect intolerance.

The manic individual exaggerates his sense of control over positives, believing that his desire for an outcome will usually translate to a successful result. Furthermore, the manic differs from the depressive who believes that gains are aberrations and, therefore, carry gravity that will lead to crushing disappointment. The manic, indeed, believes that current gains are the portent of greater gains to come: Once rewarded, always to be rewarded. Like the gambler, he believes he is on a roll, with accelerated speed, ever moving "onward and upward."

Example

Peter, a young man in a manic episode, viewed almost everything as a terrific gain. A hamburger was the greatest meal he's ever had. Every venture he considered taking on was a sure thing. He indicated that he was willing to put in whatever it takes to make his business ideas work, but he became easily distracted to the next possibility. Peter had considerable difficulty recognizing the lack of contingency—that is, the lack of relationship between his effort and outcome. Although he was putting in many hours to get his business venture going, nothing appeared to be happening. He also believed that he would be able to control all positive outcomes—that is, he would be able to control whether a woman wanted sex with him, whether his investments worked out, and whether he would get caught smuggling drugs in an airport.

Risk Denial in Mania

Decision-makers manage their risk of exposure to loss by utilizing a variety of strategies. I have suggested that depression often involves excessive risk-aversion and the utilization of strategies that will minimize either exposure to loss or the personal relevance of loss (Leahy 1997a, b, c). For example, depressed individuals can manage their risk by increasing *waiting time* or *demands for information*: If they wait long enough, they may find that the problem resolves itself or they may feel more "ready" to solve the problem. Similarly, if they demand more information, they may feel more secure about the outcome. The tradeoff against waiting and high information demands is the opportunity cost of not engaging in the behavior under consideration. However, since the depressed individual believes that there is a lower probability of the behavior's working out or conferring high pleasure, the opportunity cost is discounted as insignificant.

Table 2.4 Risk Management Strategies in Mania

Risk Management Concerns	Examples
Diversification	High diversification: Manics believe they have many investments and, therefore, a loss on one is compensated by a gain on another.
Duration	Variable: Manics may vary between taking a short-term view about outcome, to taking the view that they have an infinite time-horizon for gain.
Replication	High: Manics believe that they can continue in their efforts indefinitely if required.
Waiting	Low: Manics do not believe that they need to wait to obtain more information to act. They can act now.
Information demands	High: Manics have low information requirements and can move forward on a hunch.
Disappointment aversion	Low: Manics have little concern about failure and can view failure as a temporary aberration with no personal relevance.
Manipulation of expectations	Manics feel comfortable—even eager—raising their own and others' expectations about their potential.
Exaggeration of hope	High: Manics view hope as never ending and assume that it will all work out.
Over-commitment	Manics exert a maximum of effort and fails to perceive signs that things are not working out.
Advertising self-evaluation	Manics tell everyone exactly how they think they will do and do little to cover their public image should their behavior fail.

In contrast, manic individuals abhor waiting and regard information demands as impediments to be ignored. In this sense, they fail to utilize any risk management for these dimensions. Because the depressed individual views the opportunity cost to be high for losing the alternative, he is less likely to wait or demand information. Furthermore, waiting creates greater frustration for the manic, partly because of the sense of urgency and partly because the manic sees no value in waiting or demanding information. The credibility and plausibility of pursuing a behavior is determined more by the selective focus on a few satisficing bits of information (Leahy, 1997, 1998; Simon, 1979) and on the very desire to obtain it. Thus, for the manic, the assumption guiding this is, "If I want it, I can get it," and, "The more I want it, the more likely I'll be able to get it." The manic believes that the little information that he has is satisficing. In contrast to the depressed individual who looks for reasons not to act (negative satisficing), the manic looks for reasons to take action—thereby searching for a positive satisficing criterion. While the depressive asks, "Is it possible I can lose?" and then quits if the answer is affirmative, the manic asks, "Is it possible I might win?" and then proceeds if the answer is "Yes." Both polarities reflect limited search for information that is congruent with the mood.

Depressives are held back by disappointment aversion: They tend to regret mistakes and, therefore, they do not want to get their hopes up lest they be dashed down. In contrast, the manic acts as if disappointment is unlikely (or, in fact, impossible) and, even if it occurs, there is no possibility of regret. He anticipates an infinite ability to absorb costs and views mistakes as so much insignificance that will deflect off his Teflon ego. The manic is not held back by disappointment and, therefore, cannot manage risk by this consideration.

Depressives manage the risk to their ego by managing expectations. They either attempt to lower their own expectations or those of others regarding possible success. Consequently, their reference point of aspiration is scaled downward: "I know that I won't succeed," or "I can't believe that you would think I'd be able to do that. You're so unrealistic!" In contrast to this social-cognitive strategy of depressives, manics are continually raising the expectations that they and others hold of the manic: "I'm going to set up my own company!" or "You'll be impressed when my experiment works out!" Just as the manic appears to confuse the appearance of a monetary transaction with the ability to afford the merchandise, the manic's approach to expectations confuses the strength of the desire for an outcome with its inevitability. Simply wanting it to be true makes it so.

Depressives attempt to "get hope down": increasing hope may result, they believe, in greater risk for exposure and disappointment. Better to expect less and not be surprised. Better to be safe than sorry. In contrast, the manic is a beacon of hope—again, often confusing the wish for an outcome with the probability of its occurrence: "I know it'll work out. I can make things happen!" Riding hope as if it is a reality, the manic believes that the more he hopes for the richer and more successful he will become. This emotional reasoning component is one that manics defend vigorously in therapy—partly because of their certainty that they are correct and partly because of their fear that, if they agree with the caution advocated by therapists, they will be defeated in their essential goals.

Individuals often manage their risk exposure by either straddling or hedging. Straddling involves exerting minimal effort and, then, quitting early: "I went to the gym, worked out for fifteen minutes, and didn't feel any better. So I went home." Hedging involves putting down competing bets—literally, betting against yourself. The anxious and depressive dependent patient may hedge by having more than one therapist, maintaining a relationship outside of marriage, or put up with an abusive relationship simply as a protection against loneliness. Manic individuals may appear to straddle—they may have several therapists, lovers, relationships, or other interpersonal investments. They may appear to have their hands in many deals, any one of which has a high probability of collapsing. But it would not be accurate to view this as straddling or hedging. Rather, it reflects a perception of unlimited resources available to invest in unlimited opportunities. The intention behind the behavior is not to protect against risk—it is to avoid losing opportunities for profit and pleasure. After all, from their point of view they have unlimited energy and resources, they believe each alternative is a sure bet. They are focused on maximizing gains and they are indifferent to loss. They are always ready to be dealt in.

Depressed and anxious individuals manage risk by "hiding." They may isolate themselves from coworkers, fail to go to appointments, withdraw from interactions when they are present, and remain taciturn and aloof. No one kicks a sleeping dog, they believe, utilizing a low-profile strategy. They avoid tasks or jobs that place them in a position of public exposure of failing. In contrast, manics seldom hide—unless they retain enough reality testing to recognize the illegality of their schemes. They enjoy bragging about their plans and behavior, since each plan represents a certain triumph for which they will take all the credit. They will call friends or even near-strangers to share their enthusiasm about their successful exploits. In fact, it is this lack of hiding—the extensive public display of manic boasting and bravado—that is often a point of regret once the manic mood has passed.

Similarly, the manics fail to obscure self-evaluation. They fail to hide their role in their behavior; they have publicly predicted and publicly exposed their plans and behavior. They act as if they do not care what anyone sees or hears, discounting other's esteem for them as less important than their enthusiasm or esteem for themselves. Whereas depressives may minimize their effort, fail to show up, and utilize self-handicapping strategies like lack of preparation or alcohol to obscure his true potential, manics believe that they will devote all their energy, resources, and the public domain of themselves to their true potential. Since they believe that what is possible is positive they want to be viewed as the sole protagonists. Promethean manics see themselves rising from the fire that engulfs them, whereas depressivse see themselves as the ashes that have been consumed.

Structural Similarities of Mania and Depression

Thus far, I have emphasized substantial differences between manic and depressed individuals in the cognitive schemata underlying decision-making, attitudes toward gains and losses, and risk taking. Yet, implied by this comparison, is another assumption—that is, that manic and depressed individuals are characterized by distortions in their thinking. This more general similarity reflects underlying structural similarities between these apparently polar opposites. In fact, the shift from one pole to the other may be mostly reducible to the emphasis on pessimism versus optimism.

What are these structural similarities? First, both polarities are characterized by selective information processing—including attention, recall, recognition, and reproduction of information. The difference is that the depressed individual selectively focuses on the negative and the manic focuses on the positive. Second, both individuals have a bias toward evaluating information. For the depressed individual, the evaluation of a loss or gain is consistent with pessimism and scarcity, while for the manic individual; the evaluation is marked by unbounded optimism and abundance.

Third, both polarities attribute inordinate personal causation to events, with depressed individuals blaming themselves for negatives and manic individuals overattributing personal causation for positives. Although this chapter has not focused on schematic content, I would suggest a fourth structural similarity. I refer to this as *schematic polarity,* by which I mean a tendency for mood to affect the directional valence of a schema. Thus, the same individual whose schema is one of incompetence and unlovability, in the depressive phase, will manifest a schema of overcompetence and exaggerated attractiveness in the manic phase. Thus, the schema itself does not change, only the polarity of its manifestation. Furthermore, whereas in the depressed phase individuals avoid or compensate, in the manic phase they approach and undercompensates (that is, act like a risk lovers). Again, the polarity of the schema, not its dimensionality or content, remain similar.

A fifth structural similarity may be found in the nature of automatic thoughts and assumptions (see Leahy & Beck, 1988). As I have previously suggested, depressed and manic individuals appear to be exceedingly different in these areas—perhaps, to play on words, they are polarized. The depressed individual believes that he fails at everything, whereas the manic believes that he succeeds at everything. Yet, the similarity is that both are using dichotomous thinking. Thus, the fifth similarity between these apparently polar opposites is in their nonnormative thinking—that is, their consistent epistemological errors. These include the lack of differentiation, the dependence of thought on emotion, the inferential leaps beyond the information, the exaggerated personal causation, the selective focus on schema-relevant information, the tendency to mislabel—and, thereby, overgeneralize—and the overuse of faulty inductive reasoning. For depressed (D) and manic (M) individuals, respectively, these errors are represented by the following contrasts:

- "I fail at everything" (D) versus "I succeed at everything" (M)—lack of differentiation
- "I feel like a loser, therefore I am a loser" (D) versus "I feel omnipotent, therefore, I am God" (M)—dependence of thought on emotion
- "If I fail at this, then I can't do anything" (D) versus "If I succeed at this, then I am a genius"—inferential leaps
- "The relationship fell apart entirely because of me" (D) versus "I can make any relationship work, if I want to" (M)—exaggerated personal causation
- "She doesn't like me, therefore I'm a loser" versus "She likes me, therefore I'm wonderful" (M)—selective focus on schema-relevant information
- "I'm an idiot" (D) versus "I'm a genius" (M)—mislabeling/overgeneralizing
- "If I fail at this, then I am a failure" (D) versus "If I succeed at this, then I am a superior and wonderful person" (M)—faulty inductive reasoning.

The contrast between these poles is more in the hedonic content and valence (negative versus positive) than in the difference in logic or structure. Neither is normative.

CLINICAL IMPLICATIONS IN THE TREATMENT OF MANIA

It is beyond the scope of this chapter to provide a model for the treatment of mania. The interested reader is directed to Basco and Rush (1996), and Newman, Leahy, Beck, Gyusalai, and Reilly-Harrington (2001). However, there are specific conceptualizations and interventions that may be derived from the model proposed here. Let us briefly explore them.

Preliminary Considerations

The approach taken here is in the treatment of the bipolar patient when he is euthymic—that is, between episodes and not mood-symptomatic. Once the manic phase is activated, it may be difficult to implement these interventions, unless the patient and therapist have arrived at a case conceptualization and plan of treatment before the episode. A hallmark of the mania is the lack of insight and the perception that one does not need help, but rather needs help getting rid of help givers. Consequently, in the euthymic phase, it is useful to review previous manic phases (What can be learned?) and to plan future phases and how the risk will be minimized.

Case Conceptualization

A central component of the treatment of mania is the medicalization of the disorder: "This is an illness—a chronic illness—for which you need continued treatment. Treatment will focus on the management of the illness through medication and therapy. Medication will help reduce mood variability and therapy will help you manage the moods when and if they occur." The case conceptualization, based on the model outlined above, focuses on the typical cognitive distortions during the manic phase. The patient is asked if, during the manic phase, he recalls believing that he had unlimited resources and had the belief that he would be able to achieve unlimited benefits in the future. His beliefs that he can predict with certainty, control all outcomes, and act without costs are examined. His love of risk, during the manic phase, and the specific risks that he

Table 2.5 Clinical Implications

Portfolio Concern	Manic	Interventions
Assets available	Unlimited	Focus on limits of current resources and how actions will risk depleting valued assets
Future earning potential	Unlimited	Examine how future earnings are limited and, in fact, may be compromised if manic action is carried out
Market variation	Certain predictability	Examine how outcomes are often unpredictable and uncontrollable and that a sudden loss may wipe an investor out
Investment goal	Maximize gain, indifferent to loss	Focus on trade-offs and risk of loss and indicate how potential gains may be offset by enormous costs or losses
Risk-orientation	Risk lover	Indicate that loving a risk is not the same thing as achieving an outcome. Indicate how emotional reasoning ("I think it will work out") is not a good predictor of outcomes.
Functional utility of gain	Very high	Indicate that anticipated rewards that may seem highly useful have seldom, in the past, maintained their appeal: Past rewards achieved in a manic state are now viewed as unrewarding.
Replications of investment	Unlimited	Indicate that one does not have an infinite number of "tries" or "hands" to play and that each "hand" will cost more than he may have available.
Duration of investment	Short term	Indicate that to achieve outcomes, the manic may have to put in more effort and time than is available.
Portfolio diversification	Very high	Point out to manics that they may not have sufficient assets to offset losses in one area. Moreover, indicate how rewards in certain areas (e.g., family, friends, and job) may be compromised if they act out.

pursued are also examined. His overemphasis on energy and enthusiasm as proof that his high motivation will lead to positive outcomes is identified. His time-urgency and rejection of disappointment or regret, during his manic phases, are also examined. Underlying schemas of control, entitlement, competence, or sexual gratification are examined, as these relate to risks encountered during the manic phase.

Precommitment Strategies

All of us recognize that there are certain temptations that we cannot resist. If we wait to resist until the tempting stimulus confronts us, then we are lost. Some people have part of their salary withheld every month, since they know that they will spend it if they have it. Others demonstrate a precommitment to avoid temptation by avoiding environments that tempt with liquor, drugs, or even an occasional high calorie pastry. Precommitment simply reflects our recognition of our all-too-human weakness to act myopically on our emotions and appetites.

The manic patient is a good candidate for precommitment. For one patient whose mania was characterized by excessive spending, the precommitment agreement included the following: "Do a mood check daily (for mania). If the mood includes more than three manic symptoms, then leave the credit card with my husband, don't go to the mall, don't spend more than $100 without first reviewing it with my husband, and wait 24 hours after two nights of good sleep before shopping" (see Newman et al., 200,1 for detailed descriptions of these self-control strategies). For other patients, precommitment strategies include, before a manic episode, promising not to drive, not to call prostitutes, or review unconventional decisions with the therapist and two friends. The essential point for the patient to commit to is that, during a manic episode, there may not be sufficient control to make these decisions. Thus, enlisting a contract with the therapist before the episode may enhance greater compliance and reduced risk. The therapist and patient can later refer back to the precommitment agreement once the patient becomes manic. Although this may be a desirable approach, the reader correctly recognizes that it will not always work.

Inoculation Against Distorted Manic Thinking

As indicated, interventions to reduce manic risk are better initiated during the euthymic phase. During this calmer period, the therapist can examine the idiosyncratic symptoms of mania, including the "case conceptualization," noted above. The therapist and patient can weigh the costs and benefits of acting out mania and the consequences of prior manic episodes. The patient's specific cognitive distortions regarding justification of acting out behavior, perceptions of unlimited resources and power, emotional reasoning, time urgency, and selective focus on the positive may be identified. As indicated, manic cognition is polarized toward the positive extreme, thereby ignoring real risks. The goal in the inoculation stage is finding the normative middle.

This implies that reality is often located somewhere within the shades of gray between the polarity of unlimited power and unrelenting failure. I refer to this as the normative middle to focus the bipolar patient away from extreme, rigid, and emotionally laden cognition. The normative middle recognizes differentiation ("I am not entirely powerful or power-less"), independence of events ("A success [or failure] on one task does not always generalize to other tasks"), and distribution of causal forces ("It's not entirely my fault or entirely my credit"). The goal of the inoc-ulation phase is to encourage patients to avoid the belief that they are either superior or inferior—but, rather, equal to the norm.

Inoculation entails active role-plays in which the therapist alternates between the tempting energizing distortions of mania and the rational response. The patient plays the alternative. Thus, the therapist can "barb" the patient with the perception of unlimited assets and risk-enthusiasm, while the patient disputes these distortions:

Therapist: Let's imagine that you're feeling manic. You've slept two hours a night for the last two nights; you feel energized, you're irritated, and you want to go to the mall. I'll be the automatic thoughts. You have a tremendous amount of money. Just go to the mall and buy whatever you want.

Patient: I don't have a lot of money. I'll regret it.

Therapist: You're manic, you don't regret anything.

Patient: I'll come out of the manic mood, and then I'll get depressed about what I've spent.

Therapist: But you feel invincible. Just go with your feelings.

Patient: When I'm manic, my feelings are a poor guide.

Therapist: You have to have those things now!

Patient: No, I can wait. The mood will pass. Then I won't want them.

The patient is encouraged to write these self-instructions on cards and review them daily. Further role-plays are useful in addressing the desire to tell everyone how wonderful one is, to challenge perceptions of the ability to predict and control outcomes, and to challenge the belief that one has unlimited ability to make up for any losses.

Developing Realistic Decision-Processes

Once the mania has unfolded, it may be difficult to help the patient recognize the distortions in her decision-making. Consequently, it is useful to direct the manic's attention toward these distortions once she is euthymic. Implied by the mood-dependent model of portfolio concerns, the manic individual is distorted in the overly optimistic direction. This positive-valence results in exaggerations of resources, predictability, control, indifference to regret, and need for information. If we return to Table 2.1 above, which highlights the portfolio concerns that characterize mania, we can see that the clinical task is to focus the manic on the following realizations:

- Your current resources are limited. What are they?
- Your future resources—especially in the near future—are also limited. What are they?
- You think that you can predict the future. How wrong have you been in the past about your predictions?
- You think that you can control events. How wrong have you been in the past about your ability to control outcomes?
- When you are manic, you think that risk is low. But what has really happened when you did risk things? Are there even worse things that could have happened, but you were lucky to avoid them?
- You have thought that things that you achieved, bought, or consumed were going to be terrific? How valuable were they—in reality? Now that you are not manic, do you think they were worth the risk or price that you paid?
- You thought you could just keep going. Nothing would stop you. In reality, have you learned that you do not have unlimited energy or time to make things work out?
- You often think when you are manic, that you have an unlimited range of different resources and rewards in your life. Has it turned out that the losses that you experienced when you were manic have had a negative impact on you?

CONCLUSIONS

Individuals contemplating change estimate their current and future resources, their ability to predict and control outcomes, the functional utility of gains and disutility of losses, their tolerance of risk, and their capacity for regret. But individuals differ in their perceptions of these elements—that is, individuals maintain different portfolio theories. These portfolio theories constitute a major component of the cognitive schemata of individuals who are manic, depressed, or euthymic. The hesitancy of the depressed individual in taking a risk—or making a change—follows the internal logic of the depressed individual's perception of scarcity, depletion, unpredictability, low hedonic value of gains, and tendency toward regret. Given their portfolio theory, inhibition and withdrawal follow a "psycho-logic" that makes eminent sense to the depressed patient, but may seem self-defeating to the therapist. In fact, unwillingness to engage in apparently rewarding behavior may, for the depressed person, appear to him as the best method to avoid further losses.

In contrast, the manic individual is viewed here as maintaining an exaggerated-positive portfolio theory. This is based on his assumption of unlimited resources—currently and in the future—and the ability to control and predict outcomes. The aggressive hedonism of the manic, coupled with his indifference to regret and his sense of entitlement, constitute his perception that he—and, perhaps, he alone—can perceive the merit in what appears to others, on the sidelines, as a long shot. When confronted with a long shot, which appears to others to be a foolish risk, the manic responds with the sense of certainty in his ability to predict, control, enjoy or tolerate any foreseeable outcome.

The potential advantage of a portfolio model of decision-making is that it assists us in understanding why depressed individuals fear changing their pessimism and why manic individuals feel entitled to their optimism. There are structural similarities between these two polarities—that is, the dichotomous, emotionally fused, syncretic, and intuitive quality of thought. Yet, while structurally similar in certain ways, these polarities are diametrically opposed in their approach to risk. The portfolio model advanced here may be useful in suggesting cognitive interventions that may assist the manic individual in controlling the risk-potential that follows from his exaggerated sense of resources, predictability, and control.

CHAPTER **3**

Depressive Decision-Making: Validation of the Portfolio Theory Model

Cognitive models of depression have emphasized biases or distortions in information processing, perception of noncontingency, attributional style, and underlying schematic processes that confer vulnerability to further depression (Abramson, Metalsky, & Alloy, 1989; Beck, 1987; Beck, Rush, Shaw, & Emery, 1979; Clark, Beck, & Alford, 1999; Ingram, Miranda, & Segal, 1997). Depressed individuals show a bias toward recalling and predicting negative events, blaming themselves for negative outcomes, not taking credit for positive outcomes, and maintaining negative assumptions and schemas even when the individual is not symptomatic. Cognitive models of depression propose that depressed individuals have distortions or biases in their thinking, such that they selectively attend to negative information (Beck et al., 1979), attribute negative outcomes to themselves and positive outcomes to external or situational factors (Abramson, Seligman, & Teasdale, 1978), or ruminate about negative experiences (Nolen-Hoeksema, 2000). Although there is considerable empirical evidence supporting these different cognitive models of depression, there are little data on the factors that affect the willingness of depressed individuals to change.

Normative models of decision-making propose that individuals would consider all alternatives, objectively weigh the costs and benefits of each option, and focus on future utility rather than past disutility (or "sunk costs") (Baron, 1994). However, individuals seldom follow the normative model in their mundane decisions that are determined more by heuristics and regret-aversion than by exhaustive searches and hedonic calculus (Baron, 1994; Kahneman & Tversky, 1979; Simon, 1979). Although cognitive models of depression have established biases in information processing, judgment and explanatory style, there has been little focus on the issue of how depressed individuals make decisions. An exception to this is the work on helplessness and hopelessness depression that does address the issue of how depressed individuals view their future prospects for rewards (Abramson et al., 1989; Abramson et al., 1978; Alloy, Abramson, Metalsky, & Hartledge, 1988). According to these models, individuals will manifest hopelessness about future positive outcomes if they believe that their current negative outcomes are due to stable and internal causes (such as lack of ability) and if they believe that positive outcomes are due to luck or low task difficulty (Abramson et al., 1978).

Portfolio Theories and Decision-Making

Decision-making may be viewed as a core problem in depression, since depressed individuals may either persist in nonrewarding patterns or may prematurely give up in the face of helplessness (Beck, 1987; Leahy, 1997a). Depressed individuals may forgo the opportunity for rewarding behavior because of their negative predictions about outcome. The present study was guided by a more general model of decision-making that takes into consideration a range of assumptions that individuals make that affects their view of the desirability of making a decision.

The model of decision-making that is proposed here is an economic, or functional-utility, model that attempts to draw on the schematic and attributional models, but that also introduces additional considerations in decision-making. I shall argue that depressed and nondepressed individuals may be viewed as differing in their underlying behavioral investment strategies—strategies that, in the current model, are referred to as "portfolio theories"(Leahy, 1996; 1997b; 1999; 2001).

According to modern portfolio theory—a financial-decision model—individuals utilize different assumptions and goals in considering how they will allocate their resources and how much risk they will tolerate (Bodie, Kane, & Marcus, 1996; Markowitz, 1952). The original formulation of portfolio theory as a model of decision-making was advanced by Markowitz (1952) to account for investor strategy in considering variance in performance of securities. In this chapter, I have attempted to utilize the portfolio model as a means of conceptualizing nonfinancial decisions—an approach that has proven to be useful in other areas marking the interface of psychological and economic concepts (Becker, 1976; 1991; Becker, Grossman, & Murphy, 1991; Kahneman, 1995; Kahneman & Tversky, 1979).

A portfolio theory is the individual's perception of his or her resources, ability to produce future resources, diversification, emphasis on maximization of rewards or minimization of costs, potential for regret, hedonic utility for gains and losses, and risk-tolerance. For example, optimistic and rational individuals, who view themselves as having abundant current resources and potential for future earnings with a long duration, would be likely to tolerate greater risk in their investments than would individuals lacking current and future resources or who would view themselves as having a shorter duration of investment. Presumably, individuals who have abundant current and future resources can absorb a loss, should it occur, especially if they believe that there is a long duration in which this recovery could occur. Furthermore, greater risk tolerance would be assumed if individuals believed that they had many potential replications of behavior—for example, many potential "hands" to play in order to win. It is important to emphasize that one can be pessimistic *and* rational if underlying assumptions about scarcity of current assets and future rewards are accurate.

Modern portfolio theory proposes that individuals will tolerate greater risk if they are more highly diversified, since a loss in one investment may be offset by the performance in other investments. Thus, diversification may be viewed as a way in which costs may be contained or compartmentalized, avoiding the risk of overgeneralizing a failure. Given the negative cognitive schemata of depressed individuals, we would anticipate that these individuals would view losses as having a spreading activation effect, such that they would trigger other losses, thus adding to risk aversion.

Although modern portfolio theory is mute on the issue, one would expect greater willingness to take a risk if the individual perceives gains as having high hedonic utility—for example, providing pleasure or pride. The value of a gain (utility) determines the motivation and incentive to achieve that gain according to Atkinson's expectancy value model (Atkinson, 1957; 1983; Atkinson & Raynor, 1978). Expected value of gain is similar to the reinforcing potential of an outcome, implying that individuals who expect to enjoy an outcome are more likely to exert effort to pursue that outcome. Since depressed individuals are often characterized by anhedonia, the utility of a gain is diminished.

Similarly, we would expect that individuals would be less tolerant of risk, and less likely to change, if losses had high disutility—that is, that losses are suffered. Although a common observation in decision-making is that individuals often suffer their losses more than they enjoy their gains (see Thaler, 1992), this differential of disutility-utility would be expected to be higher in individuals who are risk-averse. Consequently, we might expect that risk-aversion and depression would be related to a tendency to be less concerned with maximizing gains and more concerned with avoiding further losses. This expectation is based on the view that depressed individuals, characterized by anhedonia and a tendency to blame themselves for failures, will place less emphasis on gains and more emphasis on avoiding losses. This question is addressed in the current study.

Individuals who adapt a pessimistic portfolio model would assume that the "market" for rewards is characterized by scarcity—especially, scarcity of rewards for the self. This pessimistic or Malthusian view would be expected to result in a tendency to define losses at the margin—that is, to view any small decrease as a potentially larger loss and, therefore, to stop-out or quit, early. This is, of course, reminiscent of the helplessness model (Abramson et al., 1989; Abramson et al., 1978; Dweck, 1975; Dweck, Davidson, Nelson, & Enna, 1978). Also, given a view of scarcity, gains would be perceived as aberrations from the market norm and, therefore, would not be trusted. Consequently, pessimistic portfolios would imply that only a very large gain would be counted as a gain and that gains could be viewed as having gravity—that is, regressing toward the assumed low mean of the market. Thus, pessimistic portfolios would result in stopping out quickly with losses and "selling," or abandoning, gains rapidly.

Portfolio Theory of Depressive Pessimism

Leahy (1997a; 1997b; 1999; 2001) has proposed that depressed individuals utilize a negatively biased portfolio theory in considering their options. Consistent with other cognitive models, the portfolio theory model stresses the negative cognitive bias of depressive schemata. The portfolio theory of depression, based on investment models of decision-making, proposes that individual variation in risk-tolerance is related to the depressed individual's assumptions of scarcity and depletion, regret-orientation, criteria for defining losses and gains, rules for quitting, and information demands prior to making decisions. This model proposes that depressed individuals are risk-averse and tend to place less emphasis on maximizing gains and more emphasis on minimizing losses.

The portfolio theories of depressed and nondepressed individuals are displayed in Table 3.1. The depressed individual has a pessimistic port-

Table 3.1 Portfolio Theories of Depressed and Nondepressed Individuals

Portfolio Concern	*Depressed*	*Nondepressed*
Assets available	Few	Some/Many
Future earning potential	Low	Moderate/high
Market variation	Volatile	Low/predictable
Investment goal	Minimize loss	Maximize gain
Risk-orientation	Risk averse	Risk neutral/risk lover
Functional utility of gain	Low	Moderate/high
Replications of investment	None/few	Many
Duration of investment	Short term	Long term
Portfolio diversification	Low	High

folio theory and is expected to view himself or herself as having few current assets available, low future earning potential (few rewards forthcoming). In addition, the market is viewed as volatile and characterized by scarcity, the goal is to minimize loss rather than maximize gain, risk is avoided, gains have low hedonic value, there are few opportunities expected to repeat behavior to produce reward, there are high demands for an immediate return, and there is little diversification of rewards (see Leahy, 1997a). In contrast, the nondepressed individual, having a more optimistic portfolio theory, is expected to see himself or herself as having more current assets (present and future); the market is viewed as relatively predictable and as marked by sufficient reward, the goal is primarily to maximize gains rather than minimize losses, there are future opportunities to replicate behavior, there is a longer duration on the horizon, and potential rewards are diversified.

The depressed orientation toward loss is displayed in Table 3.2. Depressed individuals, according to the portfolio model, would be expected to have a low threshold for defining loss, to stop-out quickly, to view the market as characterized by scarcity. Purposeful behavior would be depleting, one loss would trigger other losses (cost-cascades), and there would be a greater tendency toward regret. The pessimistic depressive portfolio would view gains as requiring a high threshold for definition, low valuation and low probability of occurrence, and lack of control (see Table 3.3).

Our study was an attempt to investigate how depressed and nondepressed individuals perceive their current and future assets or resources and how these factors are related to their perception of decision-making. The portfolio theory of depressive decision-making leads to several predictions. These predictions are that nondepressed individuals would be more likely than depressed individuals to

Table 3.2 Loss Orientation in Depression

Loss Orientation	Example
Low threshold	The slightest decrease is viewed as a loss of significant proportion.
High "stop-loss" criteria	A small loss leads to termination of behavior. Consequently, the depressive gets stopped out early.
Scarcity assumptions	The world is viewed as having few opportunities for success. This is generalized to a zero-sum model of rewards for self and other.
Depletion assumptions	Losses are not simple inconveniences or temporary setbacks. They are viewed as permanently drawing down resources.
Cost-cascades	Losses are viewed as linked to an accelerating linear trend of further losses.
Temporal focus	The depressive takes a short-term focus, viewing his investments only in terms of how they will pay off or lose in the short-term.
Reversibility and revocability	Losses are viewed as irreversible and not compensated or offset by gains. Negative investments are irrevocable—he cannot see himself as able to pull out easily.
Regret orientation	Losses are followed by regret that one should have known better. His hindsight bias is focused on the assumption that he should have been able to make perfect decisions with limited information.

1. Have more current and future resources;
2. Be more focused on a strategy to maximize positives rather than minimize negatives;
3. Be more likely to take credit for their achievements;
4. Be more willing to take risks and be less likely to be cautious;
5. Be less likely to generalize negative outcomes;
6. Be more likely to perceive positive changes more easily and less likely to perceive negatives.

In addition, the investment model proposes that the willingness to take risks, or to be less cautious, will be related to the perception of the self as

1. Having many current and future resources;
2. Being able to predict and control outcomes;

Table 3.3 Gain Orientation in Depression

Gain Orientation	*Example*
High threshold for definition	A major change is required to be considered a gain.
Low valuation	Gains are viewed as having little hedonic or personal value. They are often discounted.
Low probability	Future gains are viewed as unlikely and unpredictable.
Immediate demand	There is little ability to delay gratification. The depressive is "myopic," tending to get caught in the immediate consequences of an action.
Contingency traps	Focusing on short-term frustration, the depressive will continue to avoid or engage in pointless behavior simply because it provides short-term reduction of anxiety.
Lack of control	Gains are viewed as noncontingent—out of the control of depressives. Although they believe that they can produce losses, they do not believe that they have control over producing gains.
Gravity of gains	Since the norm is negative, gains are viewed as self-correcting toward the negative—that is, they have gravity.

3. Taking a maximization rather than minimization strategy;
4. Taking credit for positive outcomes;
5. Being persistent, even in the face of a negative outcome;
6. More likely to generalize positives and less likely to generalize negatives;
7. Demanding less information before making a decision;
8. Less likely to need to build a consensus to make a change.

Participants

Participants consisted of 153 patients (59 males, 94 females) in a mental-health clinic in a large urban center. The mean age was 37.13 years ($sd = 9.59$) with the youngest and oldest participants at 19 and 62 years, respectively.

Measures

All patients were tested at the intake, when they were provided with a series of self-report measures, including the Beck Depression Inventory

(BDI) (Beck & Steer, 1987), Beck Anxiety Inventory (BAI) (Beck & Steer, 1990), Symptom Checklist 90–Revised (SCL-90–R; (Derogatis, 1977), Structured Clinical Inventory Diagnostic Scale-Axis II (SCID; Spitzer, Williams, Gibbon, & First, 1990), Locke-Wallace Marital Adjustment Scale (Locke & Wallace, 1959). In addition, the Decision Questionnaire (DQ), which was developed for this study, was administered. The Decision Questionnaire assesses 25 dimensions related to a variety of issues derived from the portfolio theory described above (see Appendix). Patients responded using a 6-point scale, ranging from (1) "very untrue of me" to (6) "very true of me." Only the data for the DQ and the BDI are reported here. The means, standard deviations, and dimensions of the DQ are shown in Table 3.4.

Correlations were calculated among all items on the DQ and for depression scores and two-tailed tests of significance were employed. These correlations are shown in Table 3.5. Two subjects did not complete the BDI, resulting in a final sample of 151 for the BDI. The mean score on the BDI for the sample was 16 ($sd = 11.96$), with no significant difference between males and females on this measure. Females were more likely than males to blame others if things don't work out ($p < .001$) and to claim that a small negative change often seems like a big negative change, while males were more likely than females to say, "when I achieve something, I do not enjoy it that much" ($p < .002$).

Depression and Portfolio Dimensions

The *depressive portfolio theory,* which is presumed to be risk-averse, was largely supported in the current study. As inspection of Table 3.5 indicates, more depressed patients utilized a negative portfolio theory, with depression significantly related to beliefs that current and future resources are scarce, outcomes are unpredictable and uncontrollable, there is a low utility for gains, and a high disutility for losses. Depressed individuals were more inclined to blame themselves for failures and less likely to internalize success. They generalized negatives, stopped-out early, had a high criterion for defining gains and a marginal criterion for defining losses, and they had a greater demand for certainty and consensus building before taking action. Depression was negatively associated with the goal of maximizing gains but was unrelated to the goal of minimizing losses, caution, blaming self for failure, and waiting a long time before making a decision. Less depressed individuals were more willing to take risks.

There was strong confirmation for the portfolio model of risk, which largely paralleled the findings for depression and portfolio concerns indi-

Table 3.4. Means and Standard Deviations of Decision Questionnaire Items

	N	Mean	SD
I have little to offer in a relationship	142	2.12	1.68
I have many skills and abilities at work or school	141	5.03	1.44
I have many sources of reward in my life	140	4.34	1.70
I expect that in the future my relationships will improve	142	4.65	1.53
I expect that in the future my skills and abilities will improve	142	4.73	1.36
I expect that in the future I will have many rewarding experiences	142	4.62	1.56
Most things in life seem unpredictable	142	3.97	1.34
I am usually able to make things turn out the way I'd like	142	3.75	1.48
I don't mind taking risks	142	3.89	1.57
I focus much of my time and energy on trying to achieve positive things	142	4.52	1.36
I spend much of my time and energy avoiding negative things	139	3.93	1.40
When I achieve something, I do not enjoy it that much	142	3.29	1.66
I take credit for my achievements	142	4.23	1.30
I blame myself if things don't work out	142	4.43	1.40
I blame others if things don't work out	142	2.77	1.44
I am very cautious	142	3.94	1.49
If I don't get what I want immediately, I doubt that I'll ever get it	141	2.87	1.57
I get discouraged more easily than others	141	3.37	1.77
If something doesn't work out, I tend to think other things won't work out	133	3.47	1.72
If something does work out, I think other things will work out	133	3.96	1.42
When things improve, I have a hard time seeing the improvement	133	3.35	1.60
A small negative change often seems like a big negative change	133	3.92	1.54
I need to know for certain that something will work out before I try it	133	3.02	1.67
I often wait a long time before I do things to help myself	132	3.56	1.75
I feel it is important for me to convince others or myself that my decisions are correct	133	3.69	1.81

Table 3.5 Correlations of BDI Score and Decision Questionnaire Items

	bdi	bai	I have little to offer in a relationship	I have many skills and abilities at work or school	I have many sources of reward in my life	I expect that in the future my relationships will improve	I expect that in the future my skills and abilities will improve	I expect that in the future I will have many rewarding experiences	Most things in life seem unpredictable	I am usually able to make things turn out the way I'd like	I don't mind taking risks
bai	.544[2]										
I have little to offer in a relationship	.387[2]	.115									
I have many skills and abilities at work or school	-.249[2]	-.142	-.146								
I have many sources of reward in my life	-.467[2]	-.171[1]	-.467[2]	.315[2]							
I expect that in the future my relationships will improve	-.490[2]	-.243[2]	-.487[2]	.275[2]	.544[2]						
I expect that in the future my skills and abilities will improve	-.455[2]	-.206[2]	-.372[2]	.353[2]	.474[2]	.790[2]					
I expect that in the future I will have many rewarding experiences	-.484[2]	-.206[2]	-.478[2]	.414[2]	.551[2]	.831[2]	.758[2]				
Most things in life seem unpredictable	.298[2]	.204[1]	.124	-.139	-.142	-.175[1]	-.098	-.215[1]			
I am usually able to make things turn out the way I'd like	-.382[2]	-.050	-.400[2]	.211[2]	.568[2]	.511[2]	.458[2]	.660[2]	-.251[2]		
I don't mind taking risks	-.255[2]	-.115	-.254[2]	.178[1]	.380[2]	.382[2]	.357[2]	.294[2]	-.170[1]	.259[2]	
I focus much of my time and energy on trying to achieve positive things	-.453[2]	-.205[1]	-.317[2]	.390[2]	.529[2]	.596[2]	.627[2]	.603[2]	-.093	.446[2]	.430[2]

Additional column headers (no data values in the displayed rows): I spend much of my time and energy avoiding negative things; When I achieve something, I do not enjoy it that much; I take credit for my achievements; I blame myself if things don't work out; I blame others if things don't work out; I am very cautious; If I don't get what I want immediately, I doubt that I'll ever get it; I get discouraged more easily than others; If something doesn't work out, I tend to think other things won't work out; If something does work out, I think other things will work out; When things improve, I have a hard time seeing the improvement; A small negative change often seems like a big negative change; I need to know for certain that something will work out before I try it; I often wait a long time before I do things to help myself

Table 3.5 (Continued)

	bdi	bai	I have little to offer in a relationship	I have many skills and abilities at work or school	I have many sources of reward in my life	I expect that in the future my relationships will improve	I expect that in the future my skills and abilities will improve	I expect that in the future I will have many rewarding experiences	Most things in life seem unpredictable	I am usually able to make things turn out the way I'd like	I don't mind taking risks	I focus much of my time and energy on trying to achieve positive things	I spend much of my time and energy avoiding negative things	When I achieve something, I do not enjoy it that much	I take credit for my achievements	I blame myself if things don't work out	I blame others if things don't work out	I am very cautious	If I don't get what I want immediately, I doubt that I'll ever get it	I get discouraged more easily than others	If something doesn't work out, I tend to think other things won't work out
I spend much of my time and energy avoiding negative things	-.069	-.106	-.097	.054	-.006	.105	.091	.071	-.064	-.086	-.053	.173[1]									
When I achieve something, I do not enjoy it that much	.371[2]	.081	.452[2]	-.122	-.418[2]	-.352[2]	-.300[2]	-.327[2]	.217[2]	-.321[2]	-.139	-.298[2]	-.053								
I take credit for my achievements	-.271[2]	-.201[1]	-.321[2]	.255[2]	.332[2]	.397[2]	.416[2]	.475[2]	-.305[2]	.388[2]	.350[2]	.234[2]	.037	-.284[2]							
I blame myself if things don't work out	.139	.012	.207[1]	-.094	-.060	-.045	.035	-.038	.259[2]	-.108	-.073	.012	.107	.169[1]	-.182[1]						
I blame others if things don't work out	.203[1]	.043	.179[1]	-.069	-.136	-.247[2]	-.188[1]	-.260[2]	.187[1]	-.138	-.005	-.152	-.022	-.058	.160	.032					
I am very cautious	-.043	-.140	.020	-.225[2]	-.112	-.053	-.159	-.098	.074	-.171[1]	-.329[2]	-.087	.351[2]	-.057	-.070	-.046	-.086				
If I don't get what I want immediately, I doubt that I'll ever get it	.319[2]	.257[2]	.347[2]	-.348[2]	-.451[2]	-.348[2]	-.350[2]	-.366[2]	.278[2]	-.343[2]	-.121	-.411[2]	-.076	.255[2]	-.387[2]	.128	.245[2]	.180[1]			
I get discouraged more easily than others	.460[2]	.273[2]	.419[2]	-.233[2]	-.434[2]	-.371[2]	-.309[2]	-.317[2]	.300[2]	-.396[2]	-.224[2]	-.341[2]	-.110	.374[2]	-.276[2]	.199[2]	.214[1]	.114	.686[2]		
If something doesn't work out, I tend to think other things won't work out	.394[2]	.187[1]	.393[2]	-.211[1]	-.491[2]	-.431[2]	-.414[2]	-.464[2]	.239[2]	-.578[2]	-.234[2]	-.234[2]	.235[2]	.371[2]	-.367[2]	.336[2]	.183[1]	.194[1]	.493[2]	.474[2]	
If something does work out, I think other things will work out	-.251[2]	-.141	-.292[2]	.024	.418[2]	.403[2]	.310[2]	.417[2]	-.140	.437[2]	.318[2]	.377[2]	.103	-.333[2]	.249[2]	.004	.139	-.122	-.145	-.285[2]	-.111

Table 3.5 (Continued)

	bdi	bai	I have little to offer in a relationship	I have many skills and abilities at work or school	I have many sources of reward in my life	I expect that in the future my relationships will improve	I expect that in the future my skills and abilities will improve	I expect that in the future I will have many rewarding experiences	Most things in life seem unpredictable	I am usually able to make things turn out the way I'd like	I don't mind taking risks	I focus much of my time and energy on trying to achieve positive things	I spend much of my time and energy avoiding negative things	When I achieve something, I do not enjoy it that much	I take credit for my achievements	I blame myself if things don't work out	I blame others if things don't work out	I am very cautious	If I don't get what I want immediately, I doubt that I'll ever get it	I get discouraged more easily than others	If something doesn't work out, I tend to think other things won't work out	If something does work out, I think other things will work out	When things improve, I have a hard time seeing the improvement	A small negative change often seems like a big negative change	I need to know for certain that something will work out before I try it	I often wait a long time before I do things to help myself
When things improve, I have a hard time seeing the improvement	.248[2]	.087	.311[2]	-.246[2]	-.367[2]	-.333[2]	-.258[2]	-.432[2]	.421[2]	-.369[2]	-.178[1]	-.217[1]	.060	.372[2]	-.419[1]	.186[1]	.133	.306[1]	.355[2]	.458[2]	-.302[2]					
A small negative change often seems like a big negative change	.365[2]	.156	.332[2]	-.131	-.271[1]	-.321[2]	-.163	-.306[2]	.355[2]	-.351[2]	-.222[1]	-.101	.157	.255[2]	.290[2]	.200[1]	.427[2]	.539[2]	-.189[1]	.610[2]						
I need to know for certain that something will work out before I try it	.200[1]	.094	.309[2]	.003	-.323[2]	-.223[1]	-.061	-.149	.291[2]	-.259[2]	-.530[2]	-.158	.065	.097	.267[2]	.149	.310[2]	.361[2]	.433[2]	.414[2]	-.211[1]	.394[2]	.505[2]			
I often wait a long time before I do things to help myself	.075	-.042	.300[2]	-.399[2]	-.329[2]	-.151	-.052	-.194[1]	.208[1]	-.270[2]	-.302[2]	-.348[2]	-.061	.263[2]	-.224[2]	.217[1]	.061	.172[1]	.407[2]	.445[2]	.266[2]	.312[2]	.248[2]	.404[2]		
I feel it is important for me to convince others or myself that my decisions are correct	.323[2]	.030	.282[2]	.006	-.268[2]	-.138	-.043	-.207[1]	.324[2]	-.119	-.341[2]	-.190[1]	.074	.270[2]	-.101	.129	.146	.095	.078	.214[1]	.193[1]	.254[2]	.313[2]	.358[2]	.293[2]	

[1] Correlation is significant at p < .05 (2-tailed tests).
[2] Correlation is significant at p < .01 (2-tailed tests).

cated above. Risk-aversion was associated with almost all of the deci-
sion-dimensions. The only exceptions to the portfolio model of risk taking was that willingness to take a risk was unrelated to avoiding negatives,
enjoying a positive gain, blaming self or others for negative outcomes, or
doubting that one will achieve a positive after failing to achieve a goal.
Greater tolerance of risk was related to perception of more abundant
current and future resources, the ability to predict and control outcomes,
focus on maximizing positives, viewing the self as less cautious, less
likely to get discouraged, less likely to generalize negatives, more likely
to generalize positives, more likely to define a marginal gain as a positive, less likely to define a marginal loss as a negative, lower demands for
certainty and consensus building, and less procrastination.

To examine the structure of the general portfolio dimensions, a prin-
cipal components factor analysis was performed utilizing a varimax rota-
tion. Four factors emerged that accounted for 53.6% of the total variance.
The rotated factors are shown in Table 3.6. Factor I, which accounted for
31% of the variance, was a general efficacy factor, including most of the
dimensions of the portfolio model. Factor II, accounting for 9.8% of the
variance, may be described as a discouragement factor. Factor III, accounting for 6.9% of the variance, reflected an unpredictability dimension. Factor IV, accounting for 5.8% of the variance, reflected
risk-aversion. Factor scores were computed for these first four factors
and these scores were correlated with scores on the BDI. There were
significant correlations between depression and three factors, such that
general efficacy ($r = -.406$, $p < .01$), discouragement ($r = .192$, $p < .05$),
and risk aversion ($r = .220$, $p < .05$) were related to depression in a
manner consistent with the portfolio theory.

Relationships Between Portfolio Dimensions

There were numerous significant relationships within the various dimensions of the portfolio model. For example, the following questions may
be viewed as reflective of a belief in availability of current resources and
rewards: " I have little to offer in a relationship," "I have many skills and
abilities at work or school," and "I have many sources of reward in my
life," "I have little to offer in a relationship," " I have many skills and
abilities at work or school," "I have many sources of reward in my life."
The following may be considered as future resources and rewards: "I
expect that in the future my relationships will improve," "I expect that in
the future my skills and abilities will improve," and "I expect that in the
future I will have many rewarding experiences." Examining the correla-

Table 3.6 Rotated Component Matrix for Decision Questionnaire

	Rotated Factors			
	I			IV
	General	II	III	Risk-
DQ Item	Efficacy	Discouragement	Unpredictability	Aversion
I have little to offer in a relationship	-.467			
I have many sources of reward in my life	.515			
I expect that in the future my relationships will improve	.861			
I expect that in the future my skills and abilities will improve	.884			
I expect that in the future I will have many rewarding experiences	.889			
Most things in life seem unpredictable			.781	
I am usually able to make things turn out the way I'd like	.563			
I don't mind taking risks				-.782
I focus much of my time and energy on trying to achieve positive things	.671			
I take credit for my achievements			-.514	
If I don't get what I want immediately, I doubt that I'll ever get it		.825		
I get discouraged more easily than others		.799		
If something doesn't work out, I tend to think other things won't work out		.483		
If something does work out, I think other things will work out	.464			
When things improve, I have a hard time seeing the improvement			.699	

Table 3.6 *(Continued)*

	Rotated Factors			
	I	II	III	IV
	General			Risk-
DQ Item	Efficacy	Discouragement	Unpredictability	Aversion
A small negative change often seems like a big negative change		.455	.580	
I need to know for certain that something will work out before I try it		.488		.656
I feel it is important for me to convince others or myself that my decisions are correct				.613

tions of current resources and rewards indicates that these dimensions were generally associated with viewing life as predictable, controllable, risk accepting, focusing on maximizing positives, enjoying positives, taking credit for achievements, not giving up easily, not discouraged, not generalizing negatives, generalizing positives, easily noticing a positive change, not magnifying a negative change, low needs for certainty, less procrastination, and less need to build a consensus. A similar pattern of correlations was found for future resources and rewards, with the additional finding that patients who anticipated future resources were less likely to blame others if things do not work out.

The portfolio model stresses the importance of maximizing gains or growth potential as an incentive. Individuals who emphasized maximizing positives or gains viewed themselves as having current and future resources, able to make things turn out the way they wanted them to, more likely to emphasize minimizing losses, enjoying positives, taking credit for achievements, not giving up easily, not discouraged, not generalizing negatives, generalizing positives, easily noticing a positive change, low needs for certainty, less procrastination, and less need to build a consensus. Maximizing positives was unrelated to viewing life as unpredictable, blaming self for negative outcomes, caution, and viewing a small negative change as a big negative change.

Minimizing negatives was not related to most of the portfolio dimensions. The only dimensions significantly related to minimizing negatives were more emphasis on maximizing positives, greater caution, generalizing negative outcome, and viewing a small negative outcome as a big negative outcome. Predictability and control are important factors in considering decisions. Individuals who viewed life as unpredictable were less likely to believe the following: things would turn out the way they wanted them to, willing to take a risk, enjoy things that they achieved, and take credit for their achievements. These individuals were less likely to believe that they had skills and abilities, many sources of rewards in life, and that their relationships would improve. They were more likely to blame themselves and others for failures, doubt that they would get something if they did not achieve it immediately, get discouraged easily, generalize negatives, have a hard time seeing improvements when things get better, view a small negative as a big negative change, need to know for certain, wait a long time to help themselves, and need to convince others and self before taking action. Thus, predictability was generally related to a negative portfolio theory.

The belief that one can make things turn out in the future was related to most portfolio dimensions. These individuals were more likely to take risks, focus on achieving positive things, enjoy what they achieved, take credit for their achievements, generalize positives, and see positives easily. They were also more likely to believe that they have many skills and a lot to offer in a relationship, to find many sources of reward, and to expect that their relationships and abilities will improve and that they will have many rewarding experiences. A belief in being able to make things work out was related to lower scores on caution, giving up easily, discouragement, generalizing negatives, demands for information, need to convince others, and waiting. This sense of self-efficacy—being able to make things work out—was a central component of the positive portfolio model. The need to know for certain that something will work out "before I try it" was related to all of the dimensions *except* the belief that one had many skills and abilities at work and school or that these abilities will improve and to the tendency to avoid negatives and enjoying positives.

Risk-Taking and Portfolio Concerns

The investment model proposes several general and specific predictions about how individuals calculate their willingness to take risks or to perceive themselves as cautious (or risk-averse). First, generally consistent with the model, is the fact that the willingness to take risks was related to the perception of having many current and future resources. Specifically, willingness to take risks was associated with the perception that one had something to offer in a relationship, many sources of rewards in life, and the belief that future relationships, work skills, and rewards would improve. Second, risk taking was related to the self's perception of predictability and control over outcomes. Third, there was good evidence for risk taking related to the desire to achieve positive outcomes, but not for the desire to avoid negative outcomes. Fourth, consistent with the model, the willingness to take risks was related to the added hedonistic value of enjoying the achievement and taking credit for achievements. However, not consistent with the model, risk taking was not related to the tendency to blame the self for negative outcomes. Fifth, there was partial support for risk taking related to persistence: Greater willingness to take a risk was related to being less discouraged but was only marginally related to the tendency to reject the statement, "If I don't get what I want immediately, I doubt that I'll ever get it" ($p < .07$).

Sixth, individuals who were more willing to take risks were more likely to generalize positives and less likely to generalize negatives. Seventh, these individuals demanded less information before making a decision and were less likely to need to build a consensus to make a change. Eighth, the analysis of the data for the perception of the self as cautious only partially replicated the findings for the perception of the self as willing to take a risk. Interestingly, the willingness to take a risk and the perception that one is very cautious, was not *robustly* correlated (i.e., $r = -.329$, $p < .001$)—certainly, related to one another but not reducible to each other. Although this relationship is statistically significant, one might have expected logically that risk and caution are tapping the same dimensions. They are not. In fact, the perception of the self as cautious was not significantly related to depression.

Except for one item that indicated that cautious individuals were less likely to believe that they had many skills in work or school, caution was unrelated to the perception of current positive resources. Caution was related to a tendency to view the self as less able to "make things turn out the way I'd like, to "spend much of my time and energy avoiding negative things," and to blaming others "if things don't work out." In addition, caution was related to the following beliefs: "If I don't get what I want immediately, I doubt that I'll ever get it," "if something doesn't work out, I tend to think that other things won't work out," and the view that a small negative change seems like a big negative change. Not surprisingly, caution was related to the need to know for certain that something will work out before trying it and the tendency to wait a long time before trying to do things to help the self. In summary, caution appeared to be more related to the perceived inability to control outcomes, externalizing blame, attempts to minimize negatives, giving up easily, generalizing negatives, and to general inhibition.

Risk taking and caution might appear to us, if we take a logical analysis, as reflecting the same construct. However, the empirical data do not support the equivalence of these factors. As expected, risk-taking was related to a range of portfolio concerns, whereas caution was unrelated to many of these portfolio concerns. A preliminary interpretation of this difference is that risk taking is an appetitive strategy, whereas caution is a defensive strategy. One possibility is that individuals, when asked about their willingness to take risks, consider the current resources that they have and their future "earning" potential. They focus on how a risk will produce a positive outcome. However, when individuals think about their caution, they consider how much they can control outcomes and how likely they will be to avoid negatives. Caution calls for a defensive strategy of thinking—one in which the individual wonders, "How can it go wrong?" Moreover, caution may mean different things to different people. For some, caution may reflect being prudent and planful, while for others it may mean inhibition and fear.

CONCLUSIONS

Our study offers general support for a model of depressive decision making based on modern portfolio theory. First, a generally pessimistic portfolio theory is supported by the finding that 21 of the 25 dimensions were significantly related to depression. Moreover, the factor analysis suggests that depression is related to 3 factors that reflect lower self-efficacy, discouragement, and risk-aversion. Second, within the dimensions of the portfolio theory there were significant relationships across responses, suggesting that individuals consider numerous factors simultaneously in contemplating change and investment of resources.

Third, this study also offers support for a model of risk taking based on the individual's consideration of concerns identified in portfolio theory. Of 24 dimensions, 19 were significantly related to willingness to take risks. Risk tolerance was related to the perception of higher self-efficacy in the present and future, emphasis on maximization strategy, not stopping out quickly, more internal attribution for success, low generalization of failure, high generalization of success, lower information demands, and lower need for consensus building. Some of these dimensions are related to the attributional models of learned helplessness and hopelessness—such as the emphasis on internal attribution and generalization for success (Abramson et al., 1978; Alloy et al., 1988). However, the current model substantially augments the attributional and other cognitive models by emphasizing perception of current resources, quitting strategies, criteria for delta change up and down, information demands, and consensus building.

If we return to Table 3.1, which depicts the hypothesized portfolio theories of depressed and nondepressed individuals, we find that the data from this study offer general support for the model. More depressed individuals did believe that they had fewer current and future assets, that the "market" is volatile (unpredictable), that they were less likely to have maximization as a goal (but, contrary to prediction, minimizing losses was not their goal). They were more risk-averse, they had less utility (pleasure and pride) in gains, they were less likely to replicate behavior (e.g., they gave up more easily), they were less likely to stay a longer duration, and they believed that had low diversification (variety of resources).

It is important to note that one factor, self-efficacy, accounted for a substantial amount of variance in the questionnaire. This may be because more items on the questionnaire tapped self-efficacy than any other dimension. In addition, it may be possible that self-efficacy may not only be a baseline of how one feels about the ability to absorb a loss, but it also may be indicative of the perception of producing positive outcomes. Thus, the perception of risk may differ for individuals high and low in self-efficacy, such that the subjective risk may not be the same. Risk may be considered an indicator of subjective probabilities of outcomes, not objective circumstances.

The current study has several limitations. First, contrary to the portfolio model, the desire to minimize negatives and the tendency to be cautious were not significantly related to depression. Although the desire to maximize gains was related to both depression and risk taking, minimization of negatives was unrelated to these variables. It may be that the perception of minimizing negatives and caution may mean different things to different people. Some individuals may view either avoiding negatives as maximizing positives or being risk averse. In other words, there may be contradictory meanings for this for different people. Perhaps a better way of testing this would be to ask, "Would you be willing to accept some negative outcomes in order to have a chance to achieve a positive outcome?" Of course, the objection to this rephrasing is that it appears to be reducible to the meaning of risk, thus leading to a tautological test of the portfolio model. Caution was related to risk-aversion but unrelated to depression. Again, it may be that some individuals interpret caution differently from others. For example, some people may view caution as careful and productive, whereas others may view caution as being unwilling to expose oneself to potential costs, irrespective of possibilities of positives.

A second set of limitations of this study is the absence of a behavioral index of risk taking. In the current investigation, we relied on the individual's report of risk taking, rather than measuring their actual behavior. Future research could explore the validity of this issue. Third, the current study assessed perceptions of self-efficacy, without assessing actual self-efficacy. Thus, it is difficult to know if the individual's perception of low self-efficacy is accurate and, therefore, that it may represent a valid reason for risk-aversion. The clinician would need to examine whether the goal of therapy is to increase self-efficacy (for example, train the individual in social skills and assertion) or modify the self-perception of efficacy—or, indeed, do both). Fourth, the current study does not allow causal interpretations for these dimensions. For example, we cannot determine from these data if lower self-efficacy leads to greater information demands or whether greater information demands lead to lower self-efficacy. Similarly, it could be that risk-aversion results in lowered self-efficacy. Sequential time-sampling would allow us to assess the causal links among these variables.

Despite these possible limitations, the current study suggests substantial support for the portfolio model of depressive decision-making. As Leahy (2001) has suggested, each of these dimensions in decision making provides a possible point for intervention in clinical practice. Similar to Beck's (Beck et al., 1979) model of depression, the current model provides a detailed description of how depressed individuals may think about mundane issues that may make them vulnerable to maintaining their depression.

APPENDIX

Decision Questionnaire

Please indicate *how you generally feel* using the scale below. Place the number you chose in the space provided for each statement. There are no right or wrong answers

Scale: 1 = Very untrue of me   4 = Slightly true of me
        2 = Somewhat untrue of me   5 = Somewhat true of me
        3 = Slightly untrue of me   6 = Very true of me

1. _____ I have little to offer in a relationship.
         ASSETS-RELATIONSHIP
2. _____ I have a lot of skills and abilities at work or school.
         ASSETS-WORK
3. _____ I have many sources of reward in my life.
         ASSETS-GENERAL

4. ____ I expect that in the future my relationships will improve.
   FUTURE-ASSETS-RELATIONSHIP
5. ____ I expect that in the future my skills and abilities will improve.
   FUTURE-ASSETS-WORK
6. ____ I expect that in the future I will have many rewarding experiences.
   FUTURE-ASSETS-GENERAL
7. ____ Most things in life seem unpredictable.
   PREDICTABILITY
8. ____ I am usually able to make things turn out the way I'd like them to.
   CONTROL
9. ____ I don't mind taking risks.
   RISK PREFERENCE
10. ____ I focus a lot of my energy and drive at trying to achieve positive things.
    MAXIMIZATION OF GAIN
11. ____ I focus a lot of my energy and time avoiding negative things.
    MINIMIZATION OF LOSS
12. ____ When I achieve something, I do not enjoy it that much.
    HEDONIC VALUE
13. ____ I take credit for things I do achieve.
    POSITIVE PERSONAL ATTRIBUTION
14. ____ I blame myself if things don't work out.
    NEGATIVE PERSONAL ATTRIBUTION
15. ____ I blame others if things don't work out.
    NEGATIVE EXTERNAL ATTRIBUTION
16. ____ I am very cautious.
    CAUTION-INHIBITION
17. ____ If I don't get what I want immediately, I doubt that I'll ever get it.
    FUTURE NEGATIVE
18. ____ I get discouraged more easily than others do.
    STOP OUT EARLY
19. ____ If something *doesn't* work out, I tend to think other things *won't* work out.
    GENERALIZED NEGATIVE
20. ____ If something *does* work out, I think other things *will* work out.
    GENERALIZED POSITIVE

21. _____ Even when things improve, I have a hard time seeing the improvement.
    HIGH THRESHOLD FOR GAIN
22. _____ A small *negative* change often seems like a big negative change.
    LOW THRESHOLD FOR LOSS
23. _____ I need to know for certain that something will work out before I try it.
    CERTAINTY DEMANDS
24. _____ I often wait a long time before I do things to help myself.
    PROCRASTINATION
25. _____ I feel it is important for me to convince others or myself that my decisions are correct.
    CONSENSUS SEEKING

CHAPTER 4

Decision-Making and Personality Disorders

The cognitive model of personality disorders has emphasized the thematic content of personal schemas—that is, habitual patterns or biases in viewing the self and others. For example, Beck and Freeman (1990) propose that the avoidant personality views the self as vulnerable to depreciation and rejection, and views others as critical and demeaning. According to this model, avoidant individuals utilize strategies to either avoid or compensate for their schematic vulnerability. For example, persons with avoidant characteristics tend to avoid evaluative situations and avoid unpleasant thoughts. In addition, Millon and his colleagues (Davis & Millon, 1999; Millon, Davis, Millon, Escovar, & Meagher, 2000) maintain that avoidant individuals compensate for a lack of interpersonal rewards by developing a rich fantasy life. A similar conceptual model has been advanced by Young (1990), who argued that personality might be understood as the persistence of early maladaptive schemas for which the individual utilizes avoidant, compensatory, and schema-maintaining strategies. Thus, individuals who view themselves as defective may avoid situations that are challenging or that could lead to rejection, could compensate by deferring to others, or might pursue experiences that maintain the schema, such as self-defeating relationships.

Review of Portfolio Theory

I have advanced a model of decision-making based on how individuals compute their current and future resources, their ability to tolerate risk, their regret orientation, and their perception that they can replicate be-

haviors with a long duration (Leahy, 1997, 1999, 2001). Pessimistic decision-making is based on a "portfolio theory." Portfolio theory suggests
that individuals with a pessimistic portfolio believe that they have low
current and future resources, low ability to predict and control outcomes,
low utility for gains and high disutility for losses, high stop-loss rules for
quitting early, high regret, and high demands for information. In contrast,
an optimistic "portfolio" includes the assumption that one has considerable current and future resources, considerable ability to predict and
control outcomes, high value for positives, low disutility or suffering for
losses, the ability to tolerate loss, and low demands for information.
Individuals with manic, or overly optimistic and grandiose portfolio theories, tend to overestimate current and future resources, predictability,
control, and hedonic value, while underestimating potential costs and
risks (Leahy, 1997, 1999, 2001).

Portfolio theory of decision-making may help us expand our understanding of the phenomenology of different personality disorders. This
theoretical model of decision-making proposes that individuals differ in
their assessment of current and future resources in 5 ways: (1) in interpersonal and task-oriented domains, (2) in estimates of predictability and
control, (3) in perceived utility of gains and losses and how they are
defined, (4) in tolerance of risk, and (5) in demand for information before making decisions. Evidence of the relationship between these various dimensions and depression was found in a recent study (Leahy, 2001).
A pessimistic portfolio theory was supported by the finding that, of the
25 dimensions of decision making, 21 were significantly related to depression and 19 were significantly associated with risk-aversion.

Portfolio Theory and Personality Disorders

Decision-making models may be especially important in understanding
the different personality disorders. Some individuals with personality
disorders are assumed to be highly avoidant and indecisive, others are
viewed as impulsive, others may require considerable information prior
to making a decision, and others may not enjoy the benefits of rewards.
For example, persons with avoidant personality disorder (APD) are characterized by low self-esteem, sensitivity to rejection, and demands for
guarantees before entering into a relationship. The portfolio-decision-
making model suggests that these individuals will be low in current and
future self-efficacy, have high information demands before making a
decision to change, high stop-loss criteria (i.e., quitting early), internal-
ization of negatives, and lack of generalization of positives.

Dependent personality disorder (DPD) is characterized by the reliance on others for decisions and resources as a reflection of lower self-efficacy. Consequently, persons with DPD have a tendency to stay in bad situations or relationships simply to maintain security and to avoid abandonment. These individuals are also seen as risk-averse and are likely to rely on others for important decisions. As a corollary of their dependency, they are often inclined to blame others when things do not work out.

Individuals with obsessive-compulsive personality disorder (OCPD) tend to have relatively intact self-efficacy, but are viewed as indecisive and risk-averse. Typically, they require considerable information before making a decision. Self-defeating individuals often reject positive outcomes, blame others for their failures, and quit early. These individuals might be reasonably expected to have low self-efficacy.

Paranoid personality disorder (PPD) is characterized by distrust and blame of others, which has been viewed as symptomatic of either inflated self-esteem or as a defensive avoidance of low self-esteem (Zigler & Glick, 1984, 1988). Zigler and Glick have offered a model of paranoia that stressed the dynamics of self-protective externalization of blame to avoid self-criticism. According to Zigler and Glick's model, individuals with paranoid personalities are more likely to blame others if things do not work out and are expected to blame themselves as well. They could be characterized by a pessimistic model of decision-making that is, low self-efficacy, high information demands, low generalization of success, and high generalization of failure.

Persons with histrionic personality disorder (HPD) are characterized by their lack of self-awareness or insight, their need to impress others, and their impulsivity. Thus, these individuals are more likely to be risk-takers, or even risk-lovers, unlike the other personalities described here.

Individuals with narcissistic personality disorder (NPD) are characterized by their lack of empathy and their grandiose sense of themselves, often devaluing or blaming others for their problems. However, psychodynamic models of narcissism (Kernberg, 1974; 1975; 1998a; 1998b) emphasize the emptiness of the interior lives of these individuals, such that they may mask their privately experienced low self-esteem with grandiose public displays of their worthiness. Thus, evaluation of how persons with NPD regard their decision-making processes may cast some light on our understanding of their perceptions of self-change and self-efficacy. A similar model has been advanced as a schema-focused model by Young and Flanagan (1998), suggesting that those with narcissistic personalities use grandiosity to protect against their experience of "injured" or "defective" aspects of the self. In the present study, I investigated the perception of self-efficacy and decision processes in patients who varied in narcissistic characteristics.

Borderline Personality Disorder (BPD) is characterized by unstable affect, feelings of emptiness, chaotic interpersonal experiences, self-destructive behavior, and self-loathing. Individuals with BPD can be risk-averse or risk-seekers, depending on their volatile moods. However, it is generally expected that they possess low self-efficacy, a tendency to blame others, a general sense of helplessness and hopelessness, and a high degree of procrastination. Linehan's (1993) dialectical-behavioral model of BPD emphasizes the multiple facets of the borderline personality (e.g., relentless crises, feelings of emptiness, difficulty modulating affect, hopelessness, and anger). The current study on decision processes allow us to examine how these factors may be reflected in portfolio theories or decision strategies.

Finally, antisocial personality disorder (APD) is characterized by a lack of concern for the rights of others as well as difficulty assessing negative outcomes. Individuals diagnosed with APD, lacking empathy, often present with a history of cruelty toward others and violations of the law. Their self-esteem may remain intact, since their standards of conduct for themselves leave little capacity for guilt. These individuals generally have low frustration tolerance, leading them to give up early, and they are expected to blame others. Given their impulsive nature, we would expect higher risk-taking behavior from these individuals.

METHOD

In order to explore the relationship between personality disorders and the decision making model of portfolio theory, 101 adult patients in a private practice clinic were asked to complete a variety of self-report forms including the Beck Depression Inventory (BDI; Beck & Steer, 1987), Beck Anxiety Inventory (BAI; Beck & Steer, 1990), Symptom Checklist–90–revised (SCL–90–R; Derogatis, 1977), Locke Wallace Marital Adjustment Test (Locke & Wallace, 1959), and a 25 item Decision Questionnaire (Leahy, 2001). The Structured Clinical Interview for DSM–III–R (SCID–II; Spitzer, Williams, Gibbon, & First, 1990) was administered by staff psychologists. The SCID–II was used as a measure of personality disorder. Rather than classify individuals categorically as avoidant, dependent, or other personality disorders, it was decided to score individuals dimensionally on each scale. The rationale was that many individuals often simultaneously score high on several personality disorders (Livesley, 1998; Livesley, Schroeder, Jackson, & Jang, 1994; Millon et al., 2000).

There is no á priori basis on which to decide that one categorization of a personality disorder should take precedence over another. There is also little rationale for using an arbitrary cut-off point for a personality disorder, since individual variation would be lost in such a categorical system. By using a dimensional rather than categorical approach, more of the data can be utilized, with an evaluation of the same individual along a variety of personality dimensions. However, one consequence of using a dimensional scoring system is the necessity of recognizing that we are describing variations in a personality trait or style and not fixed categories of individuals.

RESULTS AND ANALYTIC COMMENTARY

Individual correlations were calculated for scores on each personality disorder on the SCID–II and the 25 dimensions of the Decision Questionnaire that assesses the various portfolio dimensions described earlier. The means and standard deviations for the scores on the different personality disorders are shown in Table 4.1 and the correlations between scores on the personality dimensions and the decision questionnaire dimensions are shown in Table 4.2. In addition, factor scores were derived for the 25

Table 4.1 Means and Standard Deviations of the SCID-II Personality Dimensions

Personality Dimension	Mean	Standard Deviation
Avoidant	2.98	2.12
Dependent	2.42	1.92
Obsessive Compulsive	4.79	2.02
Passive-Aggressive	2.65	2.09
Self-Defeating	3.64	2.57
Paranoid	2.45	1.73
Schizoid	1.35	1.12
Schizotypal	1.37	1.26
Histrionic	1.97	1.63
Narcissistic	4.56	2.59
Borderline	4.02	2.60
Antisocial	.88	1.36

Note: N = 101.

Table 4.2 Correlation Matrix of Decision-Making Dimensions and Personality Disorders

	Avoidant	Dependent	Obsessive Compulsive	Passive-Aggressive	Self-Defeating	Paranoid	Schizoid	Schizotypal	Histrionic	Narcissistic	Borderline	Antisocial
I have little to offer in a relationship	.339**	.290**	.136	.181	.405**	.240*	.137	.131	-.004	.161	.275**	.132
I have many skills and abilities at work or school	-.188	-.306**	-.033	-.072	-.302**	-.166	-.228*	-.223*	-.172	.020	-.228*	-.181
I have many sources of reward in my life	-.338**	-.349**	-.173	-.149	-.353**	-.280**	-.056	-.020	-.150	-.077	-.261*	.015
I expect that in the future my relationships will improve	-.191	-.416**	.035	-.071	-.306**	-.150	-.123	-.159	.012	.109	-.032	-.030
I expect that in the future my skills and abilities will improve	-.217*	-.295**	.019	-.132	-.231*	-.072	-.021	-.122	.046	.110	.046	.049
I expect that in the future I will have many rewarding experiences	-.276**	-.425**	.059	.006	-.286**	-.114	-.080	-.084	.020	.098	-.142	-.035
Most things in life seem unpredictable	.294**	.295**	-.070	.225*	.368**	.322**	.156	-.116	.150	.281**	.329**	.195

Table 4.2 *(Continued)*

	Avoidant	Dependent	Obsessive Compulsive	Passive-Aggressive	Self-Defeating	Paranoid	Schizoid	Schizotypal	Histrionic	Narcissistic	Borderline	Antisocial
I am usually able to make things turn out the way I'd like	-.362**	-.255*	.091	-.047	-.236*	-.183	.020	-.033	.013	-.009	-.325**	.006
I don't mind taking risks	-.117	-.233*	-.060	-.177	-.077	.092	.242*	.089	.216*	.022	.066	.195
I focus much of my time and energy on trying to achieve positive things	-.208*	-.308**	-.103	-.060	-.216*	-.127	-.040	-.057	-.158	.086	-.225*	-.123
I spend much of my time and energy avoiding negative things	.206	.107	.140	.103	.020	.061	-.085	-.152	.063	.305**	-.005	-.127
When I achieve something, I do not enjoy it that much	.493**	.123	.252*	.168	.501**	.366**	.138	.102	.239*	.245*	.339**	.133
I take credit for my achievements	-.251*	-.317**	.067	-.092	-.526**	-.106	-.150	-.237*	-.006	-.114	-.067	.053
I blame myself if things don't work out	.206	.209*	.121	.138	.341**	.285**	.088	-.095	.054	.380**	.391**	-.028

Table 4.2 *(Continued)*

	Avoidant	Dependent	Obsessive Compulsive	Passive-Aggressive	Self-Defeating	Paranoid	Schizoid	Schizotypal	Histrionic	Narcissistic	Borderline	Antisocial
I blame others if things don't work out	.093	.260*	.008	-.103	.034	.187	.092	.080	.098	-.006	.078	.201
I am very cautious	.157	.131	.246*	.189	.080	-.038	-.113	-.057	-.026	.064	-.059	-.077
If I don't get what I want immediately, I doubt that I'll ever get it	.345**	.513**	-.049	.107	.418**	.282**	.198	.285**	.260*	.097	.276**	.156
I get discouraged more easily than others do	.453**	.350**	-.032	.192	.371**	.476**	.208	.212*	.246*	.191	.404**	.330**
If something doesn't work out, I tend to think other things won't work out	.594**	.403**	.132	.338**	.484**	.343**	-.060	.015	.001	.327**	.277*	-.064
If something does work out, I think other things will work out	-.233*	-.013	.101	-.099	-.189	-.063	.031	-.156	-.079	.061	-.179	.112

Table 4.2 (*Continued*)

	Avoidant	Dependent	Obsessive Compulsive	Passive-Aggressive	Self-Defeating	Paranoid	Schizoid	Schizotypal	Histrionic	Narcissistic	Borderline	Antisocial
When things improve, I have a hard time seeing the improvement	.443**	.198	.154	.138	.513**	.267*	.154	.180	.245*	.166	.260*	-.067
A small negative change often seems like a big negative change	.411**	.219*	.069	.104	.300***	.337**	.134	.005	.211	.150	.228*	.014
I need to know for certain that something will work out before I try it	.368**	.098	.256*	.197	.183	.082	-.175	-.044	.045	.239*	.159	-.151
I often wait a long time before I do things to help myself	.294**	.307**	.220*	.209	.473**	.226*	.123	.344**	.268*	.237*	.505**	.285**
I feel it is important for me to convince others or myself that my decisions are correct	.225*	.337**	.388**	.116	.233*	.097-	.168	-.169	.100	.305**	.086	-.075

Note. Two-tail tests. *$p < .05$. **$p < .01$

decision-making dimensions, which yielded four factors—Self-efficacy, Discouragement, Unpredictability, and Risk Aversion. For the sake of brevity, I will limit my discussion to several personality disorders, excluding discussion of the data on schizoid, schizotypal, passive-aggressive, and antisocial personality characteristics.

Avoidant, Dependent, and Self-Defeating Personality Disorders

According to Millon and others (Davis & Millon, 1999; Millon et al., 2000), avoidant individuals are characterized by low self-esteem, sensitivity to rejection, and caution when approaching others. Dependent individuals also are expected to have low self-esteem, but their focus is on concerns regarding abandonment, presumably because they believe that they cannot provide for their own needs. Self-defeating personalities also are expected to have low self-esteem, to view rewards as unsatisfying and to become anxious when things improve. We examined some of these issues by correlating scores on the SCID–II, using it as a dimensional scale rather than as a categorical measure. Thus, patients could score relatively higher or lower on each of the personality scales for the DSM–III–R.

Decision dimensions were significantly correlated with avoidant, dependent and self-defeating personality. Of 25 dimensions, 18 were correlated for avoidant and dependent scales, and 19 of 25 decision dimensions were correlated for self-defeating personality characteristics. Substantial similarities between these 3 personality disorders were observed in the correlation matrix between the decision-making dimensions and personality disorders (see Table 4.2). Individuals in these groups generally believed that they had few resources in current and future relationships, at work or in personal relationships. All believed that they had little ability to control and predict outcomes. Dependent Personality Disorder and self-defeating personality type were related to self-blaming if things did not work out. All 3 personality types were less likely to take credit for positives, all predicted that negatives would continue and be generalized, and all quit early. Individuals with Avoidant Personality Disorder and self-defeating personalities tended to have a high threshold for defining positives and a low threshold for defining negatives. They procrastinated and felt the need to build consensus before making decisions. Examination of the relationship between the factor scores and these personality dimensions suggested that Avoidant and Dependent Personality Disorders are related to Discouragement ($r = .373$, $p < .01$; $r = .245$, $p < .05$, respectively), and Unpredictability ($r = .333$, $p < .01$; r $= .229$, $p < .05$, respectively). Self-defeating personality type was also related to Discouragement ($r = .343$, $p < .01$) and Unpredictability ($r = .422$, $p < .01$).

It was interesting to observe how the avoidant and dependent personalities differed. Dependency was related to risk-aversion, but avoidance was not related to risk. Those with avoidant personality characteristics also reported that they did not derive much pleasure from positive events, and were less likely to generalize positives when they did occur. The reliance that persons with Dependent Personality Disorder have on others was supported by the finding that they are more likely to blame others if things do not work out. Those with Avoidant Personality Disorder reported that they demand more information before making decisions—a finding consistent with the meaning of "avoidance." Self-defeating personality type was associated with being less likely to maximize positives, less likely to generalize positives when they did occur, and high demands for information.

These findings are consistent with a schematic model (Beck & Freeman, 1990), which suggests that people with dependent and avoidant personality characteristics view themselves as incompetent and weak, respectively. These individuals utilize a pessimistic portfolio that is based on their low estimation of current and future rewards, low perceived personal efficacy, and a hesitant style of decision-making.

Obsessive-Compulsive Personality Disorder

Individuals with OCPD were assumed to have relatively intact self-esteem, but to have difficulty making decisions. OCPD was not significantly related to most of the decision dimensions, except for those associated with caution, waiting, and information demands. OCPD was related to deriving little pleasure from positives. OCPD was significantly related to the decision factor, Risk-Aversion ($r = .284$, $p < .01$). These data support the view that persons with OCPD inhibit their impulsivity and have higher demands or requirements for information before making decisions. However, the current study did not support Millon and his colleagues' (2000) view that these individuals are inclined to blame themselves or others because of their relatively greater emphasis on rules and responsibility. The data reported here imply that individuals with OCPD demonstrate their conscientiousness by demanding more information, and perhaps this is a manifestation of their reassurance-seeking tendencies. These data suggest that OCPD individuals are better characterized by self-doubt, caution, and demands for information than by rule-seeking attitudes.

Paranoid Personality Disorder

The cognitive model of paranoia stresses the moralistic and control dimensions of the paranoid personality. Zigler and Glick's (Zigler & Glick, 1984; 1988) model of paranoia views the paranoid style of distrust and grandiosity as a cognitive defense against feeling low self-esteem and the perception that they will be rejected and fail. PPD was related to viewing oneself as having few positive resources in current relationships and few resources in general. In addition, PPD was related to low predictability, blaming oneself, receiving low pleasure from positives, having a low threshold for defining negatives, a high threshold for defining positives, quitting early, and generalizing negatives. Thus, individuals with PPD believe that they will not be effective in producing positive events (which they do not much enjoy when they are achieved), and that negative events will only continue. They scored relatively high on procrastination. Thus, paranoia is a constellation in which the individual is pessimistic, views himself or herself as less likely to predict outcomes, has a hard time seeing positives (but sees negatives easily), procrastinates, and self-blames. PPD was significantly correlated with the decision factors of Discouragement ($r = .393$, $p < .01$) and Unpredictability ($r = .259$, $p < .01$).

Histrionic Personality Disorder

According to the cognitive model, individuals with HPD tend to view themselves in terms of glamour and impressive display. Millon et al. (2000) suggest that persons with histrionic characteristics use dramatic and demanding appearance and behavior to obtain rewards and attention from others, but interior is empty and prone to depression. Rewards for the histrionic person would seem to be temporary, always requiring a new dramatic display to promote further self-aggrandizement. Millon suggests that these individuals lack insight, which may result in their inability to develop a self-critical reflection. Only a few of the decision dimensions were related to histrionic personality characteristics.

Interestingly, individuals with HPD viewed themselves as more likely to take risks. In addition, they tended to derive less pleasure from positives, were more likely to predict negatives, more likely to quit early, had a high threshold for defining positives, and procrastinated more. Persons with HPD scored higher on the decision factor of Discouragement ($r = .274$, $p < .01$). These data are consistent with Millon's view of the person with histrionic traits as lacking self-reflection and the ability to delay gratification. They are easily frustrated, give up, and demand a lot to reward themselves. Interestingly, there was no significant relationship between measures of perceived competence, or current and future resources, and histrionic personality characteristics. Consistent with Millon's view, these individuals are not suffering from a self-critical voice and are willing to take risks to achieve their transitory goals.

Narcissistic Personality Disorder

The cognitive model of NPD stresses the inflated and grandiose schema about the self. However, other formulations, such as that of Millon (Millon et al., 2000) and Kernberg (Kernberg & Senia, 1995), emphasize the view that individuals with narcissistic personalities experience a sense of emptiness and meaninglessness—indeed, feelings of worthlessness. They attempt to compensate for these feelings of emptiness by inflating their self-views and surrounding themselves with admiring and deferent need-gratifiers. Persons with NPD may have difficulty deriving any lasting pleasure and satisfaction, both because of feelings of emptiness and because nothing quite lives up to their grandiose expectations.

The data in the present study indicate that narcissism is unrelated to perceptions of present and future resources—that is, individuals with narcissistic personality characteristics do not view themselves as lacking self-efficacy in the present or future. However, NPD was related to six decision factors: (1) low predictability of future events, (2) attempts to minimize negatives, (3) generalizing negatives, (4) high demands for certainty, (5) procrastination and (6) the need to build consensus. However, persons with NPD tended to blame themselves when things did not work out. They also scored higher on the decision factor of Unpredictability ($r = .282$, $p < .01$). Thus, the view of narcissistic personality that emerges from these data is of someone who is generally pessimistic, anhedonic, and indecisive. Essentially, this is someone who tries to avoid making mistakes, perhaps because self-criticism will follow.

Borderline Personality Disorder

No study of personality disorders would be complete without some description of the borderline personality. These individuals are characterized by instability in every area of their lives, with such variability that Beck and Freeman did not even describe their core schemas in their book on personality disorders. In the current study, BPD was related to the perception of few current resources but was unrelated to the perception of future resources. Thus, for those with BPD, although events may vary from day to day, the current situation always seems bad. Individuals with BDP believe that they cannot predict or control future outcomes, they predict and generalize negatives, and they place less emphasis on maximizing positives. They do not take pleasure from positives, they have a high threshold for defining positives, a low threshold for defining negatives, and they blame themselves when things do not work out. Persons with BPD frequently claim that they procrastinate.

The overall view of borderline personality is of an individual who believes that he or she has few resources and little personal efficacy and is anhedonic, and highly self-critical. Higher scores on BDP were related to higher scores on the decision factor of Discouragement. This is consistent with Linehan's (1993)view that these individuals often believe that they are incompetent and have difficulty deriving pleasure from events.

CLINICAL IMPLICATIONS

Avoidant, Dependent, and Self-Defeating Personality Disorders

The decision model appears to describe many of the characteristics of avoidant, dependent and self-defeating personality types. As noted earlier, 18 of 25 dimensions were significantly correlated for avoidant and dependent, and 19 of 25 dimensions correlated with self-defeating personality. The decision-model, based on portfolio theory, appears to be a good description of how these individuals contemplate decisions. These individuals believed that they had few current or future resources, little control or predictability of outcomes, were less likely to take credit for positives, more likely to predict and generalize negatives, and more likely to quit early. We develop a picture of those with avoidant and dependent personality traits as believing that they have low competence, are easily discouraged, lack self-control, and crave predictability.

Clinical implications from this study suggest that these patients need to be assisted in improving their general level of social competence and to learn to take credit for their positive achievements. Their general pessimism about negative outcomes may be reinforced by their tendency to quit early or to procrastinate before helping themselves. Clinical interventions include training in persistence, examining the costs and benefits of giving up early, and graded task assignments. Individuals with avoidant personality are associated with requiring more information before making decision can be addressed. These hesitant patients can be helped to recognize the opportunity costs in waiting for additional information. Hesitancy may reduce the opportunities for reward. The data also indicated that DPD was related to risk-aversion and blaming others. Clinical interventions should focus on self-care and self-reliance, rather than depending on others, and should encourage having the dependent patient collaborate in assigning homework. Reassurance seeking should be discouraged in the therapeutic relationship, lest the patient come to believe that only the therapist or someone else can really help him.

The data on self-defeating personality type mirrored many of the findings for avoidant and dependent personalities. Self-defeating and avoidant personalities were less likely to define a positive and more likely to define a negative. These individuals manifest an inhibited and hesitant style in confronting change—often not seeing positive change when it is there. They are more likely to see marginal negative changes as major setbacks. Self-defeating personality characteristics were also related to the decision factors of not maximizing positives and requiring high demands for information. These hesitant individuals may appear to others as masochistic, but they may actually be employing a risk-management style that they believe keeps them from being disappointed. For example, one patient with self-defeating personality characteristics believed that her pessimism and tendency to question any positive change were good methods to avoid being disappointed and ending up as a "fool." Her belief was that looking for the dark center of the cloud, rather than the silver lining, allowed her to avoid investing too much of herself into something that would not work out. A case conceptualization that stressed the role of hedging and self-fulfilling negative prophecies allowed her to make therapeutic improvements.

Obsessive-Compulsive Personality Disorder

As indicated above, patients with OCPD do not have a general impairment in self-esteem nor do they manifest a tendency to blame others. Many individuals with OCPD believe that they are highly competent, and they maintain high standards of which they are proud. However, they do have high demands for information before making decisions, and tend to utilize waiting and caution as decision strategies. Clinical interventions that can be useful with these individuals focus on their demand for certainty by examining the costs and benefits of passing up timely opportunities to demand perfect information. Contrary to a common perception of these patients as self-critical, there was no evidence of this in the present study. OCPD individuals were inhibited in making decisions primarily because of their requirement for more complete information. Many of these individuals have excessive standards of responsibility, based on hindsight bias and the need to know for sure (see Leahy, 2001). Examining information demands and utilizing the double standard is a helpful tool with which to explore the unrealistic information requirements that are demanded. Some individuals with OCPD can recognize that many of their better decisions (e.g., choosing to purchase real-estate or to make a commitment in a relationship) have been made with incomplete information. Goals with these individuals are to help them make timelier, less conflicted decisions, and to abandon the desire to make perfect decisions in an uncertain world.

Paranoid Personality Disorder

Data from this study offer support for the model of paranoia advanced by Zigler and Glick (1984, 1988). According to this model, paranoia is a defensive response to an underlying depression, such that the person with paranoia wards off depression by bolstering the ego with a sense of grandiosity and deflects self-blame by blaming others. Although we do not need to utilize a defensive-dynamic model, the current data do indicate that persons with PPD tend to blame themselves and others, and see themselves as having low self-efficacy. These individuals also show indications of pessimism and procrastination. Although many clinicians find it difficult to work with patients with paranoid personality characteristics, establishing a trusting and collaborative working relationship is essential with any patient with any paranoid qualities, especially those with delusions (see Alford & Beck, 1994; Haddock et al., 1998).

The underlying depressive features of those with paranoid personality features suggest that the collaborative alliance should focus on enhancing these patients' sense of personal self-efficacy. This can be accomplished through behavioral activation, social-skills training, or by modifying the self-perceptions toward the positives that do exist. The cautious and inhibited style of decision-making often reflects fears that they will be taken advantage of or hurt by others. This decision-making style needs to be carefully modified toward encouraging prudent, but not risky, decision-making. All-or-nothing definitions of trust, a tendency to personalize others' behaviors, "mind-reading" others' negative intentions, and failing to perceive ones own contributions to the creation of conflict are important targets for change. The often hostile and provocative behaviors of these individuals should not blind the clinician from recognizing that this apparent "attack" mode may mask underlying depression and low self-esteem (Young, 1990; Zigler & Glick, 1988).

Histrionic Personality Disorder

The view of individuals with HPD as being impulsive was supported in the present study. Along with APD, persons with histrionic symptoms were more likely to report taking risks. These individuals also showed a lack of persistence (i.e., they tended to give up easily). Individuals with HPD predicted negative outcomes, were less likely to see a positive as a real positive, and reported frequent procrastination. Their generally poor self-direction and self-discipline is reflected in high risk taking, lack of persistence, and a tendency to derive little pleasure from positives. However, they rarely endorsed items related to low self-esteem, such as having few current or future resources that they might control. These data reinforce a view of persons with HPD as having little self-reflection and self-direction. This relative lack of self-direction suggests that the clinician could profitably focus on (a) helping the patient become more aware of risky and impulsive decisions, and (b) calling attention to the necessity of developing plans that are well thought out and giving due consideration for both the short- and long-term consequences. Many individuals with Histrionic Personality Disorder have chaotic and emotionally labile relationships—ones that begin and end with high intensity interactions. Some have serious financial problems—often the result of their inability to plan and save, and sometimes because of capricious spending habits. Clinicians can assist these patients to recognize the need to rely on well thought-out plans, rather than emotions and seductive displays, and help the patient to develop more rational decision-processes, tolerance of frustration and emotional regulation.

Narcissistic Personality Disorder

Contrary to the psychoanalytic schema-focused eclectic view that persons with NPD experience intrapsychic suffering as a result of a deflated, empty self (see Kernberg, 1975; Kernberg, 1998a; Young & Flanagan, 1998), the data reported here do not suggest impairments in their perceived ability to control current or future resources—that is essentially, self-efficacy. Nor did those with NPD present with an exaggerated view of their abilities. Narcissism was related to an inhibited style of decision-making—that is, low predictability, high demands for information, procrastination, minimization of negatives, generalizing negatives, and a need to build a consensus before making decisions. What might account for this inhibited, almost compulsive, style of decision-making? Persons with NPD tended to blame themselves when things did not work out, which suggests that they may be highly prone to regret. Thus, these individuals may utilize an inhibited and pessimistic style of decision-making to avoid feeling regret.

Many patients with NPD perform at levels less than their potential. This might suggest they have a strong fear of failure. In particular, they fear that others will humiliate them if things do not work out. In any case, these data suggest that the clinician can assist the patient in making progress by examining pessimistic assumptions such as, "I need to know for certain," and "If I don't know for certain, then it won't work out." Practice in small steps toward longer-term goals, rather than reliance on the "big hand," may help the patient experiment with progress. One patient with NPD felt trapped because he believed that he could not take an ordinary job lest it reflect his failure and humiliation. He found it helpful to look at a so-called ordinary job as the first step in a procession of more challenging jobs in the future. Indeed, taking an ordinary job was reframed by the therapist as a challenge to enhance his ability to practice being ordinary—a task that both he and the therapist viewed as very demanding.

Borderline Personality Disorder

Individuals with BDP generally utilize a pessimistic decision strategy. Data from the current study suggest that the clinician should help clarify patients' views of their current situations and lack of emphasis on achieving positives. These patients, often characterized by reporting lives that consist of unrelenting crises (Linehan, 1993), do not perceive themselves as able to predict or control events and do not take pleasure from positives. Therapists can instruct patients in competency tracking—that is, monitoring any positive behavior and positive outcome and in learning to compartmentalize or place negative outcomes in perspective. For example, the tendency of persons with BDP to count any negative as a big negative, to generalize negatives, and to blame themselves can be countered using the following techniques:

1. Offset negatives with positives.
2. View negatives along a continuum to gain perspective of degrees of negativity.
3. Utilize the double-standard technique to ask whether such a negative by another would be viewed as so terrible.
4. Help recognize that one can correct and change ones own behavior without condemning oneself.

5. Establish reasonable standards of behavior, such that one is not held entirely blameworthy for all negative outcomes.

The present study found that individuals with BPD view the current situation as bad but are neutral about the future, which suggests that they are engulfed by their current field of experience. Several techniques may be utilized to help them recognize that the present is not overwhelming:

1. Emotional regulation and cognitive distancing techniques, such as mindfulness training and radical acceptance (see Linehan, 1993; Teasdale, 1999).
2. Using the continuum technique (discussed above) to place current events in perspective.
3. Diversifying one's perception of other positives that are available to offset any current negatives.
4. Examining past catastrophic and all-or-nothing predictions to determine why they were not accurate.
5. Discourage reliance on emotional reasoning and encourage reliance on facts and how a theoretical "reasonable" person might see things.
6. Writing short narratives that describe how the current situation can be resolved in a positive manner.

SUMMARY

This study suggests that persons with different personality disorders vary in their approach to making decisions. Decision dimensions that reflect perception of resources (current and future), predictability, control, regret, threshold for defining outcomes, and demands for certainty are related to personality dimensions. Other models of personality disorders emphasize the underlying dynamics that mold the personality or stress the cognitive content of schemas. However, the current decision-model provides an empirical basis for describing how individuals who are high and low on various personality dimensions view decision-making.

The portfolio model suggests that individuals utilize different criteria in making decisions. There are 25 dimensions of a pessimistic portfolio, with factors related to self-efficacy, discouragement, unpredictability, and risk-aversion. The portfolio model allows us to examine how different individuals define positive or negative changes, whether they enjoy or excessively suffer the experience of change, and what value they place on information, predictability, and control. The correlational nature of present study does not allow the prediction of different personality disorders based on their decision-making strategies, nor does it allow us to examine the causal relationships between personality disorders and decision-making. However, important differences did arise in the empirical investigation of personality dimensions and portfolio concerns. The pessimistic portfolio closely mapped onto many of the decision criteria for diagnosing avoidant, dependent, and borderline personality disorders. Individuals with these disorders generally appear to utilize very pessimistic portfolio strategies, having perceptions of low current and future access to rewards, high information demands, quick stop-loss or quitting rules, less enjoyment of gains. They are more likely to suffer negatives and have high information demands.

The data on OCPD was revealing in that it supported the view of individuals with OCPD as inhibited and cautious, but not as lacking in self-esteem. Especially interesting are the data on paranoid personalities, which suggest an underlying negative portfolio view of the self, having low self-efficacy, being easily discouraged, and cautious about change. Persons with HPD reported a preference for risk, low frustration tolerance, and a tendency to quit easily. Finally, the findings relevant to those with NPD did not support the commonly held view that these individuals are masking low self-esteem, but rather that they are afraid of making mistakes.

The approach taken here was largely empirical and was not guided by any one theory of personality. Future research should attempt to replicate these data, possibly applying other measures of personality disorder with a different sample. However, these findings do suggest important differences among the various personality disorders that may help clinicians understand how different patients perceive themselves as capable of making positive change.

PART II

Pessimism and Self-Limitation

CHAPTER 5

Strategic Self-Limitation

For many patients entering treatment, cognitive therapy appears optimistic: it emphasizes the brighter side of things, the likelihood of solutions and hope, the personal value of the patient independent of achievement, and the possibility of rapid change and recovery. Cognitive therapists attempt to focus their patients on the evidence, the importance of rationality, and the need to change behavior to change reality. The assumption guiding the therapist's interventions is that the patient will be convinced, through a Socratic dialogue, that rationality and a hedonic calculus can only lead to the conclusion that he, the patient, should abandon his irrational and unproductive thinking and behavior and adapt new ways of functioning.

I refer to this as the rational principle, but I realize that in therapy there are limits to rationality. The limits to rationality are reflected in the tendency of some patients to maintain—indeed, even strengthen—beliefs that have already proven to be a failure. Most of us have seen patients who argue vigorously that change for them is impossible, that the therapist is naive and that there are no rewards available. Indeed, when hope seems just around the corner, the patient appears to become anxious, get angry with the therapist, and threaten to give up. Often, we observe in therapeutic frustration that the patient argues more forcefully for the negative the more the therapist presents a positive alternative. Is the patient masochistic, as Freud suggested in his interpretation of depression (Freud, 1917)? Are there substantial secondary gains that the patient covertly adheres to and about which the patient and therapist are unaware? What could account for this motivated negative cognition? I shall argue that negativity and hopelessness often have a purpose—primarily to avoid further loss, humiliation, or regret.

THE RISKS OF CHANGE

Therapists are in the business of producing change. However, the patient may be committed to avoiding risk. I refer to this as the difference between maximization *strategies* that emphasize producing as many rewards as possible (the therapist's position) in contrast to a minimization strategy that attempts to avoid loss at all costs (this is the patient's position) (Leahy, 1996; 1997a, b, c). Maximization of rewards is an appetitive strategy that, in many cases, may carry greater risk. The depressed patient, resisting change, may be less focused on a strategy of maximizing rewards and more focused on a strategy of minimizing regret. Since action is more likely than inaction to lead to regret (Kahneman, 1995) and since depressed individuals are notoriously pessimistic, they may utilize a strategy of inaction in order to minimize losses. Indeed, one might view the depressive strategy as a bet that one can control losses, but not gains. The depressive strategy of inaction, so obvious in symptoms of social withdrawal, decreased energy, indecisiveness, and decreased activity level, is a commitment to an age-old belief that "no one kicks a sleeping dog."

Anxiety and depression often take the form of minimization. For example, the inhibition of movement and the collapse response of some anxious individuals may prevent them from the risks of heights, water, dangerous animals, separation from protective parents, humiliation, and interpersonal conflict (Beck, Emery & Greenberg, 1985; Bowlby, 1968; Marks, 1987; Menzies, 1997). Depressive avoidance and procrastination, marked by low energy, withdrawal, and indecisiveness, may prevent the risks of further mistakes, regrets, loss, and depletion of resources (Leahy, 1997b). One might argue that a maximization strategy aimed at gaining more rewards makes sense in an environment with high resources and low danger, whereas a minimization strategy aimed at avoiding further loss makes sense in an environment with low resources and high danger. The resistant patient views the world as low reward–high danger. Attempts to push him or her in the direction of change are viewed as putting him at greater risk for a low benefit.

Risk-Reward and Decision-Making

I have proposed that depressed individuals are less likely to follow a maximization of reward strategy in making decisions about future change (Leahy, 1996, 1997a, b). In advancing this model of mundane decision-making, I have suggested that the individual's decisions are directed toward considerations of risk-reward calculations where we might employ traditional economic concepts, such as assets, diversification, risk-tolerance, and future-earning potential.

This investment model of decision-making, derived from microeconomic theory and modern portfolio theory, proposes that individuals consider their current assets, future ability to produce rewards (future earnings), ability to diversify, and other factors that shall be described shortly. For example, consider an individual who is optimistic or nondepressed. He views himself as having the ability to enjoy future rewards, as someone who makes good decisions, as having the ability to produce rewards in the future, as having a variety of other resources to fall back on and as not highly motivated by regret should things not work out. We would expect this individual to take a maximization strategy in making decisions, such that he is willing to tolerate some risk in the hope of gaining some rewards that he could enjoy. If his decision does not work out as anticipated, he believes that he can absorb the cost since he can produce alternative rewards or because he has other assets. Consequently, the optimistic individual is more willing to tolerate risk because he believes that he will not be devastated by loss and because he places greater hedonic value on rewards.

In contrast, the depressed or pessimistic individual approaches decision-making as if he has few assets available, little or no future earning potential to offset losses, high regret in the face of failure, and a low enjoyment of rewards that are achieved (low hedonic value). Moreover, the pessimistic individual is less likely to define a reward as rewarding, since his focus is more on the downside potential and because of his anhedonia. Consequently, the pessimistic individual, calculating risk-reward ratios, anticipates more to lose than to gain and, because of his regret-orientation, demands greater certainty before he makes a decision.

Pessimistic and optimistic individuals differ in terms of their risk-management concerns. The optimistic individual views decisions as less risky and, should a loss occur, he views himself as better able to absorb the loss. In contrast, the pessimistic individual views risk as highly problematic. Losses are interpreted as setting off chain reactions of other losses (which I have referred to as cost cascades) (Leahy, 1997b), with the cost of loss enhanced by the tendency of pessimistic individuals to attribute the cause to personal inadequacies that are viewed as stable and generalizable to other areas of his life (Abramson, et al., 1995).

In a recent study, most of these predictions were confirmed (Leahy, 1999). The Beck Depression Inventory and a 25–item, 6-point scale, questionnaire that assessed the dimensions identified above were administered to 75 clinic patients. As predicted by the portfolio/risk-management model, greater depression was associated with greater risk-aversion,

more demanding criteria in defining gains and with high stop-loss standards for quitting. Risk aversion was associated with a perception of
fewer current and future sources of rewards, higher information demands,
greater self-criticism, and the tendency to generalize loss to other areas.
Both risk-aversion and greater depression were associated with less of a
demand for maximizing positives as a goal.

Inaction and Risk-Management

An implication of the portfolio risk-management model, and the findings
obtained in support of it, is that depressed individuals should utilize strategies to minimize risk. As Kahneman (1995) has found, action rather than
inaction is more likely to evoke regret—that is, is more likely to add to the
cost of risk. Therefore, depressed individuals, more prone to regret or self-
criticism than are nondepressed individuals, should place greater emphasis
on strategies emphasizing *inaction* rather than *action,* since inaction confers
less regret. According to this model, resistance to change is a risk-management strategy. The patient does not enjoy the suffering of depression or
anxiety, but change may be viewed as producing even more difficulty. If the
patient has experienced recent losses and we urge him to make some positive
changes, we may be viewed as the Pollyannaish visitor who tells someone
who suffered a fire recently, "Ignore the fire alarm you are hearing. It's a
false alarm. Better to respond to false alarms than to lose all the rest."

Consider the following case: A single male complains excessively
about his lack of a girlfriend. He spends most of his time in his apartment
and, when he comes to therapy, he complains that women are bitches
who only want a man who is a financial success. He periodically visits
prostitutes with whom he feels less threatened. When the therapist suggests that he may view women in all-or-nothing terms, he claims that the
therapist does not understand the women in the city, that there is no
chance for him, and that cognitive therapy is naive and simple-minded.
When the therapist suggests alternatives of how to meet women, he becomes simultaneously more angry, depressed, and hopeless, attempting
to prove to the therapist that he is too old, has nothing to offer, and that
the therapist should fire him as a patient. On the occasions when he
carries out some behavioral homework, he shows partial compliance, but
then gets angry that he has not achieved immediate success and uses this
as further evidence of his hopelessness.

In the pages to follow, I shall illustrate how the risk-management
model of resistance can be helpful in treating these apparently negativis-
tic and seemingly provocative patients. I should indicate that the therapist

should become aware of his or her own vulnerability inadvertently to confirm the patient's hopelessness by becoming angry with the patient, punishing the patient, or buying into the hopelessness of the patient by concluding that treatment cannot work. To address these countertransference issues, the therapist should attempt to accomplish the following: (a) develop a curiosity about the resistance—and share this curiosity with the patient and with colleagues, (b) do not personalize the patient's resistance—the patient had these problems prior to entering therapy, (c) develop a case conceptualization of the resistance by examining how previous life-events, recent losses, maladaptive assumptions, and behavioral adaptations contribute to the resistance, (d) recognize that the resistance to change maintains the patient's suffering and that people who suffer deserve our help and empathy, and (e) do not fear confronting the resistance in an empathic, collaborative, but direct manner—if the resistance is not resolved, the patient is unlikely to get better and will probably quit therapy anyway. With these counter-transference issues in mind, let us examine what concerns the patient may have that lead him to activate a strategy of resistance.

Risk-Management Concerns in Self-Limitation

Because of the emphasis on risk, the resistant patient attempts to inhibit change by focusing on several concerns that, he believes, reduce risk. As indicated earlier in my discussion of the investment model of decision-making, the resistant patient believes that losses are imminent, volatile, and catastrophic and that these losses have a spreading-activation quality setting off cost-cascades of a chain-reaction of other losses. Second, the depressed-resistant patient equates uncertainty with risk and volatility, whereas uncertainty can logically be considered as neutral regarding loss. For example, I am unsure as to how valuable my house will be next year, but this does not necessarily imply that my house will increase or decrease in value. Uncertainty is really an index of our ability to know what will definitely happen, but it is neutral about the direction of change. However, due to the negative schemata of the depressed patient, uncertainty is a "marker" of loss.

Similar to uncertainty, the depressed individual views uncontrollability as a marker or indicator of loss. Research demonstrates that people are willing to tolerate higher levels of shock if they can be sure of when it will be administered and if they can control it (Geer, Davison & Gatchel, 1970; Geer & Maisel, 1972). Again, controllability is not logically an indicator of loss or danger. For example, as a passenger on an airplane, I have no control over the safety of the plane, but this is irrelevant to whether it is safe. Individuals with specific phobias attempt to increase the ability to foresee and control through hypervigilant, superstitious safety behaviors (Salkovskis, 1997; Wells, 1997), paralleling the demands for certainty and control that resistant-depressed patients manifest.

Sunk Costs

Another factor affecting risk-taking among resistant patients is self-consistency. A variety of cognitive-consistency theories attest to the tendency of individuals to not only perceive consistency where it may not be present, but to seek consistency of their beliefs and actions. This may include attempts to reduce cognitive-dissonance (Festinger, 1957), maintain preexisting schemas (Beck, 1967; 1987; Beck, Freeman and Associates, 1990), or to verify beliefs about the self, even when these beliefs are negative. The resistant patient may explain his current hesitancy to change by reifying the lack of change: "The reason I don't change is that I've never changed." Thus, what needs to be explained is reduced to an observation of a pattern that becomes the explanation for itself. This is similar to what I would describe as the commitment to sunk-costs. Anyone who has bought a computer and upgraded it, only to find that within a year the computer appears obsolete, has the ambivalence of just having spent money on something that is worth less than all the prior investments made in it. I recall my own ambivalence in taking the advice of a colleague. After I had spent money the previous year on a computer that was now obsolete, he said "toss it over a cliff." My commitment to my sunk-cost was that I would have to finally realize that I had thrown good money after bad. The depressed patient, who has committed substantial behavior in useless pursuits, recognizes that he has substantial sunk-costs to justify.

An important feature of sunk-costs, as a factor in resistance, is that rational decision-making is (ideally) forward-looking for utility. Thus, we say to the patient, "What are the costs and benefits of carrying out this action?" We are looking for future utility ratios. However, many depressed individuals (and, in fact, individuals in general) are backward-looking in their decisions: "How can I walk away from something I've spent so much time and effort on?" One only needs to think of the peripatetic justifications of the Vietnam War to recognize that sunk-costs carry substantial dissonance motivation that keeps our decisions looking backward rather than facing forward. Sunk costs are a significant contributor to resistance.

Table 5.1 indicates some of the typical "risk" concerns of depressed and anxious patients. As indicated earlier, depressed individuals view

Table 5.1 Risk Management Concerns in Self-Limitation

Concern	Example	Self-Handicapping Strategy
Loss	Patient views loss as intolerable, setting off a chain reaction of other losses (cost-cascades) that will be catastrophic.	Avoid any change that can produce any loss. Look for loss or danger. Ask, "Is it possible that loss can occur?" —If so, stop out quickly.
Uncertainty	Patient views uncertainty as indicative of risk and volatility: "Anything can happen—probably the worst will happen."	Require total reassurance, demand perfect information, delay making decisions. Patient argues against hope, attempting to prove he is helpless and hopeless.
Uncontrollability	Patient believes, "If I don't have perfect control, then it must be dangerous."	Patient manifests negative control by non-compliance with homework and self-help, focusing on avoidance and escape as factors he can control.
Self-Inconsistency	The patient is committed to maintaining a consistent view of himself. "I've been doing this all along, so I must have some good reasons for my decisions."	Patient defensively argues in favor of his depressive choices as rational and the only reasonable alternative. He views the therapist's endeavors as criticisms, invalidation, and naiveté.
Regret-aversion	The patient believes that if he makes a mistake he should or will criticize himself.	The patient demands certainty of positive outcomes, believes that if things get better it proves he was a fool for not having changed before, or if things get worse, then it proves he is worthless.
Commitment to sunk-costs	The patient has already invested time, energy, and suffering pursuing a life-course of failed action. To give this up implies that all of past behavior was wasted.	The patient claims, "I've already committed too much of myself to this to give up on it."

Table 5.1 *(Continued)*

Concern	Example	Self-Handicapping Strategy
Self-evaluation	The patient views change as a risk of negative self-evaluation wherein he will be proven incompetent.	The patient avoids true self-evaluation by minimizing his effort, proving that the task is impossible, or blaming others. Patient either sets standards too high (i.e., so that anyone would have failed) or too low (i.e., so that he is assured of success).
Excessive Ego-Ideal	The patient's goals are idealized as perfect in work, romance, and experience. Nothing less than perfect is satisfactory.	The patient discounts alternatives less than perfect since they are viewed as further proof of his mediocrity. He takes pride in his unwillingness to compromise as proof that, even though he has not achieved much, he has not lowered his standards—that is, at least he is not just average.

change with a negative portfolio—that is, they have the assumption that they are likely to lose, that there is great uncertainty and uncontrollability, and they are regret-oriented. Further, resistant and depressed individuals, like others, are committed to self-consistency and are reluctant to abandon a behavioral pattern unless they are highly compensated for change—that is, unless there is considerable predictability of a more positive outcome. Resistant individuals are committed to past behavior as a sunk-cost that they justify by trying to make the unworkable work.

Consider the risk-aversion of a resistant, depressed patient, confronted with the therapist's recommendations for a change in behavior, for example, to get out of a bad relationship. The patient has a satisficing search for information focused on the question, "Can I lose?" (see Leahy, 1997; Simon, 1979). The self-limitation strategy is to stop searching for alternatives once a negative outcome is identified. Similarly, the patient equates uncertainty with the downside and, therefore, demands greater information to make a change. For example, depressed individuals claim that they demand greater consensus from others before making a decision (Leahy, 1999). Emphasis on self-consistency, similar to self-verification processes, leads the patient to defensively argue in favor of a losing position. Self-limitation is also reflected in the fact that the patient is backward-looking for disutility—that is, focused on sunk-costs that cannot be reasonably recovered. Since the abandonment of a previous position carries the added burden of self-criticism, the depressed individual is paradoxically *more* committed to the lost cost: "I've put too much of myself into this to walk away now."

An example of these self-limitation processes is indicated in the case of a single woman who had considerable difficulty giving up on a three-year relationship with a married man. She indicated that she would get into long arguments with him in which she insisted that he would never leave his wife, but he insisted that there was a good chance that he would (he never did). I asked her what she hoped to accomplish in these apparently futile arguments. She responded, "I hope that he wins the argument and convinces me that he will leave his wife." I asked, "What would that mean to you if he did?" She responded, "Because then I would not have wasted all those years. I would have been right to have stayed in it."

Attributional Maneuvers and Self-Handicapping

Self-handicapping often focuses on avoiding direct evaluation of ability or self. The assumption of self-handicapping is that individuals attempt to protect their self-esteem, in conditions of uncertainty, by obscuring evaluation by engaging in excuse-generation, creating impediments of performance, or barriers to attribution of ability (Arkin & Oleson, 1999; Berglas & Jones, 1978; Jones & Rhodewalt, 1982; Snyder, Higgins, & Stucky, 1983). According to attribution theory, we are more likely to make personal attributions in the case in which the individual's behavior is distinctive, consistent, and not in consensus with others (Kelley, 1971). Similarly, we are more likely to make personal attributions if the individual has expended effort, but failed at a task that is relatively easy for others (Weiner, 1974, 1985). Depressed individuals, already suffering from low self-esteem, may employ attributional maneuvers to prevent direct evaluation of their optimal abilities. Thus, the individual may pursue unusual and low probability outcomes, since failure at these outcomes does not reflect true potential (i.e., anyone would have failed). Minimizing effort, quitting early, provoking others, and setting excessively high standards are also attributional strategies to avoid being measured by the standard that others are measured. Thus, a depressed individual rejected the feasibility of smaller steps toward success, since failure at any smaller step conferred greater implication of less ability, whereas failing at the "grand scheme" might only mean that he set his goals higher than others did.

For example, a college student, who often compared himself to his father, who had achieved considerable fame as an intellectual, appeared committed to drinking and playing pool, rather than studying, and to taking the most difficult courses. His attributional self-handicapping was that if he failed, he could attribute it to his independence from the grind of meaningless courses, whereas if he succeeded it proved he was a genius. Either way, there was no direct assessment available of his true potential. Both failure and success were within his attributional control.

Protective Perfectionism

Perfectionistic standards may also underlie the overinvestment in the ego-ideal of self-critical depressives. A severely depressed woman strongly resisted abandoning her demand for a perfect partner, partly because of the sunk-cost phenomenon described earlier and partly because of her belief that these perfectionistic standards maintained her self-esteem: "If I gave up my standard then I would be just like everyone else. Even though I don't have the perfect partner, I still have my standards." From her perspective, abandoning perfectionism would relegate her to a world of all-or-nothing nobodies. Once she abandoned her excessive ego-ideal regarding a partner and a career, she was able to make significant changes that helped decrease her depression.

Similar to the attributional self-handicapping illustrated above, perfectionism allows the individual to avoid being measured on a normal curve. If he fails to be 100%, then the only conclusions that are warranted are that he is not perfect (which is not informative since it is not distinctive) and he has high standards (which he considers admirable). The perfectionist avoids being measured on a standard scale in order to avoid determining his relative standard.

Tactics of Self-Limitation

I have identified some of the general strategies of self-limitation and self-handicapping. I now turn to a description of typical tactics by which the resistant patient attempts to undermine the process of change in therapy. These are shown in Table 5.2. Inspection of this table indicates that the depressed individual engages in both direct and indirect maneuvers in therapy. For example, direct maneuvers include motivated negative cognition, devaluation of alternatives, and attempts to prove hopelessness. A writer, with considerable talent, insisted that everything was lousy in his life (his apartment, his relationships, his writing), that any changes sug-

Table 5.2 Self-Limitation Tactics

Tactic	Example
Motivated Negative Cognition	Argues vigorously for hopelessness, becomes angry or despondent when confronted with positive information.
Devaluation of Alternatives	Views positive alternatives as naive, dangerous or pointless.
Off-task Distractions	Changes the subject in session to irrelevant discussion, trivializes the therapy session with complaints.
Readiness Demands	Insists that he must feel like changing or be ready to change before he is willing to change. Focuses on his lack of motivation or discomfort.
Perfectionism Procrastination	Demands a perfect solution before he is willing to try new behavior.
Proving Hopelessness	Despite positive resources or progress, attempts to show that everything is hopeless.
Minimal Compliance (Hedging)	Complies with minimal effort in self-help and then concludes that therapy does not work.
Somatic and Vegetative Preoccupation	Frequent complaints and overfocus on how badly he feels physically or how exhausted he feels.
Blaming Others	Focuses on how others are the cause of his problems, either currently or in the past.
Provoking Therapist	Insults therapist, questions therapist's competence, or is sexually provocative.
Disattribution self-handicapping	Creates "barriers" to self-evaluation by self sabotage (e.g., getting drunk), minimal effort, or taking on impossible tasks.
Hiding	Comes late to sessions, infrequent attendance, hypersomnia, and withdrawal.

gested were naïve and stupid and that hopelessness was the only reasonable alternative. The therapist can recognize motivated negative cognition because the patient energetically argues the negative, often to the point of bringing up extraneous material completely unrelated to the topic at hand. By proving the negative and embracing hopelessness, the patient can rest assured within his cocoon of controllable safety. Once the writer was confronted with his investment in proving the negative, he was able to recognize that he was attempting to avoid more public failure and humiliation that he feared would occur once he completed his project.

Readiness demands are also central for resistant patients. These individuals utilize emotional reasoning to guide them in making a decision to change. They would rather talk about their problem than make a change. "I have to feel ready for a relationship" or "I have to feel ready to move out on my own" are examples of self-limitation that limits risk. Talking about their problem is often viewed, by them, as a means whereby they may feel ready at some unforeseen point. The patient can be asked, "What would happen if you took this action and you were not ready?" or "Have you ever exercised when you were not ready to exercise?" Individuals focused on readiness may be told that motivation often comes after behavior rather than before it. Behavior is a warm up exercise for motivation.

Some patients utilize minimal compliance (straddling) as a self-limitation tactic. They invest a small amount of effort and quit early. From the patient's perspective, straddling has a number of advantages. First, the patient can claim that she tried. Second, straddling allows one to test the waters. If it is unpleasant, one can quit early and not run any further risks. Third, the patient can appear to please the therapist, but maintain his risk-management strategy. Some patients modify the agenda by focusing entirely on somatic and vegetative complaints: "My legs ache. I'm tired. I feel spaced out a lot." These preoccupations not only elicit sympathy from some—especially if the patient is a "doctor-shopper"—but they also make his concerns immediate, concrete, and unrelated to self-esteem. The patient often operates with the assumption, "If my problems are really medical, then there is nothing wrong with who I am." One patient, confronted with significant problems in his work and relationships, dwelled on the possible diagnosis of chronic fatigue rather than attempt to solve real-life problems. Another patient whose self-critical thoughts were (apparently) being addressed by the therapist, shifted the topic suddenly to claim, "My legs have been very tired recently." This individual indicated later that he was afraid of getting his hopes up, because he might be disappointed. Focusing on the fatigue he experienced would allow him to change the subject and preserve the hopelessness that he believed protected him from taking foolish, optimistic actions.

Finally, a common method to resist change is "hiding"—simply not showing up. Many patients come late to sessions, attend infrequently, withdraw, or become silent, or engage in no-show behavior. In many cases, this behavior reflects the patient's ambivalence about the value of therapy, but in some cases, it may also reflect the patient's belief that therapy requires too much change. For example, one patient, contemplating separation from his wife, was fearful of separating but unmotivated to work on improving the marriage. He claimed that therapy sessions were very helpful in making him confront his fears but that he often utilized hiding as a technique both in therapy and in his marriage.

Modifying Resistance

The Therapist as Negotiator

Many therapists are ambivalent about confronting resistance. Some believe that the therapist's role is similar to a consultant: the patient sets the agenda, tells the therapist what he wants to accomplish, and the therapist responds to these requests. If the patient resists change, according to this model, then the patient is viewed as not ready for change. Other therapists may view resistance in personal terms—the patient is in a power struggle or the "patient is devaluing me." These observations may be true, of course, but they may obscure the purpose that these maneuvers serve. Many therapists are fearful of confronting resistance because they view resistant patients as unmotivated and fear that confrontation will drive the patient out of therapy.

I view the therapist's role differently. The patient implicitly indicates his desire to change by coming to therapy, but he may also be unable to bring about this change. We can view the patient as locked in the classic neurotic conflict—that is, trying to achieve two goals simultaneously that appear to him to be self-contradictory. For example, the patient may want to feel less depressed, but fear that change will make him more depressed. In a sense, the patient's conflict is with himself and only incidentally with the therapist. The therapist's role is to help the patient negotiate change within himself. The patient is encouraged to examine this dialogue with himself—the part that wants change and the part that resists. I have found that most resistant patients are fully aware of their resistance and the confrontation of this resistance is sometimes refreshing. It feels authentic, they may say, and it may help them address the confusing dialogue going on within themselves: "I want to change, but I am afraid that this will only make matters worse."

I have identified a number of interventions that may be used to modify resistance (see Table 5.3). As in *principled negotiation* (Fisher & Ury, 1981), the therapist mediates this negotiation by helping the patient identify his primary goal and examines, collaboratively, how subsequent behavior is related to the goal. For example, the patient's primary goal may be set in the initial treatment planning sessions: "What do you want to accomplish in our work in therapy?" The patient may indicate that his

Table 5.3 Modifying Self-Defeat

Intervention	Example
Agenda-setting	"What problem would you like help with today? Can you specify exactly what you want from this session?"
	When patient goes off-task: "How does this relate to your making progress on the problem you put on today's agenda? What are the costs and benefits of not working on this problem?"
Identify patterns of self-defeat	"Have you noticed that you put a small amount of effort into things and then quit? This seems to be a pattern. Is it possible that you have a vested interest in keeping yourself from moving forward in certain areas?"
Examine costs and benefits of self-defeat	"Every pattern that we have has costs and benefits. What could be the costs and benefits to you of hedging (failing, provoking, hiding, etc.)?" "How would your life have been different if you never hedged (failed, provoked, etc.)?"
Monitor self-defeat	"Let's keep track of when and how often you hedge (fail, provoke, hide, etc.)." "What situations or thoughts seem to trigger your self-defeat?"
Examine the negative implications of success	"Let's imagine that you succeeded at (something). Perhaps this has some negative implications for you. What could they be? What would happen next? Higher expectations, more public failure, let yourself or others down, have to maintain success, not deserve success?" "How would you handle these consequences of success?"
Examine fear of self-evaluation or self-exposure	"Sometimes we try to avoid finding out what we could do under the best of circumstances—that is, when we have put all our effort into something we might fear finding out that we are not as good as we think we are. Do you ever have that fear? Do you do things to make sure that you don't get a clear evaluation of yourself? What do you expect or demand of yourself? What would you think of yourself if you found out you were not as good (or as great) as you think you should be?"

Table 5.3 *(Continued)*

Intervention	Example
Examine the minimization strategy	"Some people aim for achieving positives, but other people try to avoid loss and defeat. Are you the kind of person who tries to avoid loss and defeat? Do you look for how you might fail and try to quit early? Are you afraid that if you experience one loss, then many other losses will follow?"
Examine reasons for and against success in the future	"Let's examine all the possible reasons why you might (or might not) have success in the future. Are any of these potentially within your control? What if you persisted at something for a long time?"
Recall previous successes	"You have had some success at some things in the past. What have you had even partial success at? How did you do that? What did you say to yourself? Can you apply any of that to your current problems?"
Externalize the self-defeat voice	"Let's practice arguing against the negative self-defeat voice. I'll be the negative voice, you argue against me. Therapist: It's too good to be true. You may as well quit now and not be a fool. Patient: I can make progress on some things. I'm not a bad person. I deserve some good things in life.
Experiment with success	"Let's set up some experiments with small amounts of success and see what it triggers for you. Do you become anxious, angry, sad, confused, regretful, etc? What are your automatic thoughts? How would you challenge them?"
Contract against self-defeat	"Would you be willing to put off sabotaging yourself until you speak with the therapist?"
Slow down success	"Rather than become demanding and impatient with success, would you be willing to experience success only in small doses and pull back momentarily from too much success?"
Lower the idealization of success	"Some people get too far ahead of themselves when they think of success—in fact, they think of perfection. Is this what you do? Do you get disillusioned? Would you be willing to consider progress not perfection as the goal? What are the costs and benefits of accepting progress rather than demanding or needing perfection?"

Table 5.3 *(Continued)*

Intervention	Example
Write a success script	"Describe, from beginning to end, how you could succeed at something. At what points in the script do you feel anxious, angry, depresses, confused, etc. What's going through your mind?"
Self-reward for success	"You have had mixed feelings about progress, so it's important to reward yourself when you experience positives. Make a list of ways of praising yourself when you pursue positives."

goal is to feel less depressed and to get out of a bad relationship. These goals become the reference point for evaluating resistance. Later, as the patient resists change by attacking the therapist or not doing homework, the patient's attention may be referred to the initial goals: "How will attacking me help you become less depressed?" or "How will not doing homework help you resolve this relationship problem?" The patient's resistance should be conceptualized as a "battle within the self" rather than "a battle with the therapist"—that is, a conflict between the principle goals and the resistance.

Agenda setting is useful in establishing the primary goal for the session. Nevertheless, patients may resist by not setting an agenda. The therapist may refer back to the primary goal: "How will not setting an agenda help you overcome your depression?" or "What are the costs and benefits of not having an agenda?" One patient indicated that the cost of setting an agenda was that he would then be committed to change. If the therapist imposed an agenda, he reasoned, then he could reject the agenda as irrelevant, thereby avoiding change, or he could explore the agenda to see if it was "safe." Patterns of self-defeat in other areas of life may also be directly identified: "I have noticed that you do not have an agenda for our sessions. I wonder if this is a pattern that you may have in other areas of your life. For example, do you find yourself reacting to events rather than actively making them change?"

Straddling strategies may be identified and examined for costs and benefits. For example, a woman who would remain aloof and distrustful with men, even though she claimed she wanted a relationship, indicated that by holding back (straddling) she was able to "test out" the man's true intentions. It had not occurred to her that her aloofness was perceived as cold rejection by men that then led men to withdraw, thereby confirming her negative predictions about men. The therapist was able to convince her to temporarily abandon straddling and to focus on monitoring any positive attention from men. She was also instructed to reward positive attention. This offset the straddling, which then helped disconfirm (partially) her negative view of interacting with men.

Although cognitive therapists often engage in "competency tracking," by having the patient self-monitor positives, I have also found it useful to have patients monitor their self-defeating behavior. For example, a patient who complained, thereby alienating friends and coworkers, examined the costs and benefits of complaining and self-monitored his complaining. This led to an increased awareness that he was complaining far more than he thought he was and eventually led to a proactive self-control script: "If I find myself complaining, I should immediately stop, tell myself that this accomplishes nothing and annoys people, and focus on what I can control that is positive." Other self-defeating behavior, such as provoking others, can also be monitored. A woman recognized that she would provoke her partner when she began feeling closer to him. This then led to his withdrawal or counterattack, which then confirmed her negative view of men. Her instruction was to catch herself provoking and replacing it either with a positive or with no behavior. This allowed her to disconfirm her negative view of him and to recognize her self-verifying negative behavior.

Some individuals self-defeat because they fear that they cannot adapt to the "costs" of success. These individuals believe that further movement forward may demand greater intimacy (and rejection), greater success (and a more precipitous fall to failure), and greater public recognition (and a higher risk of humiliation). Motivated negative cognition and vigorous arguments favoring hopelessness often reveal these fears of success. (I view this as a fear of the consequences of success, rather than a fear of success per se.) These fears can be examined directly by asking about the fears of greater demands, higher expectations, greater exposure, or greater disappointment, which might accompany greater success. The therapist may ask how the patient has handled success in the past. For example, one patient indicated that she did well on her graduate exams, leading to an increase in her hopes, only to be rejected by all the schools to which she applied (given her perfection, she had only applied to a few elite schools). Another woman indicated that she had become very close to a man she planned to marry and then he suddenly broke off the engagement. This resulted in her future relationship choices: she either chose men who were less successful than she was, thereby allowing her to devalue them as marital choices, or she would act out through infidelity when she was involved with men whom she viewed as plausible marital partners. Her ultimate fear was that she would end up in a marriage that would not work and that this would lead either to a man betraying her or to her sense of failure. By self-sabotaging, she was able to achieve her goal of preventing success from moving forward into the risks of ultimate betrayal and failure. As indicated, moving forward, for many of these people, may confer greater risk.

The patient may have fears of greater exposure. The writer mentioned earlier feared that, once he completed his work, it would be rejected by either the publisher or result in public humiliation once it was published. This individual utilized marijuana smoking as a self-handicapping excuse: "I'll get around to my writing once I get a handle on my smoking." The inflated ego-ideal—of being a famous writer—resulted in his utilization of numerous self-defeating strategies, hypersomnia, conflicts with his partner, and fixing his apartment. Once these fears of self-evaluation were exposed, he was able to finish his writing.

The emphasis on minimization of loss as a strategy is central for many individuals resisting change. For example, the patient may only search for possibility of failure and, once he finds this "evidence," he quits. This stop-loss approach may result in the patient saying, "I've tried all these things before, but they do not work." The patient has really tried straddling in order to minimize losses. The patient may be asked to self-contract for continued effort or longer duration in a situation (for example, a relationship), before quitting is allowed. Normalizing loss, rather than catastrophizing it, may also help the patient overcome the minimization strategy. For example, viewing loss as a learning experience, a normal step toward later rewards, the cost of doing business, or as compartmentalized, may be helpful in allowing the patient to view experience and loss as investments in the future.

Some patients act like binge-eaters when success occurs. They jump into relationships too quickly and too intensely and then are bitterly disappointed when they do not work out. The therapist may introduce the idea of a deprivation-hunger model to highlight the increased demand for immediate and great success. The patient can examine the costs of demanding more success immediately—for example, the tendency to over-commit too early to problematic relationships, thereby confirming the belief that his or her relationships never work out. In many cases, the hunger-deprivation process may alienate others, thereby resulting in the self-fulfilling prophecies of the depressed patients. One useful analogy is that of rappelling ropes in climbing; short changes in height or descent are accompanied by readjustments to the safety ropes. I have found it helpful to have patients slow down success so that they do not get their hopes up too high or demand too much from others.

Many self-defeating individuals have been busy creating stories about their possible failures. Detailed narratives are helpful in assisting the patient in imagining success and making it plausible. In contrast, cognitive therapy homework may often appear too intellectual and dry—it may lack a real-life feeling. Stories tend to be memorable, which may account for their popularity in cultures in conveying important lessons. The patient may be asked to write out brief (say two-page) stories about specific details about how she or he can be successful in developing a relationship. For example, one woman found it helpful to write out a short story of meeting a man, going out on a date, getting to know each other, and developing a meaningful relationship. Even though she had been in relationships before, she indicated that this was a totally novel exercise for her since she seldom visualized things working out. Narratives are valuable as a way of concretizing the plans that the patient can imagine executing in solving a problem and achieving a goal. These narratives may also reveal the points when the patient becomes anxious or depressed: "I became anxious in my story when we talked about sex because then I realized that I thought he was just trying to use me." The patient's fears of this "exploitation" may be addressed by asking the patient, "What would it mean to you if all he wanted was sex?" One woman indicated that it meant that he was superior and she was worthless. Her anticipation of this exploitation often led her to provoke the man aggressively and, thereby, avoid the risk of intimacy.

CONCLUSIONS

Many individuals in treatment will work collaboratively with the therapist and will find that behavioral and cognitive interventions rapidly modify mood and modify preexisting beliefs. However, many patients who have experienced long commitment to no-win relationships and dysfunctional beliefs and behavior may find it difficult to abandon these prior commitments. I have compared this to the phenomenon of sunk cost, since the patient is more concerned with making sense of past disutility than with increasing future utilities. Furthermore, for many depressed individuals, the choices that they consider are perceived as carrying greater risk than potential reward and their inhibition in moving forward may often be understood as a risk-management strategy.

Given the commitment to sunk costs and risk-management, resistance has an internal psycho-logic—that is, it actually makes sense, given the patient's assumptions. Inhibition of movement is often very adaptive, such as the inhibition to sail in heavy winds or to cross a swaying bridge. The approach presented here allows both patient and therapist to collaborate in understanding the value of resistance and to explore the implications of change. By examining what it means to abandon sunk-costs and well held beliefs, the therapist and patient may reframe change as the flexibility and ability to be strong enough to be wrong about the past and right about the future. Furthermore, by examining the negative self-verification of straddling, hedging, hiding, and provoking, the patient and therapist can reattribute failure to too much risk management rather than to personal and permanent inadequacies. Conceptualizing resistance as self-protective adaptation is considerably less pejorative for patients than to view them as unmotivated. Resolving the internal conflict, between the self that seeks improvement and the self that fears loss, allows resistant patients to understand how getting in their own way has appeared to them necessary for self-protection.

CHAPTER **6**

Sunk Costs and Resistance to Change

Normative models of decision-making (i.e., how rational people should make decisions) propose that individuals consider all relevant alternatives, collect information regarding the costs and benefits of each alternative, weigh these alternatives irrespective of primacy and recency effects, and focus on enacting a decision regardless of past investments and committed actions (Baron, 1994; Plous, 1993). Thus, decision-makers examine all the relevant information with the hope of maximizing their search and with the ability to weigh information dispassionately as to its relevance toward a goal. The normative model argues that decisionmakers should ignore the order of information presented and should give considerable emphasis to base rate information in the population at large, rather than choose the first alternative that comes along. The normative model stipulates that decisionmakers should not place greater emphasis on a personal anecdote rather than on abstract, but objective, data.

Normative models are based on Subjective Expected Utility (SEU), such that individuals are assumed to calculate the probabilities of future utilities of various possible actions, compare these utility ratios, calculate the uncertainty involved, and consistently choose the alternative with the best ratio (Bell, Raiffa, & Tversky, 1988). Normative models assume a decision-maker whose choices are dictated by hedonic calculus, with alternatives compared along an ordinal continuum of transitivity, such that, if A is preferred to B and B is preferred to C, then A is preferred to C. Thus, the normative model, emphasizing subjective expected utility, describes how a coldly rational person ignores past history of behavior and only focuses on future utility (Kahneman & Tversky, 1972; 1979; Tversky & Kahneman, 1972; 1981).

There is now considerable evidence that the normative model does not adequately describe actual decision-making. Descriptive models of how actual decision-making is carried out indicate that individuals utilize satisficing rules (Simon, 1956; 1979, 1988; 1992). Individuals consider only a small subset of possible alternatives and often base their decisions on a primacy effect, such that the first alternative that satisfies minimum criteria will be accepted (Simon, 1988). Decisionmakers may violate the law of transitivity, preferring C to A, even when A is preferred to B and B is preferred to C (Kahneman & Tversky, 1979). The violation of transitivity raises questions of the generality of SEU, since utilities appear to be nonfungible. Individual decision-makers may also ignore the rules of probability, placing considerably greater weight on information that is salient, personal, and accessible (Tversky & Kahneman, 1972).

Furthermore, individuals are seldom neutral about their past decisions and behavior. If they have invested considerable time and energy, they will utilize this past cost, or disutility, in determining their future course of action (Staw, 1976; 1981; Staw & Ross, 1987; Thaler, 1980; 1992). Thus, rather than rely on cold rational calculations of future utility (or disutility) of a course of action, a forward-looking decision, they will focus on past costs that have been incurred—a backward-looking decision.

Sunk Costs

There is substantial evidence that individuals may place greater emphasis on their prior costs and use these costs to determine whether they will continue to pursue action that already has proven to be unrewarding (Arkes & Ayton, 1999; Garland, 1990; Staw, 1976; 1981; Staw, Barsade, & Koput, 1997; Staw & Fox, 1977; Staw & Ross, 1978; 1987; Thaler, 1980). The *sunk-cost effect* is defined as the tendency to consider prior costs as facilitative of future commitments to that alternative. Consider the following, unfortunately common, experience. You have purchased a necktie that was on sale at a 70% reduction. You thought you got a good deal. You notice that the tie is not quite up to your demanding standards of taste, but you cannot pass up such a bargain. It does not occur to you that the reason that it is marked down below its cost is that all other potential buyers thought is was not worth the lower price. In fact, up to this point, you may be the first person willing to buy this tie. You take it home, put it in your closet, and never wear it. Although years go by, you still cannot find the right jacket or shirt to wear with this tie. Regardless of your lack of utility in this tie, you refuse to throw it out.

Now consider the following more serious problem. Susan has been involved with Bill for four years. He continues to say that he will leave his wife when the time is right. Susan has claimed that she loves Bill, that there is no one like him, but that she knows that the relationship is going nowhere. She agrees with her therapist and friends who point out the lost opportunities, Bill's manipulative nature, and Susan's ability to attract better prospects. All of this seems to go nowhere with Susan who continues to argue that no one can understand the special relationship that she and Bill share. Moreover, Susan indicates, "I've already put in four years. I can't just walk away from it."

Sunk-cost effects are a major barrier to change. The person looks to the past for the reasons to maintain a course of action that has now proven to be a failure. Rather than claiming that the past costs are reason enough to abandon a losing strategy, the individual may escalate his justification and investment to continue the course of action. Rather than thinking "I don't want to throw good money after bad," the individual may claim, "I've invested too much to give up on this now."

Ideally, in making a decision, we consider the future benefits that may be achieved by a course of action—that is, we consider the expected utility. For example, the woman who had already committed substantial behavior, at high cost, to a relationship that seemed to be going nowhere, might be expected to consider these costs as a learning experience and anticipate further trouble ahead. Classical learning theories, guided by a reinforcement or extinction model, would imply that she would abandon the relationship, even if no other rewarding relationship were available. From reinforcement theory, the reinforcements would be seen as diminishing as the costs increased. Longer learning history in the relationship would predict even greater impetus to abandon the relationship. However, she resisted abandoning the high-cost, long-history relationship. Individuals are not always guided by reinforcement history, nor are they easily convinced by cost-benefit analysis. Her current decision-point, whether to continue or quit, is determined by her prior investment in the relationship.

Commitment to Sunk Costs

According to normative models of decision making—that is, how a rational person would make a decision—individuals should evaluate future utility in making current decisions. Thus, an individual deciding to sell her house, should ignore the money spent on improving her house and should consider the current market for selling the house. If Carol bought the house for $100,000 and put $50,000 into the house, she should not demand that she get at least $150,000 in the sale of the house, but she should try to get what the market will pay, say, $125,000. However, individuals often act as if past investments—sunk costs—demand recovery, thereby leading many people to stick with a losing proposition (Leahy, 2001).

Consider the following from one of several studies by Arkes and Blumer (1985). Subjects are told,

> As the president of a company, you have invested ten million dollars of the company's money into a research project (a plane that cannot be detected by radar). When the project is 90% completed, another firm begins marketing a plane that cannot be detected by radar. In addition, it becomes apparent that their plane is much faster and far more economical than the plane your company is building. The question is: should you invest the last 10% of the research funds to finish your radar-blind plane?

The authors found that 85% of the subjects in the study recommended finishing the airplane. However, another group, who was not told about the prior investment, overwhelmingly decided not to invest the money. Consequently, having a prior investment, which was a mistake, became an overwhelming justification for honoring sunk costs.

There have been a number of attempts to explain the sunk-cost effect. Honoring sunk costs can be explained by commitment theory (Kiesler, 1969), cognitive-dissonance theory (Festinger, 1957; 1961), prospect theory and loss frames (Kahneman & Tversky, 1979), fear of wasting (Arkes, 1996; Arkes & Blumer, 1985), attribution processes (for example, Jones & Davis, 1965), and inaction inertia (Gilovich & Medvec, 1994; Gilovich, Medvec, Chen, 1995). Commitment theory predicts that individuals will persist with a commitment to past actions, sometimes ignoring future utility ratios. Cognitive dissonance theory argues that prior losses for a somewhat unrewarding commitment results in cognitive conflict which may be resolved either by overvaluing the prior behavior or by increased hope that the sunk cost will be redeemed, thereby justifying the past behavior. Prospect theory suggests that individuals suffer losses more than they enjoy their gains and that changing from a sunk cost may be experienced as a loss. Thus, by delaying the acceptance of the loss, there is an attempt to deny that the loss really exists. Fear of wasting would imply that as long as the individual remains committed to the sunk cost, and the hope of redeeming the prior investment, there is no finality to the recognition that it has been wasted. Thus, if the individual continues in the sunk cost, he may conclude that the prior investment was not wasted. This, of course, implies that he does not view future commitments to the sunk cost as increased wasting. While continuing a commitment to the sunk cost, he delays the recognition of wasting and takes an option on hope. Hope springs eternal as long as the sunk cost is not finalized as a loss.

Attribution processes may be involved in sunk-cost effects in that the individual may observe his own behavior and conclude that a high investment must be due to a worthwhile cause. This might be true for justifying sunk costs incurred by the self and by others: People only invest a lot if there is a good reason to do so. Finally, inaction inertia is based on the fact that there is asymmetrical regret for inaction and action: thus, in the short run, individuals experience more regret for new actions taken than continuing in a course of inaction (Gilovich & Medvec, 1994). By continuing in the sunk cost, the individual avoids an increase of regret in the short run.

A number of factors affect the magnitude of the sunk-cost effect. Increasing an individual's sense of personal responsibility for the original action increases the sunk-cost effect (Staw, 1976; Whyte, 1993), but making the individual accountable to others for a decision decreases the sunk-cost effect (Simonson & Nye, 1992). If an individual is able to attribute part of the responsibility to someone else, then he is less likely to honor the sunk cost. Thus, accountability and disattribution may be helpful in reversing the sunk-cost effect. Staw and Ross (1987) found that bifurcating (or separating) the initial and subsequent decision-making decreased sunk-cost effects, presumably because the individual considered the utility functions of each decision independently of the other. Staw and Ross (1987) also suggest providing the individual with corrective negative feedback for their decisions in an attempt to establish clearer contingencies for decision-making.

Research and theory on the sunk-cost effect indicates that, the greater the prior cost has been, the more likely individuals are to continue on a course of behavior (Arkes & Blumer, 1985; Garland, 1990). Furthermore, if they view a change as having high cost relative to their existing assets, they will continue longer in the behaviors (Garland & Newport, 1991; Kahneman and Tversky, 1979). This may imply that the longer they are in costly relationships, the *fewer* their remaining assets may be, since the relationship undermines self-esteem and decreases opportunities to pursue alternatives. This may be one reason why people stay in abusive relationships longer than objective observers can comprehend (see Dutton, 1999).

Modifying Sunk-Cost Effects

Many therapists can identify with the experience of having patients, who are locked into repeated patterns of self-defeat, argue vigorously that they cannot give up on their behavior. No-win relationships, dead-end jobs, training or education that leads nowhere, and investments in property with declining value all elicit sunk cost effects. The patient claims, "I can't walk away from four years of a relationship", "I've already put seven years into this company—I can't give up on it now"; "I'm so close to getting my degree and even though I don't want to do that kind of work, it's too close to give up"; or, "I've invested so much in this property I won't sell it for less than I paid for it." Each of these positions reflects a sunk-cost effect and each is irrational and impedes change. We will now examine how the therapist can assist the patient in overcoming commitment to sunk costs.

Educate Patients About Sunk Costs

Although the idea of sunk costs is derived from decision-theory and investment models, it is far from arcane and abstract. Everyone has a tie, blouse, computer, or relationship that reflects a sunk cost effect. Mundane, nonthreatening, examples such as a tie or blouse can be helpful for patients to understand that they may hold onto something that they would never buy again. Paying exorbitant costs to fix an old car or computer that would best be left at a junkyard are familiar sunk costs that people can readily see. The therapist can ask, "Have you ever had the experience of throwing good money after bad? Of putting more effort or investment into something that you know is not worth much? And feeling compelled to do so?" The therapist can explain that people often find themselves committing more behavior to choices that have become very costly. The prior losses and costs that are experienced are known as a sunk cost and the decision to continue in that course of action may be called "commitment to a sunk cost."

Examine the Costs and Benefits of Continuing in the Sunk Cost

Few courses of action are without some benefit. The individual who has difficulty leaving a job may still derive some significant benefits from the job; he knows what is required of him, he receives a paycheck, and he may derive some sense of competence from the work. Similarly, the woman who was described as being in a no-win relationship may point to the romance, companionship, and fun that she derives. Costs and benefits should be examined in terms of "ultimate goals"—for example, "To have a job that I can feel proud of" or "To feel that my relationship makes me feel better about myself" or "To have more stability in my life."

The costs and benefits should be examined in terms of their intensity, value, duration, and trend—that is, how strong or what is the magnitude of the reward, how important is the reward relative to your ultimate goals, for how much time do you experience the reward, and are the rewards following an upward or downward trend? Many times the individual may recall a benefit that lasts one hour ("I saw him at lunch"), but that the costs last considerably longer ("I missed him all week"). A reward may be enjoyable, "I had a good time goofing off at work," but may conflict with ultimate goals—"I'd like to have a job that challenges me."

What are the Costs and Benefits of Pursuing Different Alternatives

The first problem posed here is developing alternatives. Every commitment involves an opportunity cost—that is, a loss of a chance to pursue alternative behaviors. The man who is in an unrewarding relationship can consider the loss of opportunities to pursue other relationships. The woman who is unhappy with her job may consider the lost opportunities to pursue other training or other work. Since behavior is engaged in real time, there is the accompanying cost of lost time, which can never be recovered.

The investment trap of sunk costs implies that the individual is retrospective (about costs) rather than prospective. Expected utility theory proposes that individuals (should) consider the costs and benefits for the future for a current decision. The patient can examine the costs and benefits of basing current decisions on past sunk costs vs. the costs and benefits of basing these decisions on future utility ratios. Furthermore, the therapist can ask the patient, "Would you feel comfortable if the current situation continued for one year? Where would you like to be a year from now?" By extricating the individual from the experience of a recent sunk cost, the decision can become more prospective than retrospective. Future backward looking is more effective than current backward ties.

As with the costs and benefits outlined above, the patient may be asked to consider a range of alternatives in terms of tradeoffs for their intensity, value, duration, and trend. Often, individuals trapped in a sunk-cost commitment are myopic in considering alternatives. For example, the woman who is considering changing jobs may overvalue the inconvenience in pursuing new training or new challenges on a different job, not recognizing that these options may become easier the longer she pursues them.

Developing alternatives to a sunk cost is not always a simple matter. The sunk cost may contribute to pessimism, thereby undermining the ability to escape from the prior commitment. The therapist may inquire as to whether other friends or family members believe that there are alternatives that the patient does not see. In addition, the therapist may articulate some possibilities. The therapist may inquire as to whether the patient saw more options to leave earlier, suggesting that continuing in the sunk cost may contribute to a decline in alternative construction and an increase in hopelessness. This is especially apparent in abusive relationships.

Bifurcate the Current Decision From the Past Decision to Commit to an Action

People seldom make a decision ignoring their prior decisions and behavior. Decisions are sequential rather than unitary events calculated at a single point in time. The difficulty in escaping from a sunk cost is that you are focused on justifying your past sequence of decisions and behavior—thereby leading to an escalation in commitment. The therapist can separate, or bifurcate, the present decision from prior decisions by asking the following: "If you had never gotten into this behavior, would you make a decision to get into it now?" For example, the woman who is living with a man who is neglectful and abusive can be asked, "If you had never met John before today, but you knew how things would end up, would you make the decision to get involved with him now?" Separating the current decision from prior decisions and commitments helps the patient realize that a negative answer to the foregoing question illustrates that the patient is no longer looking at rational self-interest in the future but is now attempting to justify a past series of mistakes.

The therapist may indicate that bifurcation of decisions may imply that the higher cost ironically leads to a tendency to justify a prior commitment. The therapist may inquire why there is a difference between the first decision to get into the relationship (or behavior) and a different decision if the individual had known beforehand what the costs would be. This may lead the patient to articulate assumptions such as, "I have too much invested to walk away"; "I now have a responsibility to make it work out"; or, "I'm not frivolous; I don't walk away from my commitments." These assumptions may be examined utilizing cognitive therapy techniques. "What if you looked at your prior investments as lost costs that you can never recover? How would putting more of yourself into this help you achieve your ultimate goals? Don't you have a responsibility to yourself that is greater than your responsibility to this behavior or relationship? Wouldn't it mean that you take yourself and your future seriously if you admitted that something was not working out for you?"

Put the Decision in the Hands of Other Decision-Makers

Most therapists can attest to the fact that they may be better at giving advice than at taking their own advice. Similarly, the patient, committed to his or her past actions and decisions, has too much at stake to make the decision for the future. The woman who is living with the neglectful and abusive man can be asked, "If we asked three enlightened strangers what would be the best decision for you, what advice would they give?" "Why would their advice differ from your inclination to continue in this course of action?"

   Often the patient may respond with the truism, that casts little light, by saying, "It's always easier to see someone else's problems more clearly." But the more enlightening question is, "Why?" The patient's attention can be drawn toward the cognitive dynamics of the sunk-cost effect; strangers have not incurred a cost that they need to justify. They can focus exclusively on self-interest as defined by future utilities and costs. Their decisions are forward looking, not backward justifying.

Utilize the Double-Standard Technique

We are often quite reasonable and objective when giving other people advice, but fail to utilize objectivity when it comes to our own decisions. The patient's sunk cost dynamic may be illustrated and challenged by asking him, "What advice would you give a friend who was in this decision?" Alternatively, to elicit even greater protectiveness of self-interest, the patient may be asked, "What advice would you give your child if he or she were in this position?" The therapist may role-play all of the patient's self-justifications and ask the patient to pretend that the patient is arguing with his or her son or daughter, who is justifying the sunk-cost decision. Again, the patient's attention may be drawn to the conflict between justifying his own sunk cost and vigorously challenging the friend or child's sunk-cost arguments.

What are the Automatic Thoughts Associated with Honoring a Sunk Cost?

Some of these automatic thoughts may be elicited by examining the costs and benefits of continuing in a sunk cost. The therapist should carefully follow up with the use of the "vertical descent" technique (Burns, 1990)

Therapist: "What would it mean to give up on this relationship?"
Patient: I had wasted four years
Therapist: What would that make you think?
Patient: That I failed. That I can't make any decisions. That nothing will ever work out. That I'm doomed to be unhappy.

Another patient might respond with a different sequence of thoughts, such as "All my friends will think that they were right about what a lousy relationship I had. Everyone will think I was an idiot. No one could ever respect me again."

Or, the overly conscientious patient may think: "I should have been able to make it work. I was irresponsible. I can't be trusted to do the right thing. I'm reprehensible."

What are Some Rational Responses to the Automatic Thoughts?

As shown in Table 6.1, the automatic thoughts illustrated above may be examined in terms of rational or positive alternatives.

Examine the Overvaluation of What is Known or Possessed Versus What is Not Known or What is to Come

Decision theory research indicates that people often overvalue what they already have or possess, requiring a higher price to give up something for which they paid a lower price. Whether we call this "loss aversion" (Tversky & Kahneman, 1988) or the "endowment effect" (Thaler, 1992), individuals will find themselves preferring what they have to what they could obtain. This may be one of the reasons why investors will ride a loser and sell of off winners, perhaps hoping to redeem a losing invest-ment by watching it rise from the ashes of their portfolios (see Thaler, 1997).

Abandoning a sunk cost may activate loss aversion, since the individ-ual is giving up something that he or she possesses. This immediate

Table 6.1 Rational Responses to Automatic Thoughts.

Automatic Thoughts	Rational Responses
I have wasted four years.	This is all-or-nothing thinking. There were many positive things as well as negative things in the relationship. Giving up on something that is not working for you now does not mean that it was an entire waste. If it was a waste, then better to get out of it now.
I failed.	You didn't fail. You had some positives and negatives. The job or relationship may have failed to live up to your expectations. You can make a successful decision now to make a change.
Nothing will ever work out.	First, many other things have been rewarding to you in the past and many things are currently rewarding to you. Second, "working out" is an all-or-nothing expression—it's really about trade-offs, costs, and benefits. Third, you can examine the relative trade-offs of other options that you have.
I can't make any decisions.	You have made many decisions in the past— some have been better than others, some worse than others. Making a decision to make a change implies that you are looking at the future trade-offs for you. Making a decision to stay where you are indicates that you may think that the trade-offs are better in the current situation. Are they?
I'm doomed to be unhappy.	You have had happiness before and you have times when you are happy now. Again, this is all-or-nothing fortunetelling. No one is doomed to anything. The real question to ask yourself is, "Are the tradeoffs better in staying or in leaving?"
All my friends will think that they were right about what a lousy relationship I had.	If they are right about your making a change— that it is a good idea for you—then it may be wise to admit when someone else has good advice.
Everyone will think I was an idiot.	You friends probably want what is best for you, so they may be happy if you make a change. If they are critical of you, you might want to be assertive with them.

Table 6.1 *(Continued)*

Automatic Thoughts	Rational Responses
I should have been able to make it work.	When things don't work out it usually means that both people have contributed to the problem. What was the contribution of the other person? It also may mean that you were not in a position to make it work—perhaps the two of you are different people.
I was irresponsible.	When decisions don't work out and you make a change later, it implies that you are willing to recognize and accept reality for what it is. That is being responsible to yourself. You are not responsible for outcomes—you are not all-knowing and all-powerful. There are many examples of your acting responsibly. Perhaps you now have a greater responsibility to your legitimate self-interest.
I should have known it wasn't going to work out.	You can't know everything. You can only know the information that is available at the time. When you initially made the decision, you went with the information that you had. Perhaps the information changed over time—and perhaps you changed.

sense of loss, resulting in grief and deprivation, may be exaggerated by the individual confronting a choice. The therapist may examine the patient's beliefs about the sense of loss—"How bad do you think you will feel and for how long will you feel this bad?" "How bad do you think you will feel six months from now? A year from now?" Loss-aversion may be contrasted with the experience of gaining—"What can you gain?"

Tversky and Kahneman (1988) have proposed a model of choice—called *prospect theory*—that suggests that individuals may ignore expected utility because of how decisions are framed. Thus, the sunk-cost decision may be framed by the individual as a loss; "I will lose this relationship," rather than as a potential gain; "I will gain opportunities to have freedom and other relationships." Framing effects may be large, but they can be overcome by proposing changes as positive opportunities, with various degrees of probability; "What is the probability that you will be happy if you stay in the current relationship? What is the probability that you will be happy if you pursue something different?"

Another way of looking at this is that individuals may prefer the hell they know to the hell they do not yet know. Although, logically speaking, uncertainty is neutral in regard to outcome or valence; pessimistic individuals often infer that uncertainty implies a large negative. Thus, the statement, "The outcome is uncertain for tomorrow," does not have any definite valence—it could be positive, negative, or neutral—but the pessimistic individual will conclude, "It sounds like something bad will happen." The sunk-cost decision may be to avoid change because the uncertainty implies a negative outcome, whereas the current costs are discounted—"I know I can handle these costs. I may not be happy, but I could be worse off."

The therapist may indicate to the patient the illogical assumption that uncertainty is negative and ask the patient to predict the most positive, the most negative, and the most likely outcome as well as a neutral possible outcome of making a change. The patient can assign subjective probabilities and be asked to write out a narrative of how each of these possible outcomes may unfold.

What Would it Mean to Accept Sunk Costs as Lost Investments?

Riding a loser is a way of preserving the future option that it might become a winner. As long as the individual holds onto the decision of the sunk cost, he can hope to either redeem the sunk cost or delude himself into believing that there is still substantial potential. A common self-delusion in financial commitments is the illusion, "It's only a paper loss." Certainly, if your stock drops 30%, it is a real loss—just try to sell the stock and you will find out.

The therapist may utilize the vertical descent procedure to evaluate the meaning of accepting a sunk cost. For example, a woman, attached to a man who was an alcoholic and with whom she shared a six-year relationship, had difficulty ending the relationship:

Therapist: What would it mean to accept that the relationship is not worth continuing?
Patient: It would mean that I've wasted all that time, all those years.

Here, like many people committed to a sunk cost, the perception is about dichotomized gains and losses: "If I accept it's not working, then it was a total waste." Regret often entails all-or-nothing thinking about a past behavior as if there were no rewards in the relationship.

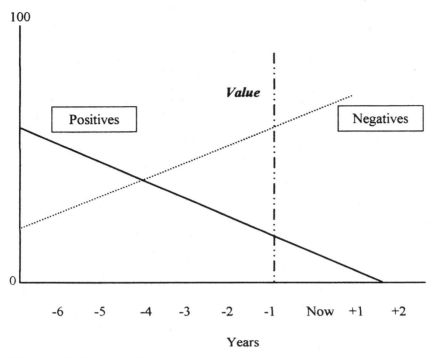

Figure 6.1 Cost-Benefit Trends and Sunk Costs

Therapist: So, if you decided now that the relationship was not worth
           pursuing, then it means that it was entirely a waste of time.
           That sounds like all-or-nothing thinking. I wonder if you can
           think of a shifting balance of positives eventually outweighed
           by negatives?

The therapist then drew the following graph for the patient:

Examine the Need to be Right

Cognitive therapy is based on a rational principle, such that the assumption is that patients will be motivated by logic and evidence to modify
their opinions. There are notable exceptions to this principle, such as the
patient's emphasis on validation, moral responsibility, or cognitive consistency (Leahy, 2001). Many individuals who are suffering in their current situation may demand validation for their suffering rather than
solutions to their problems (Leahy, 2000, 2001). If the therapist is overly

confrontational and points out how the patient may be better off making a change, the patient's validation concerns may be activated, leading the patient to conclude, " You don't understand how bad I feel". The patient may believe that he has to prove to the therapist that the pain is unbearable, while viewing exhortations to change as minimization of the patient's difficulties in the current situation or problems in making a change.

The therapist may address these concerns directly by indicating that examining possibility to change is often experienced as uncaring and as minimizing the patient's difficulties: "I can see how bad you feel and how difficult it is to even consider making a change. When I ask you to examine other options, I do not mean to imply that making a change is easy for you or that the problems you are having are not important." The therapist may indicate that "therapy is often a dilemma—no matter what you say or do at times it is painful. To think of making a change is painful because it may mean you are thinking of leaving something that is meaningful or it may mean that you feel that your feelings are being ignored. But, not to consider change might mean that you are stuck. We can try to deal with this dilemma by reminding ourselves that your experience and feelings are important and that your options are also important."

Examine How Sunk Costs are Related to Personal Schemas

Many people who are stuck in one sunk cost are able to abandon other sunk-cost decisions without regret or hesitation. The relevant factor appears to be how the sunk cost is related to the individual's personal schemas. The woman who is stuck in the abusive relationship may find it difficult to extricate herself from the sunk cost because it may activate her personal schemas of abandonment ("Everyone will leave me"), biological helplessness ("I can't take care of myself"), or demanding standards ("I should make everything work out"). In contrast, another person may be stuck in a relationship because of the need to appear special— divorce might imply failure, mediocrity, or ridicule from others. For other people, abandoning a sunk cost in a relationship may be less of a problem, because the personal schema may be positive (desirable or special), thereby implying that future benefits may be especially appealing.

The variability of sunk-cost effects for the same person may be illustrated by asking the patient, "Are there other decisions in other areas of your life that are easier for you to make?" For example, a man who had a difficult time abandoning the sunk cost in an intimate relationship found it much easier to cut his losses in business decisions. The sunk cost in the relationship implied a sense of being a success as a husband—and divorce implied failure to him. Although he was quite successful in business and in investments, he had considerable doubts about whether he was lovable. Thus, his personal schema of being unlovable was activated when he considered making a change in a relationship, but he was flexible in decision-making in business, since his personal schema in that domain was quite positive.

The therapist may help the patient examine the origins and validity of the negative personal schema, considering how the schema may have been learned from dysfunctional parents and maintained by avoidance and compensation (Beck & Freeman, 1990; Leahy, 1996, 2001; Young, 1999). Indeed, the sunk cost effect may be considered as a schema-maintaining process and the patient may be asked what changes in his schema might have occurred had he not been trapped by sunk costs. Traditional cognitive therapy techniques, such as examining the evidence, considering costs and benefits, acting against the schema, utilizing the semantic technique, and utilizing role-plays in therapy can be helpful in modifying the schema. Of course, abandoning the sunk cost may be considered as an experiment in acting against the schema, with the patient's predictions elicited and tested.

The advantage of recognizing variability in being trapped by sunk costs allows the patient to recognize the potential for change. If change is possible in one domain in life, it can be achieved in other domains. Being trapped in the sunk cost in the domain specific to one's negative schemas may further reinforce the negative schema. The woman who is trapped in a no-win relationship may point to that relationship as proof that she is unlovable, but the fear of making a change may be impeded by her belief that her unloveability will prevent her from finding better alternatives. This self-fulfilling prophecy of sunk-cost effects further strengthens her negative schema.

CONCLUSIONS

An irony of the sunk-cost effect is that everyone knows what it is but few clinicians have considered it as a factor in change. Almost all of us know what it means to throw good money after bad and many people recognize the folly of becoming overcommitted to past decisions—such as during the Vietnam War. The fact that humans, and not animals, are susceptible to sunk costs (Arkes & Ayton, 1999), is evidence of the importance of cognitive factors and sophistication in developing impediments to change. We may be too smart for our own good.

We have examined the fact that normative models of decision making may not apply for important everyday decisions in which patients are blocked from considering expected utilities in a rational way. It may be that individual decision-makers considering mundane decisions are less concerned with being rational and more sense with making sense of their past behavior. As Festinger (1954) noted many years ago, the emphasis on self-justification and self-consistency may result in apparently counterintuitive decisions, some of which may be self-defeating.

We have examined a number of possible interventions that the clinician may utilize in reversing the sunk-cost effect. The development of a rationale for the patient, based on a decision-theory model of sunk costs, is an example of how the cognitive approach is particularly effective in involving the patient in therapeutic collaboration—that is, once the patient understands the process of sunk costs, change may be facilitated. The goal of therapy is to help the individual overcome impediments to following subjective expected utility and to make decisions that are forward-focused rather than backward justifying.

CHAPTER 7

Pessimism as Risk-Management

The cognitive model of depression proposes that individuals who predict that the future will result in negative outcomes are more likely to maintain their depression and are more likely to have recurrent episodes of depression (Beck, 1976; Beck et al., 1987). Moreover, attribution models of helplessness and hopelessness stress the centrality of negative predictions that are based on explanations of failure that refer to internal, stable attributes, such as ability (Abramson, Teasdale, & Seligman, 1978; Abramson, Metalsky, & Alloy, 1989; Alloy, Abramson, Metalsky, & Hartledge, 1988). Pessimism may result from the individual's belief that she or he lacks the ability to effect positive outcomes. Given the relationship between pessimism, low self-esteem, and depression, one can wonder about the apparent irrationality of maintaining a belief that results in such negative outcomes for the individual. The view advanced in the present chapter is that pessimism may be based on a self-protective strategy.

The "Rationality" of Pessimism

Pessimistic individuals—especially very depressed individuals—often do not view themselves as irrational. Even when confronted in cognitive therapy with a request to conduct a hedonic calculus of the costs and benefits of pessimism, the pessimistic individual may resist changing her negative outlook. Cognitive therapists are often confronted with the depressed patient's stress of the validity of negative predictions, the extremity of the negative outcome predicted, and the tendency of the patient to discount countervailing positive information. What could account for this apparent commitment to a self-defeating thought?

The theory of pessimism that I advance here is based on the view that individuals attempt to avoid further losses. All of us consider the risks of change by assessing the probability, magnitude, and desirability of positive versus negative outcomes. Cognitive therapists often appear to suggest that there are generally good reasons to be optimistic about something. However, there are many situations when pessimism is a more realistic view and many cases in which optimism would confer considerable risk. The question, then, is what are the differences between pessimistic and optimistic worldviews?

Cognitive models of depressive rumination (Nolen-Hoeksema, 2000) or worry (Wells, 2000) indicate that individuals sometimes view these processes as adaptive problem solving, preparation, or self-protection. Pessimism is a rational strategy in a world of scarce resources, unpredictability, and the chance of catastrophic consequences. For example, during the trench war of World War I it would make sense in to feel pessimistic about charging across enemy lines. It would not make sense for an impoverished family to believe that spending all their money on a vacation would be a good idea. Pessimism is the rational choice just before a stock market crash. Indeed, one might argue that the history of the human species would require a certain guarded pessimism, since for much of our history resources were scarce and there was danger everywhere.

A Theory of Pessimistic Choice

The model that I have proposed is a model of decision-making or choice (Leahy, 1997, 1997a, 1999). The main dimensions of pessimistic choice are displayed in Table 7.1. A theory of choice must consider what the ultimate purpose is of the choice—to maximize gains or minimize losses—and how the individual considers the relevance of information, resources, utility, time and regret. I have employed a model of choice drawn from economic theory—specifically, modern portfolio theory.

This portfolio theory model proposes that individuals consider their choices in light of the following: current resources available, diversification of rewards, ability to produce future resources, duration of investment, ability to replicate investments, utility of gains and disutility of losses, information available, ability to use time to collect information, predictability and controllability of outcomes, regret orientation, and risk tolerance. According to this model, individuals who are pessimistic will view themselves as having few current and future resources. That is, they

Table 7.1 Pessimistic Choice Model

Portfolio Concern	Pessimistic View
Current resources available	Low: I have few rewards available.
Diversification of rewards	Low: I have very few different kinds of things that are rewarding.
Ability to produce future resources	Low: I have little ability to produce positive outcomes in the future.
Duration of investment	Short: I can't wait a long time for a positive to occur.
Ability to replicate investments	Low: I can't repeat a behavior over and over to produce a positive. If it doesn't work out immediately, it won't work out.
Utility of gains	Low: Positives that occur are not that enjoyable anyway.
Disutility of losses	High: Negatives are very unpleasant. I can't tolerate them.
Demands for information	High: Need close to certainty in order to make a decision.
Using time to make decisions	High: I need to wait a long time to collect all the information to make a decision.
Predictability and controllability of outcomes	Low-Low: I can't predict the future and I can't control it.
Regret orientation	High: I really criticize myself for any mistakes that I make.
Risk tolerance	Low: I can't tolerate any risk.

believe that they have very few sources of rewards and very little diversification in their rewards. For example, the individual is more likely to be pessimistic if she believes that a relationship is the only source of reward and less likely to be pessimistic if she views herself as having many different current and future rewards in her life. Although pessimism involves future time perspective and hopelessness, the pessimistic individual is likely to see longer duration as simply a continuation of current deprivation, rather than viewing the current negatives as temporary. Furthermore, reliance on duration as a factor that can offset current loss is the pessimistic view that the deprivation is so great now that one cannot wait for rewards in the future. For example, someone who has not eaten in five days cannot take satisfaction in knowing that he has a reservation at an excellent restaurant next week. He may not make it to the next week.

Scarcity Assumptions, Resignation, and Avoiding Effortful Helplessness

Pessimistic individuals often maintain assumptions that rewards are scarce. These scarcity assumptions may be personalized, rather than universal, assumptions. Thus, the pessimistic individual may conclude that there are very few opportunities for him—a personal assumption—but that others may have access to these resources. For example, one woman believed there was no one available for *her,* but that other women had good relationships.

If the world were viewed as having few resources for the individual, then extending effort to obtain no reward would only add to the feeling of helplessness. I make a distinction between *effortless* helplessness, wherein the individual is resigned and simply gives up, and *effortful* helplessness, wherein the individual extends effort and continually experiences failure. Resignation, in a world in which no rewards are forthcoming, is often viewed as a better strategy than constantly banging your head against the wall.

LOSS AVERSION

My view is that pessimistic individuals suffer their losses more than they enjoy their gains. Thus, they focus on how they can lose, what terrible consequence will result, and their lack of controllability of outcomes. The loss aversion is maintained by beliefs in a lower baseline, perception of extremity of loss, biased search rules for loss potential, misperception of trends, quitting rules, and resistance to disconfirmation. We shall now examine each of these factors.

Lower Baseline

A Panglossian, Candide-like optimism might make sense for someone who has abundant resources and who views the world as a replenishing experience. Bill Gates, the richest man in the world, has a lot of reasons to be optimistic. If he makes a mistake, he can afford to lose. His baseline is in the stratosphere.

But an impoverished individual, or one who believes he has nothing going for him, must consider the fact that his baseline—where he starts from in making a decision, is a much lower baseline. Drops from a very low baseline bring you close to zero, a point where suicide seems like a good alternative.

The importance of understanding the individual's phenomenal base-line is central in considering the resistance to change of pessimistic individuals. By "phenomenal baseline"I mean the standard that the depressed individual uses in assessing change. Cognitive-behavioral therapists often believe that depressed individuals should naturally be focused on incremental improvement, since their belief that they have nothing might lead one to the conclusion that any progress is worth making. However, depressed individuals may be more focused on losing more from a low baseline than in achieving small gains at the risk of a greater loss.

Extremity of Loss

An individual approaching a cliff that drops 1,000 feet will do so with considerable caution. A mistake will be fatal. Pessimistic individuals view potential losses as not only more likely, but also as more severe. A mistake will result in a loss that can be emotionally fatal. Given the potential of extreme negative consequences, pessimism may be viewed as an adaptive strategy—the more there is to lose, the greater necessity for caution.

Search Rules for Loss

The pessimistic individual approaches events with a search for a risk of loss. They utilize "satisfaction" rules, such as "Is there any sign that this won't work out?" If the answer is, "Yes, there is a possibility," the pessimist discontinues the search and does not consider either the likelihood of positive outcomes or the probability of the negative outcome. Indeed, the possibility of negative outcomes becomes psychologically equivalent to the probability of these outcomes.

Information Demands and Waiting as a Strategy

Almost all decisions in daily life are made with a degree of uncertainty. Demands for certainty in an uncertain world will result in caution, reassurance seeking, delay, procrastination, and failure to make a decision. What currently is will continue to be if the individual's information demands are too exacting.

Just as the pessimist has biased search rules for potential for loss, he also has high demands for determining the likelihood of a neutral outcome. Thus, the pessimist may believe that he needs almost perfect certainty before he takes a leap. In many cases, waiting to see what happens, or what new information comes forward, may be the strategy preferred by the pessimist. "Let's see what happens," or "I need to feel ready," or "I need to feel secure" before I make a choice become the guidelines for delaying a choice. The demand for perfect information is similar to the hypochondriac who does not feel safe unless she or her has ruled out every possibility and has complete reassurance.

The risk of excessive information demands and the use of waiting as a strategy is that opportunities are lost during the waiting period. The overly cautious person may lose an opportunity to move a relationship forward, pursue a career move, or develop new resources because of the high information demands. The demand for certainty, which the pessimist utilizes as a method to avoid risk, may continue a low-reward situation, thereby reinforcing the pessimism even further. The attempt to solve the problem by demanding more information thereby becomes the problem.

What is a "Trend"?

Pessimistic individuals are quick to see a negative trend. One or two negative events are viewed as the beginning of a trend, which in Riskind's (1997; Riskind, Long, Williams, & White, 2000) model, may be looming rapidly toward a disaster. Negative events are not compartmentalized into separate, independent, or even random occurrences. Rather, the pessimistic individual sees a trend of one negative leading to another negative in a chain reaction of negatives—very similar to a kindling effect—that once the fire gets started, it will be difficult to put it out. Consequently, the pessimist is myopic, viewing any current negative—however small—as a sign of an unfolding trend.

Positive movement—the experience of a reward—does not result in a generalization of a positive trend, since the assumption is that the scarcity assumptions dominate—that is, there are not likely to be positive trends if the world is viewed as basically unrewarding. Indeed, positive trends that begin to develop may activate an anxious, vigilant, pessimism—that is, as things improve the pessimist may become worried that he has let his guard down. This vigilant, anxious pessimism may then lead the individual to challenge the positive trend. For example, as a man became more emotionally intimate with his girlfriend, he became more worried that he was getting vulnerable. He then attempted to challenge her intentions, pick fights, and question the relationship. The girlfriend felt attacked and misled, since she had become more vulnerable, and she expressed her dissatisfaction. This then confirmed his belief that the positive trend was an aberration, that things really were negative and that he should pull out as soon as he could. This sequence of events further reinforced his view that his pessimism about relationships was a rational strategy.

Quitting Rules

Given the search rules for loss and the overgeneralization of negative or catastrophic trends, the pessimist utilizes a quick-exit quitting rule. This is similar to a stop-loss rule—any small negative will signal quitting and pulling out. Consequently, the pessimist at the first sign of a negative decreases behavior, pulls out, and loses any opportunity to achieve positives. The pessimistic view is, therefore, not open to disconfirmation since positive experiences are less likely to be achieved.

Quitting early is an important element of pessimism and helplessness. Rather than responding to frustration with increased effort the pessimist believes that quitting will help her conserve whatever meager resources are left and will prevent further disappointment.

RESISTANCE TO DISCONFIRMATION

Negative thoughts will persist unless they are disconfirmed. However, pessimistic thinking is often resistant to disconfirmation. This may be due to a number of reasons, displayed in Table 7.2.

Table 7.2 Pessimism and Use of Information

Concern	Example
Low expectations	Things basically aren't that good.
Search rule	What's the downside?
Selective valuation	Place a high value on negative, low value on positive information.
Possibility = Probability	If it is possible it won't work, it's probable.
Miscalculation of sequential probabilities	The probability of a sequence of events A, B, C, is viewed as an additive function; $.10 + .10 + .10 = .30$, rather than as a multiplicative function: $.10 * .10 * .10 = .001$
Lack of offset	The potential positives do not compensate for the potential negatives.
Selective memory	Recall all of the things that did not work out.
Hindsight bias	I should have known it would not work, given the information I had at the time.
Demands for outcomes	Decision-making is evaluated entirely by outcome rather than the process of decision-making. Thus, a negative outcome means that you were bad at making a decision, rather than evaluating the decision by the process of how you used the information available.

Pessimism May Not Be Expressed in a Precise Prediction

The pessimist may have vague predictions with an indefinite time frame—such as, "things won't work out in the future." Consequently, if positive events occur this week, they are offset by the possibility that negative events will occur sometime in the future. Indeed, much of pessimism may be experienced as a black cloud rather than as a particular occurrence or event.

The therapist should elicit predictions of specific events at precise times; "You say that you don't see yourself being happy. Can you predict that during the next week that you will have no positive experiences? If you have some positive experiences, will that disconfirm any part of your pessimism?"

Pessimistic predictions may be postulated as dispositional statements, such as "In general, things are pretty bad." These dispositional statements are difficult to disconfirm since positive events may be discounted as not affecting the general disposition, which is negative. Consequently, predictions of negative experiences, such as "It will be a bad week" (which is a general dispositional statement), may be rephrased: "What percentage of the time do you think you will experience any pleasure during the week?"

Positive Outcomes May Be Viewed as an Aberration

Pessimistic beliefs may be resistant to disconfirmation because a positive outcome may be viewed as an exception to the rule. The patient may discount these positives since they are not viewed as an example in a change in the trend. Indeed, a positive outcome may be considered a reason to increase vigilance, lest hopefulness lead to a tendency to take a greater risk.

Pessimism May Result in Self-Fulfilling Prophecies

The cautious, procrastinating and avoidant behaviors of the pessimist may result in the absence of rewards that then leads the individual to conclude that rewards are not forthcoming. The absence of rewards may result in justification for the caution, procrastination, and avoidance.

Pessimism May Be Used as a Safety Cognition

Just as the socially phobic individual may rely on safety behaviors to protect him from the risk of public exposure and humiliation (Wells & Carter, 2001), the pessimist may view his negative predictions as having protected him from disasters that may occur. Thus, the problem of pessimism actually may be attributed as the solution to avoiding further negatives. Since terrible things are not generally occurring, the pessimist may have an illusory correlation that the lack of terrible outcomes has been the result of an extremely cautious approach. Thus, ironically, neutral outcomes may be attributed to the pessimism that protects the individual.

SUMMARY

Cognitive therapy is based on appeals to rationality and hedonic calculus, yet many patients resist modification of their pessimism even when the apparent irrationality and costs are demonstrated. Taking a constructivist view, the cognitive strategy of pessimism is described as an attempt to avoid further losses in a world viewed as having scarce resources, unpredictability, and uncontrollability. Specifically, pessimism is viewed in terms of scarcity, depletion, chain-reaction of losses, volatility, myopia, and regret. The pessimistic depressive patient has a low criterion for loss and a high criterion for gains and views gains as aberrations that signify a corrective downturn. Resistance to giving up pessimism is viewed as an attempt to avoid foolish risks that expose the individual to losses that cannot be absorbed.

The theoretical model that I have advanced views pessimism as an attempt to avoid risk and loss. Arguments that focus exclusively on the fact that the pessimist is engaging in negative predictions or selectively filtering negative information may appear somewhat misguided to the chronic or rigidly pessimistic individual who views her pessimism as a protective and adaptive strategy. The model that I have proposed assists the therapist and helping the patient to recognize why the pessimism makes sense and why the pessimist resists change. This model is far less pejorative to the pessimist who may view criticisms of her negative thoughts as further criticisms of herself or himself. Moreover, the current model has the benefit of suggesting clinical interventions within a cognitive therapy model.

PART III

Acquisition and Dissatisfaction

CHAPTER 8

Insatiability

INTRODUCTION

The compulsive demand for more and more often results in anxiety, depression, and the inability to be satisfied. Individuals may appear to have achieved substantial outcomes, but may remain dissatisfied. Perfectionists may increase their stress levels beyond endurance because they can never be satisfied. Their work may drive them to exhaustion since they feel that nothing is good enough. For some, too much is never enough.

Classical models of economics rely on the idea that certain classes of demands (for rewards) are more elastic than others—"elastic" here refers to the degree to which the demand can expand or contract (Case & Fair, 1989). For example, the demand for bananas may be relatively inelastic—there are just so many bananas that one wants. In contrast, the demand for designer clothing may be more elastic—expanding during times of personal affluence and contracting during more difficult financial periods. It is also possible for a demand to be high *and* inelastic— for example, the demand for air to breathe is very high and cannot be constricted, lest one suffocate. For some individuals, the demand for exceptional success may be high and inelastic. The relevant issue, of course, is the supply. Fortunately, there is enough air for everyone, but unfortunately, exceptional success is rare.

Classical economic models of choice suggest that decreases in supply, marked by increases in cost, result in decreases in demand. However, there may be certain demands that are more elastic than others—for example, the demand for a basket of groceries to feed one's family is inelastic and, therefore, consumers perceive themselves as having to pay higher prices. However, the demand for specific grocery items may be somewhat more elastic—costly meat may lead to substitutions such as beans. The elasticity of demand and the availability of substitutes may provide individuals with opportunities to gain satisfaction during times of changing supply.

Insatiable individuals appear to act as if their demands are inelastic and that nothing can substitute for a specific goal. The old saying, "If you can't be with the one you love, then love the one you're with," has little bearing on the insatiable individual. Moreover, in some cases, the supply-demand curve appears to have paradoxical effects on these people. Thus, for these individuals, decreased supply (or rarity) may increase the individual's demand. It is as if the individual is saying, "I need to have that precisely because it is so rare."

Classical models of the utility of wealth propose that the value of an increase of wealth decreases as one moves farther along the curve (Markowitz, 1952). Thus, there are diminishing returns as one accumulates more and more wealth, leading to decreased motivation to achieve greater wealth once basic needs are realized. Insatiable individuals appear anomalous in this regard: With increased accumulation, there is a change in the standard utilized so that still greater demands are made. The insatiable individual appears to violate some of the assumptions of the utility of wealth function in that increases in accumulation do not always lead to decreases in utility or motivation. For example, a successful investor who accumulates his first million dollars—perhaps exceeding his preestablished goals—now acts with greater motivation to achieve his second million. This appears to contradict the utility of wealth rule. However, if we view this increased motivation as a function of operant conditioning, such that the achievement or investment behavior is reinforced by the first million earned, then the propensity toward the second million will be even greater. This makes sense from the operant conditioning model. Thus, what may appear to be a violation of the utility function is actually consistent with the basic law of effect in learning— behavior that is reinforced will increase in frequency.

Numerous examples of excessive appetites for drugs, alcohol, sex, and gambling may function according to these simple learning principles. The assumption in classical economics of a basic need for a basket of goods may be violated as the basic need is modified by accumulation and reinforcement. For example, families may have considered air-conditioning to be a luxury in 1950 but consider it an absolute necessity in 2002. Demands change as earlier demands are satisfied.

INSATIABLE NEEDS

In this chapter, we will examine a number of processes that may account for the apparent anomaly of individuals who cannot be satisfied. These processes reflect perfectionism, addictive behavior, behavioral momentum, operant conditioning, resistance to extinction, and the cognitive mediation of motivation. Although the focus is primarily on insatiable demands in the financial sphere, we can generalize these processes to other aspects of insatiability including drug and alcohol addiction, body dysmorphic disorder, compulsive and narcissistic disorders, marital dissatisfaction, and general perfectionism.

Financial Insatiability

Several surveys indicate a significant paradox in American culture. The per capita income has doubled in the last thirty years, but overall ratings of happiness have not increased (Myers, 2000). The correlation between income and happiness is positive, but quite low (Deiner, Sandvik, Seidlitz, & Diener, 1993). Indeed, once basic middle-class comforts are achieved, income or wealth has almost no relationship to happiness, while other factors become increasingly more important—such as relationships, leisure, and the meaningfulness of one's work (see Furnham & Argyle, 1998). Although personal income has risen by over 100% between 1979 and 1997, personal bankruptcies and personal debt have risen 400% (Sullivan, Warren, & Westbrook, 2000). The historic increase in personal wealth in the United States has not been matched by corresponding increases in personal happiness (Myers & Diener, 1996). Indeed, the increase in personal income also is associated with a decrease in the savings rate. These surveys and studies suggest that, while money can increase the likelihood of happiness, the relationship between these variables is weak. Moreover, increased income has not resulted in increased financial security as evidenced by the savings and bankruptcy rates.

The focus in the present discussion is on the individuals for whom "too much is not enough"—that is, individuals who are so work-absorbed and driven to pursue money that the quality of their lives is sacrificed. Schor (1991; 1998) has described two related phenomena, which she labels the "overworked American" and the "overspent American." Increased personal income in the past 30 years has been purchased at the cost of increased hours working, dual-career families, and loss of leisure and community or family activities. Similarly, although there has been an increase in purchasing power for the average family, there is a corresponding increase in the demands to buy more expensive items—such as designer clothing, personal services, and high-technology items. These social and economic pressures are the context of our examination of the insatiable individual. However, unlike previous discussions of these social determinants, our discussion will focus on the individual psychology of the insatiable individual.

Pervasive Insatiability

I will define "satisfaction" as a feeling that one has had "enough" and that there is no pressing need for a change. For example, the feeling of satisfaction occurs when we are eating and recognize that we have no desire for more. At some point, we feel we have had enough and there is little motivation to eat more. When we drink sufficient water, our thirst is quenched, and when we are working on a paper, we are able to say, finally, "It's finished." Other examples of satisfaction include the ability to look at oneself in the mirror and say, "I guess I look OK" or to reflect on one's intimate relationship and say, "On balance, it's working fine for me." The ability to experience satisfaction, however, appears to elude many people in numerous areas of their lives. It is no small coincidence that one of the more important recent advances in couples therapy focuses less on changing the relationship and more on acceptance (see Hayes, Jacobson, & Follette, 1994).

The experience of dissatisfaction occurs in a number of areas of excessive appetites or demands. These include dissatisfaction with one's income or wealth, appearance or body, marriage, success, or mood. For example, individual dissatisfaction with income or wealth may result in increased work and loss of leisure. In the extreme, this dissatisfaction may result in work-absorption or illegal activity in order to obtain the requisite wealth. Demands for more money may lead to excessive gambling resulting in further losses and still further demands for a get-rich-quick scheme. Financial dissatisfaction may result in taking on greater consumer debt in order to possess the items that one believes he needs. Perhaps for this reason, among others, consumer debt and personal bankruptcy has increased by about 400% in the past 30 years, even though income in constant dollars has doubled. Even though we make more money, we spend far more than we can afford. For a short period, the savings rate was negative.

Concerning appearance or body image, increased age during adolescence is associated with increased dissatisfaction with weight and appearance—for both boys and girls (Gardner, 2001; Shafran, 2001).

Excessive concerns may result in body-dysmorphic image, such that the individual believes that any single imperfection is a sign of gross deformity. This is often associated with bingeing and purging behavior, in the attempt to modify the body image, or in excessive cosmetic surgery, seldom resulting in permanent satisfaction with appearance.

Dissatisfaction with marriage is reflected in the increased rate of divorce over the past 50 years in the United States and in the tendency of individuals to marry later or to never marry (see Myers, 2000). Moreover, many individuals who are married report dissatisfaction with their relationships. Occupational success is also a focus of dissatisfaction for many individuals, resulting in work absorption, absenteeism, and a tendency to quit a job to pursue work elsewhere.

DIMENSIONS OF INSATIABILITY

Insatiability cannot be reduced to any single explanation, since a variety of processes may be operative. In this section, we will examine a number of factors that may affect insatiability. Our focus, for the present, is primarily on financial insatiability, although comparisons with other excessive appetites or behaviors will become apparent.

Perfectionism

The expectations that an individual has will affect the degree of satisfaction that he experiences. Thus, on the negative side, relative deprivation reflects the belief that one is deprived relative to other groups who have more, not in terms of one's absolute level of income or wealth (see Furby, 1991). Perfectionistic individuals are prone to dissatisfaction in that their ideal standards are exceptional and their social comparisons are upward. These individuals do not use the normal distribution as a comparison standard, relying on the uppermost limits for their standards.

Perfectionistic individuals often may be driven by underlying beliefs of inadequacy—a view first advanced by Alfred Adler (1926/1964). Thus, perfectionism, or demanding standards, may be an attempt to compensate for these more fundamental beliefs of inferiority or unloveability (see Beck & Freeman, 1990; Young, 1990). Compensatory beliefs include "If I achieve this goal, then I will be loved, respected, worthwhile and happy." For example, the compulsive academic works hard to achieve the goal of gaining tenure. When tenure is achieved, he becomes despondent, realizing that he is not happier. A patient with body dysmorphic disorder has facial surgery, but two months after her face has healed, she feels unattractive and begins to focus on other aspects of her body that are imperfect.

Some perfectionists believe that they have exceptional abilities that make it possible for them to achieve what for others would be viewed as impossible. This over-valuation of one's ability results in the illusion that any amount of effort will result in accomplishing the goal. Ironically, this over-valuation of effort and ability may result in objective helplessness in that actual increases in effort will not affect outcomes.

Emotional perfectionism often underlies insatiable behavior—the individual seeks an emotional state of complete satisfaction and bliss. This is often a factor in utilizing feeling-states as a criterion for satisfaction—"When I have that perfect feeling, then I'll know it's right." This emotional perfectionism accompanies excessive standards in appearance, wealth, financial security, and romance. Since it is largely unattainable, the individual is constantly seeking more.

Earlier Deprivation

The old saying, "Once poor, never rich," has some existential truth for some individuals. Memories of earlier financial deprivation or unpredictability may be difficult to overcome—even if the individual has accumulated substantial wealth. The underlying belief, "I could lose it all," is quickly activated for these people in the volatility of the market. They may jump to the conclusion that a 20% loss in their assets threatens total financial ruin—as if a trap had been opened.

The pursuit of savings and wealth may be motivated by several factors—the desire to have money to spend, a buffer against emergencies, investment toward longer term goals or management of wealth (Lindquist, 1981). However, many individuals appear to be motivated by a desire to feel "secure" against any imagined financial disaster. Those people who have grown up in an economically deprived family, or who had experienced sudden financial loss early in life, may believe that they can never have enough money to assure against sudden loss.

A successful investment banker had accumulated substantial assets, but was compulsively driven by his fear that he would lose all his money. He described his earlier family history as one of initial financial affluence followed by the unexpected personal bankruptcy of his father and the disintegration of his family. As he accumulated more wealth, he also imagined dramatic scenarios of how he could lose it all. This then drove him to work harder to accumulate more money to offset fears of losing everything.

A similar pattern of deprivation and insatiability was observed in the case of an attractive young woman who appeared sexually provocative with her colleagues and with her male therapist. Examination of her early adolescence revealed her experience of being awkward, overweight, unattractive, and constantly teased by her adolescent peers. She attempted to compensate for this later by being sexually active, seeking out the attention of males in bars. She described a history of erotic dancing and prostitution that made her feel superior to men and desirable. However, her underlying belief that she was unattractive and unlovable was not satisfied by these compensations.

Attempts to compensate for earlier deprivation—whether economic or social—often result in insatiable motivation. The individual utilizes the compensatory mechanisms as a means whereby temporary anxieties associated with earlier deprivation are addressed. However, unless the earlier thoughts about deprivation are addressed, the individual may continue to utilize the compensatory behaviors.

I would suggest the following as a postulate regarding compensatory behavior—*Replacement Theory*: if a reward from one class is being used to replace rewards from another class, then we would expect less satiation since one class of reward will not satisfy a different class. For example, earned money will not satisfy the need to be liked or loved.

Perceived Functional Utility

Individuals will persist in pursuing a reward if they believe that the utility will be greater than zero, greater than alternative utilities, and if they believe that the utility is greater than the cost. For example, if the individual has enough money to buy a Ford, he may exert greater effort in order to purchase a Porsche. The perception of the added utility of the higher reward may prove to be an illusion once the higher reward is actually achieved and consumed. In the interpersonal domain, the individual may believe that experiencing a relationship with a beautiful woman may have great functional utility for him—thereby motivating him to exert great effort. However, once achieved, the reward may prove less than satisfactory.

Many insatiable individuals over-estimate the value of a reward or condition forthcoming. For example, the anorexic believes that she will feel wonderful once her weight drops below 90 pounds—but she realizes, at 88 pounds, that she is still dissatisfied and tries to lose more weight. The avaricious investor believes that he will feel financially secure once he accumulates 5 million dollars but realizes that even this does not seem to be enough and tries to accumulate more. These "implicit contracts" with reality, "Once I have X, then I will feel satisfied," maintain the compulsive behavior in a never-ending cycle.

The over-valuation of an expected gain may result in the willingness to replicate behavior over a long duration and to expose oneself to increased risk in order to achieve the goal. For example, competitive swimmers are taught to "Keep your goal in front of you," and athletes utilize imagery of success and idolize sports heroes, further driving them forward in their pursuits. The idealization of the lives of the "rich and famous" further enhances the over-valuation of the goals of success. However, seldom does the experience of success provide a lasting satisfaction, thereby leading either to increasing the standard of success to drive one forward or to disillusionment.

Comparison Level

Schor (1998) suggested that one of the best predictors of spending habits is the comparison level of one's peers. Individuals whose peers make more money than themselves had higher demands and spend in excess of their earnings. Moreover, Schor found that images of relatively affluent people on television results in over-spending, since the individuals on television often represent a higher standard of living than the viewer's. Most individuals compare "upwards"—that is, they compare their standard to those who make or consume more, thereby placing greater pressure to demand more.

Models of "relative deprivation" indicate that individuals are unhappier when they compare themselves upward with individuals who are doing better than they are doing (Furby, 1980). Thus, in evaluating how we are doing we seldom use an absolute standard. Rather, we measure ourselves against standards that are generally higher than our own accomplishments. This results in a sense of relative deprivation. Insatiable individuals often measure themselves against standards of perfection or exception, seldom against the average or below average.

Self-Awareness of Satiation

The most fundamental aspect of satiation is the ability to recognize that one is satisfied. This may seem a simple task for some, but for many individuals there is no satisfactory way to establish satisfaction. For example, binge eaters may not recognize that they are satisfied until they feel bloated and nauseated, and alcoholics may not feel satisfied until they have passed out. Most insatiable individuals have little in the way of a set rule to determine satisfaction. "How will you know if you have had enough?" may lead to the answer, "I'll just know." For others, the criterion of satisfaction is more linked to the pursuit of the goal than the goal itself: "I will have no more energy" or "I'll be exhausted." Moreover, many appetitive and insatiable behaviors occur rapidly, often not allowing the individual the time to recognize that satiety has occurred. Increased dissociative experiences—for example, "spacing out" or rapidly engaging in behavior without reflection—further hampers the ability to recognize satiety.

Because much appetitive behavior is not pursued with a definitive goal in mind—for example, "If I make X, I will decrease my work hours," or, "If I consume X calories, then I will stop eating." Much of appetitive behavior is determined by stimulus effects—"I was in the casino and still had some chips," or, "I was watching the screen and thought I should buy that stock." This may be one reason why a very powerful intervention for these behaviors is stimulus control, which involves removing the tempting stimuli from the individual's immediate field of experience, for example, eliminating alcohol or drugs, avoiding casinos, and avoiding stocking the pantry with high-fat foods. These behaviors often appear to be externally driven precisely because of the lack of a self-induced standard or rule for satiation.

The foregoing has been an attempt to outline a number of processes that may affect insatiability. Although not exhaustive, I believe that we have examined several interacting factors that may account for why some individuals appear insatiable. General schematics of some of these processes are presented in Figure 8.1.

Opportunity

Compulsive and manic individuals fear losing an opportunity to do more or to achieve more (Leahy, 2000). The achievement of one goal may lead to the opportunity to achieve other goals. For example, the investor who has made money in his investments may now have more money to invest and more access to opportunities for more money. The gambler may view himself as having an opportunity to achieve even greater success on the next hand, thereby conferring greater risk to himself. Again, the focus for these insatiable individuals is less on a stable need or set goal and more on the process of pursuing behaviors—in this case, pursuing more opportunities.

I would propose the following *opportunity postulate*: "The greater the perceived opportunity to create more rewards, the less likely the individ-

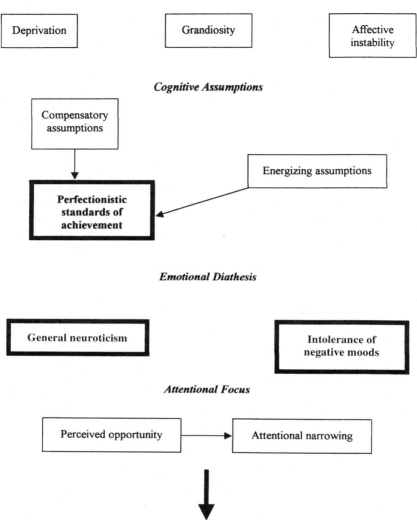

Figure 8.1a Earlier Developmental or Biological Precursors.

ual will be satiated." The focus here is less on one's needs and more on the process of achieving those needs. Implications of opportunity theory are that individuals will be more likely to seek alcohol, drugs, or gambling if the opportunity is readily available (i.e., stimulus control) and individuals will continue to take risks in their investments if they perceive that there are additional opportunities available. Many investors

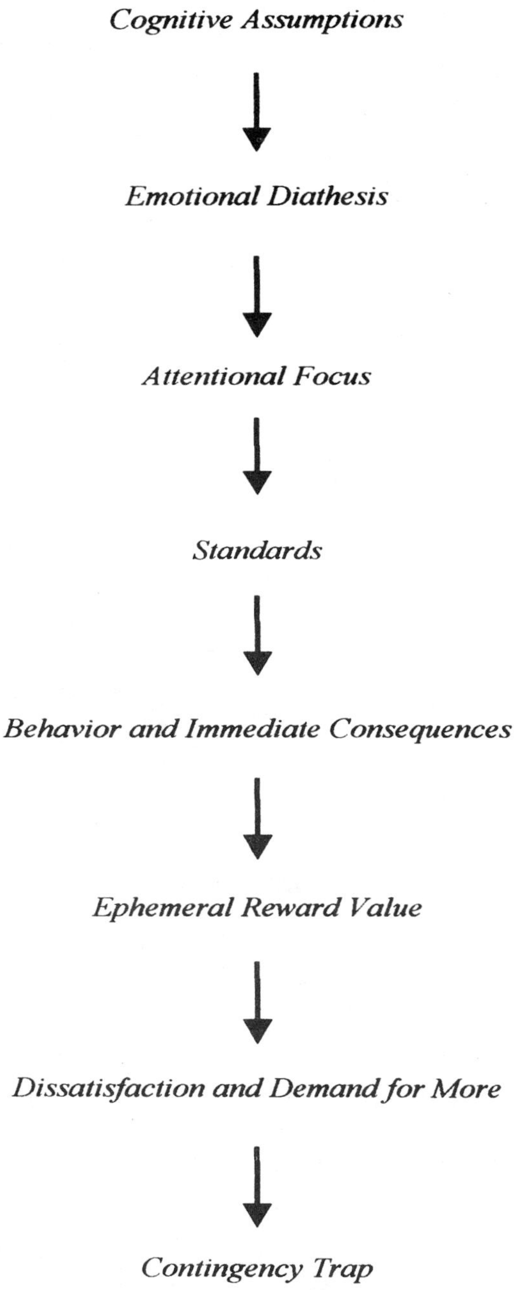

Cognitive Assumptions

↓

Emotional Diathesis

↓

Attentional Focus

↓

Standards

↓

Behavior and Immediate Consequences

↓

Ephemeral Reward Value

↓

Dissatisfaction and Demand for More

↓

Contingency Trap

Figure 8.1b Earlier Developmental or Biological Precursors.

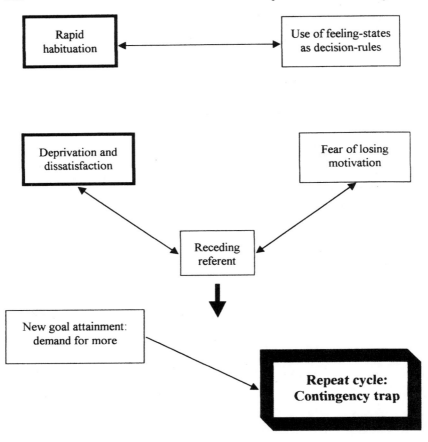

Figure 8.1a Dissatisfaction and Demand for More.

have difficulty taking their money off the table if they believe that there are still opportunities available.

Overvaluation of Effort

The insatiable individual may overestimate the power of effort to accomplish goals. For example, the speculative investor may believe that accumulating more information about companies and stocks may result in better outcomes in his investment. A common symptom of this overvaluation of effort is *screen-watching*—that is, spending excessive amounts of time checking the prices in one's portfolio or following momentary changes in the prices of individual stocks. Magical beliefs often accompany this superstitious behavior—"I'll catch something before it gets out of hand," or, even, "If I watch it, I can keep the stock up."

The attraction of effort for the individual is that it appears to confer immediate control—one can always try harder. By attributing frustration to lack of effort the individual keeps hope alive. Insatiable individuals often believe that they can gain more information about the value of companies and stocks and thereby increase their odds of making a successful investment decision. Similarly, body-perfectionists believe that they can diet more and exercise more vigorously in order to achieve their physical ideal.

Symbolic Value

Symbolic rewards are more likely to be insatiable than rewards related to biological drives. The desire for success may be less easily satisfied than hunger drive. The value of a reward may be symbolic of other needs. For example, achieving a certain financial goal may be symbolic of being successful or being a worthwhile individual, while the consumption of money is less important. Some investors look at financial returns as a way of keeping score: if you make more, then you are winning and if you make more than others do, then you beat them. Being a winner may enhance the individual's self-esteem. Similarly, having a glamorous or successful partner may be a symbolic trophy of one's personal value.

Public Display

As Thorstein Veblen (1899/1979) indicated almost a century ago, many behaviors and possessions have value because they can be displayed to others as an indication of one's social status. Images of "conspicuous consumption" might include jewelry, art, cars, clothing, and today, electronic gadgets (Packard, 1959). Romantic partners also may be displayed to others as representative of one's status and success. Pursuit of more may be driven by the fact that new objects may be displayed as signs of one's status.

The degree to which ambitious individuals engage in the public display of wealth is described in the book, *Circus of Ambition* (Taylor, 1989). Because there are an unlimited number of ways in which success may find public display, there are an unlimited number of ways in which the individual may expand his own demands for more. Insatiable individuals, in therapy, often make a point of telling the therapist about their wares—Rolex watches, expensive homes, yachts, and private jets. The ability to purchase expensive paintings that can be hung on one's walls can immediately establish the public reputation of the individual as someone with class. These individuals often find themselves in competition with other people in their social circle also driven to display their possessions.

One individual drove himself into bankruptcy attempting to display to his social circle the great success that he imagined he achieved. He leased an extraordinarily expensive car, wore designer clothing, and took expensive vacations with his wife—even though his income was modest. When we discussed the possibility of developing a budget that would guide his spending, he indicated that he resisted this because it meant he was poor and a failure. He equated the purchase of items on credit as an indication of being wealthy and successful—even though these purchases had previously driven him into personal bankruptcy.

Underestimation of Cost

The demand for more is enhanced by the tendency to underestimate the cost of pursuing the goal. It is commonplace for many individuals to underestimate how difficult it will be to obtain exceptional outcomes. The individual who fancies a glamorous partner, enormous wealth, or famed reputation may begin the pursuit informed only by naiveté. Not knowing the length of time, the improbability of the outcome, and the sacrifices that are entailed may lead the individual to drive forward toward those goals that are unlikely. Despite the old axiom that the first step is the hardest, in a long journey it is usually the steps after the first step that become more difficult.

Insatiable individuals focus on their imagination of how satisfying their outcomes will be once they are achieved. Seldom do these individuals report a realistic expectation of how difficult, if not impossible, the process will be. Few anorexics start out by stating that they believe that they will risk their lives in pursuing their body-type and few ambitious people state that they will sacrifice all of their happiness to achieve success. Some of this may be related to the overvaluation of effort—that is, the belief that increased effort will solve everything. Others are focused on the immediate experience of pleasure from momentary satisfaction (e.g., drinking or gambling) or the reduction of anxiety by engaging in compulsive work.

Perception of Satiation as Defeat or Termination

Compulsive and narcissistic individuals may perceive satiation as a sign of defeat and surrender to mediocrity. For example, a successful financial investor, compulsively driven to accumulate more, was fearful of establishing a set financial target for himself.

Therapist: How much would be enough?
Patient: I can't say.
Therapist: If you could say, "This amount would be enough," would there be a problem for you?
Patient: I would be afraid I would lose my edge. I would drift, become complacent. I would lose it all.

Interestingly, this patient came from a family that suffered substantial financial setbacks when he was a child, leaving him with the belief that all of his assets could be lost at any time. He attributed his ability to be successful with never letting his guard down and always driving for more. Ironically, his drive for more was without a specific goal—it was simply "more than I have now."

Many insatiable individuals operate with a negative motivational theory: "I must be dissatisfied in order to be motivated."

Absence of Competing Rewards

Satiation may often be viewed in terms of the alternatives available for pleasure or value. The individual who derives momentary pleasure from compulsive work—for example, the momentary sense of competence—may become so work-absorbed that alternative sources of rewards become more remote. For example, the work-absorbed lawyer may have fewer contacts with friends and family, thereby leading to the loss of these rewards, further driving him into his work. Similarly, the compulsive gambler or alcoholic may find that the result of his behavior, alternative sources of reward have been lost and that drinking and gambling are the only apparent rewards available. Further pursuing these behaviors leads to further loss of these alternatives, thereby spiraling the behavior upwards.

The simultaneous compulsive pursuit of a goal (such as drugs, body-perfectionism, success or wealth) often results in the opportunity cost of sacrificing other goals—such as leisure, health, relationships, or family. The anorexic, with her perfectionistic emphasis on controlling all aspects of her diet and with reducing her weight, will often isolate herself from others, thereby contributing to her sense of social deprivation. The work-absorbed lawyer, spending 16 hours a day working in his office, forgoes other relationships that might help him put things in perspective. As success becomes the primary goal in his mind, it also becomes the only goal available: relationships are abandoned leaving him with only work for satisfaction.

I would suggest the following hypothesis: *Competing reward theory.* If the individual does not perceive any other sources of reward from a different class of rewards, then he will persist in the first class of rewards. For example, if the individual does not believe that he can obtain rewards of being liked or loved for who he is, then he will persist in the first class of reward—namely the insatiable behavior. Ironically, most insatiable individuals engage in compulsive behavior that serves to eliminate competing rewards.

Savings and Delayed Consumption

The pursuit of symbolic and delayed rewards forestalls the consumption of the reward. One may have to work for a long time before achieving the desired outcome. The effort exerted increases deprivation that increases the perceived utility of unconsumed rewards. For example, the scientist who is working in her laboratory for years, sacrificing her personal life, hopes to obtain international recognition. This increased effort increases general feelings of deprivation. This increased deprivation may result in an even greater demand for the outcome, further motivating her to work even harder. Because she has decreased opportunities for rewards in other areas of her life—due to delayed consumption of the desired outcome (international recognition)—her selective focus on her work becomes the only perceived means to a reward. Delayed consumption, thereby, increases appetitive behaviors.

Although many insatiable individuals may appear myopically tied to their contingency traps of immediate gratification—followed by the demand for more—many insatiable individuals appear to delay gratification indefinitely. These insatiable individuals are driven by their imagination of their goals—"One day I will be proven correct!" Moreover, as these individuals invest more and more in an apparently lost cause, they are motivated further by the *sunk-cost effect,* that is, the tendency to stay with a behavior that has proven to be a failure to redeem some value from it.

I propose the following hypothesis: *Savings Theory.* The greater the opportunity to save a reward, the less satiation will occur.

Relying on "Feeling States" as "Satisfaction" Criteria

Motivational and behavioral models of overeating distinguish between satiation and hunger (Orford, 2001). How does know if one is satisfied?

When it comes to eating behaviors, the individual may rely on internal cues of fullness, absence of uncomfortable hunger feelings, or feeling bloated. Moreover, the individual may be so absorbed in the behavior of eating—and may be eating so rapidly—that he fails to attend to the physical signs of satiety. With less primary drive behavior, the satisfaction criteria may be more ephemeral. How does the individual know if he is satisfied with his partner, his success, or his wealth? For compulsive individuals and for worriers, a felt sense of satisfaction—"It just feels right," or, "I don't feel anxious anymore"—may be the criteria of deciding to cease checking or worrying (Wells, 1997).

Receding Referents

This refers to the tendency to demand more once a specified level is achieved. The individual continues to raise the bar. "Once I achieve a million, I'll want more." One individual, a founder of a well-known software company who had accumulated billions of dollars, was quoted as saying; "I'd like to have more money than anyone else—just for a short period of time." Some individuals believe that receding referents are necessary to motivate them and to prevent themselves from becoming complacent. The consequence, of course, is that the individual is necessarily never satisfied, which then leads to a demand for more.

The reliance on receding referents is due to several factors. First, the achieved goal does not live up to expectations, thereby leading some individual to think that a little more would be better. Second, success on one goal increases the expectancy that another higher goal is within reach, thereby building on the prior reinforcement. Third, the individual may believe that by having still higher goals he will be motivated to gain more—an opportunity not to be missed.

The downside of the receding referent is that there is little satisfaction in the goals that are achieved. The individual is driven to pursue more, but enjoys the benefits only for a short time. The so-called adjustment effect—such that a gain in income leads to short-term satisfaction, followed by a desire for more—may be a consequence of this receding reference process.

Contingency Traps

This refers to the tendency of behavior to be repeated simply because it leads to an immediate reinforcement. For example, much of addictive behavior can be viewed as a contingency trap, such that the behavior (e.g., drinking alcohol) is immediately reinforced by the pleasure derived, which then leads to a decrement in mood and still greater demand for the alcohol. Contingency traps are myopic in that behavior is focused on the near-term reduction of discomfort or experience of pleasure and the longer-term costs of the behavior are ignored or discounted.

Becker & Murphy (1988) have analyzed addictive behavior in terms of an increase in the price of satisfaction that maintains the addictive behavior at higher costs. Thus, the demand for a drug is inelastic and there is rapid habituation of the effect produced by the drug. This then leads to an increase of price for more of the drug, as it takes more and more to satisfy the need. I refer to these as contingency traps to highlight the idea that the individual is locked in a myopic dependency game with the substance. Every time he feels anxious, he takes the drug, which quickly habituates, which then leads to more demand for the drug.

Related to the contingency trap is the tendency of the addicted individual to rely on a short-term consequence (pleasure or relief of pain) while forgoing consequences on the longer time horizon (that is, the negative consequences of addiction). These myopic, contingently addicted individuals appear to be unable to delay gratification.

Resistance to Extinction

A reanalysis of data on reinforcement schedules suggests that the resistance to change of free-operant behavior is a positive function of the rate of reinforcement—that is, high rates of reinforcement of a behavior serve as momentum, further driving this behavior even when extinction has occurred (Nevin, 1988). Many behaviors that appear insatiable—such as alcohol abuse, gambling, smoking, drug abuse, and financial accumulation—have a long history of high rates of reinforcement and are often resistant to extinction. Even when the individual is not being reinforced during a period of abstinence, the behavioral propensity acts as a momentum (using an analogy of Newtonian physics), leading to its inevitable expression. High rates of reinforcement may, under some conditions, lead to high resistance to extinction.

Alternatively, under some conditions, behaviors that are established on intermittent schedules of reinforcement—such that the behavior is reinforced only for a percentage of behaviors—are also resistant to extinction. Moreover, intermittent schedules that are less predictable—such as variable ratio schedules (the reinforcement is given for a variety of ratios of behavior, rather than for a fixed number or time interval) are especially resistant to extinction. Thus, for the individual who engages in behavior that is intermittently reinforced and the reinforcement varies depending on different amounts of the behavior, the behavior may persist for longer periods. This may be due to the fact that the individual does not know that extinction has begun—that is, variable ratios that are thin schedules that have maintained a behavior are difficult to distinguish from extinction trials. This may be why investors (and gamblers) who have been reinforced periodically on a thin schedule of reinforcement are loathe to give up their pursuits even when the cards are stacked against them and they are losing. They do not yet know that their behavior is under extinction.

AN INTEGRATIVE MODEL OF INSATIABILITY

The foregoing has been an attempt to outline a number of processes that may affect insatiability. Although not exhaustive, I believe that we have examined several interacting factors that may account for why some individuals appear insatiable. A general schematic of some of these processes is presented in Figure 8.2.

Inspection of the schematic of the cycle of dissatisfaction indicates that we begin with individuals who are either perfectionistic or who hold unrealistic expectancies about achievement or moods. These perfectionistic or unrealistic standards may be due to attempts to compensate for earlier or current self-perceived vulnerabilities. They are supported by comparisons upwards. These individuals may overperceive opportunity to achieve their exceptional goals, maintaining beliefs that increased effort will yield better results. They then engage in appetitive behaviors (gambling, drinking, eating disorders, or compulsive work or accumulation). These appetitive behaviors yield short-term reinforcements. These reinforcements are habituated rapidly—that is, they have an ephemeral or short-lived effect, since they do not really satisfy fundamental needs. The rewards for these behaviors are further augmented by the fact that they are symbolic, intermittent, repeated, delayed, or saved—thereby maintaining the behavior. Because of the repeated nature of these contingencies—that is, dissatisfaction followed by appetitive behavior followed by quickly habituating rewards—there develops a contingency trap. The individual is caught in a cycle of repeating behaviors that lead to short-term rewards that are quickly dissatisfying.

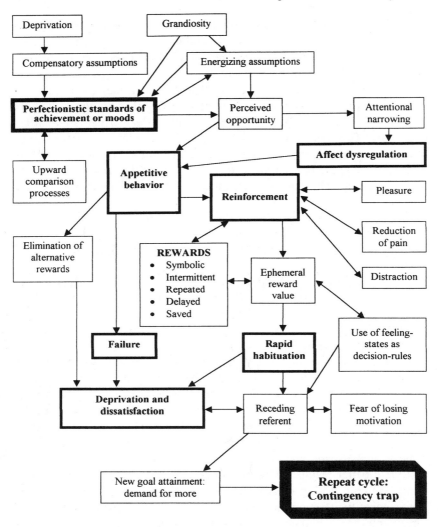

Figure 8.2 Cycle of Dissatisfaction.

These myopic repeated cycles result in the elimination of alternative behaviors and increased deprivation, accompanied by the belief that deprivation can be decreased by repeating the behaviors at a higher frequency or intensity. This repeated cycle of dissatisfaction continues unabated and, in some cases, with greater determination.

CHAPTER 9

Modifying the Cycle of Dissatisfaction

The schematic in Figure 8.2 shown in the previous chapter provides an outline for how we can assist individuals in breaking the cycle of dissatisfaction. In this chapter, we will review the numerous points of intervention that can be utilized in modifying a range of areas of dissatisfactions related to financial, physical, substance abuse, and marital problems.

Provide a Case Conceptualization

Case conceptualization is now a hallmark of cognitive therapy interventions for patients with long-standing problems (Beck, 1995; Leahy, 1996; Needleman, 1999; Persons, 1993; Persons, Davidson, & Tompkins, 2001). The case conceptualization helps the patient and therapist develop an overall understanding of the problem and how it may be addressed. The schematic in Figure 8.2 is likely to be too complicated for most patients to use. Consequently, we might use the schematic in Figure 9.1 to help guide the patient in understanding how the cycle of dissatisfaction maintains itself.

This bare-bones schematic highlights the importance of early experience in developing the demanding standards that drive the compulsive behavior. For example, one financially compulsive patient described his early comparisons between himself and his remarkably successful father and another young woman described how she could relate her body dysmorphic concerns to her mother's obsessions with weight and beauty. The therapist can help the patient identify the themes that were stressed in these early experiences. For example, success is measured by having more money than everyone else has or being lovable is determined by

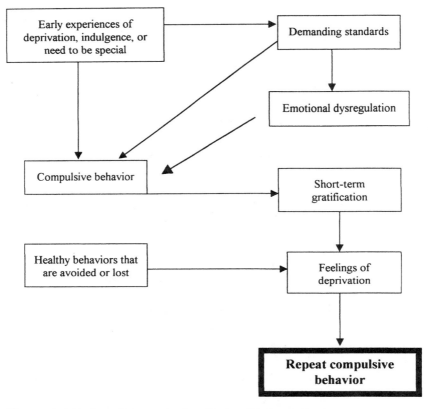

Figure 9.1 Patient Schematic for Cycle of Dissatisfaction.

being thin. Many compulsive individuals describe how they received reinforcement from parents intermittently—that is, there was not total
emotional deprivation—there was always the hope of achieving success—
that is, if one only tried harder.

The demanding standards—of financial success, beauty, emotional, or
romantic perfection are then identified. These standards then drive the
compulsive behavior. The therapist can assist the patient in identifying
the specific behavioral examples of compulsive behavior. For financially
obsessed individuals these are shown in Table 9.1. These compulsive
behaviors either produce short-term gratification or, in some cases, increase the anxiety that further drives the compulsive behavior.

Patients should examine the kinds of healthy behaviors that are lost or
avoided due to the compulsive concern about finances. These include

Table 9.1 Compulsive Behaviors Associated With Financial Concerns

Compulsive Behaviors and Concerns
Repeated checking of financial assets
Repeated checking of financial news
Watching the stock market returns over and over
Worrying that one will lose all his money
Comparing oneself repeatedly with others who have more money

time and energy for intimate relationships, friendships, sleep, proper diet and exercise, and use of leisure activity. In addition, some compulsive behaviors—for example, repeatedly checking useless financial information, such as screen-checking by investors—may take away time from more productive behaviors, such as developing professional contacts and conducting research on fundamentals.

Emotional dysregulation is a key component of the compulsive cycle of dissatisfaction. These individuals often experience intense anxiety, emptiness, and confusion that they believe they must eliminate immediately. For example, a financially compulsive individual was overwhelmed with financial worries and would address these either by compulsive checking of information, reassurance seeking, or impulsively trading in order to make up for prior losses. Another investor, beset by feelings of emptiness and boredom, due to his belief that he was not as successful as he thought he should be, visited prostitutes during the day. This served to distract him from his anxiety, but complicated his personal life and took away time from his professional work.

The short-term gratification that results from the work-absorption and preoccupation with money (and the opportunities lost for other behaviors) results in further feelings of deprivation. The underlying belief that fuels the cycle is that dissatisfaction can be addressed by repeated compulsive behaviors.

Similar analyses have been developed for individuals with eating disorders. For example, Fairburn's (Fairburn, Marcus, & Wilson, 1993; Fairburn & Wilson, 1993) cognitive-behavioral model of binge eating can be expanded to include a case conceptualization of the origins of the demanding standards of body perfectionism. In addition, the importance of affect regulation in Fairburn's model may be examined in terms of case conceptualization, as described above. For example, did the patient believe that her emotions were understood or validated in her family of origin? Was love, attention and respect contingent on accomplishments or appearance?

Identify Examples of Insatiable Conduct

To modify the behavior, we need to identify examples of the insatiable behavior or thoughts. These might include working excessive hours to accumulate money, hoarding, expressing only momentary satisfaction once a goal is attained, envy regarding the possessions of others, or spending far beyond one's realistic capacity. For example, a successful investment banker, working six days per week, complained of fatigue, dissatisfaction with work and performance, envy of her colleagues who she thought earned more than she did, and the inability to develop a social life outside of work.

Establish Motivation to Change

Many individuals with problems of insatiability complain of the stress that they experience, but are wary of scaling back. The patient should be asked to list the advantages and disadvantages of allowing oneself to become satisfied. Surprisingly, this question often results in underlying positive beliefs about insatiability, similar to the beliefs endorsed by individuals who worry (Papageorgiou & Wells, 2001; Papageorgiou & Wells, 2001; Wells, 1995). For example, positive beliefs about insatiability include the following:

- "This will motivate me to try harder."
- "If I become satisfied, I will lose my edge. I won't work hard. I'll become complacent"
- "I don't want to become average."

Beliefs about the advantages of satiation include these:

- "I'll be able to relax."
- "I'll see things in perspective—see what's important."
- "I won't drive other people crazy."

Patients should be asked to weigh the costs and benefits of being satisfied. For the patient above, the benefits of being satisfied outweighed the costs, 70% to 30%.

Examine Perfectionistic Beliefs

Compulsive individuals usually maintain perfectionistic beliefs about themselves and others. Underlying personal schemas, or beliefs, about the self often drive these perfectionistic beliefs. These schemas include beliefs that one is basically flawed and defective or that one is basically superior. For example, beliefs about personal defectiveness or flaw include self-concepts of being ugly, unlovable, incompetent, evil, or lazy. The individual may have conditional beliefs that, "If I do X, then I will overcome [or hide] my basic defectiveness." Consequently, the individual who believes that he is unlovable may believe that, "If I achieve great financial success, then people will love me." Conditional beliefs about emotions are also tied to perfectionism: "If I become very successful, I will feel good."

Grandiose or narcissistic individuals have reported earlier experiences of emotional deprivation or, alternatively, of indulgence and special status within the family (see Kernberg, 1975). In the latter case, the demanding standards of financial or occupational success, physical beauty, or romance may be a natural consequence of the earlier beliefs that life would be perfect. These individuals often have perfectionistic beliefs that drive their dissatisfaction such as, "If I make more money, I will have the perfect life" or "If I get another husband or wife, then I will achieve the happiness that I dreamed of." These individuals express their dissatisfaction through beliefs and feelings related to their entitlement—"I deserve more success," or, "I deserve to have my partner gratify me completely." These individuals often respond with anger when the therapist focuses on modifying dissatisfaction—"Do you think that I am average? That I don't deserve more?"

Examining Upward Comparisons

Perfectionistic individuals generally measure themselves against individuals who they believe are exceeding them in some valued domain. The investor who makes more money than 99% of the people compares himself with a billionaire. The 45 year-old woman with body dysmorphic image compares her current appearance with how she looked when she was 23. The therapist should ask directly, "When you evaluate yourself, you may be comparing yourself to other people. Who do you use for comparisons?" If the patient compares upwards, as almost all of them do, then the therapist can point out the importance of the normal distribution: "Is there some reason that you don't compare yourself with the entire range of people?" For example, when the therapist pointed out to a financially compulsive investor that the average family income was about $40,000, he responded, "I don't compare myself with the average person." His rationale was that he was a superior human being who should exceed everyone else. Consequently, he was often preoccupied with his feelings of envy and inferiority despite his substantial success. These upward comparisons—related to the receding referent discussed later on—can be examined for the costs and benefits and for alternative standards.

Examine Beliefs About the Benefits of Insatiability

Many compulsively driven individuals believe that insatiability provides them with the motivation to work harder—"If I become satisfied, then I won't want to work." Intuitively, this seems to make sense, but a closer inspection of this belief is that the patient is really saying, "I need to be dissatisfied to work hard." Another related belief about the functionality of dissatisfaction is the belief that "If I am not dissatisfied, then I will become complacent and lazy." Many perfectionistic individuals believe that dissatisfaction prevents them from being "average" or "mediocre." Some patients will express anger by challenging the therapist, "You are telling me I should just *settle!*"

The patient's fear of "settling" may be further examined: "What would you fear would happen if you did "settle?", " What would it mean to you?" These negative beliefs about satisfaction include, "I will become complacent, lazy, and mediocre." These beliefs about the importance of insatiability as a motivator can be examined further, as indicated below.

Evaluate and Test Beliefs About the Benefits of Insatiability

Beliefs that motivation is derived from dissatisfaction may be evaluated by the following questions and techniques:

- Have there been any activities that you pursued because you enjoyed them? What were they? How do you explain this if dissatisfaction is necessary for motivation?

For example, the patient may have pursued music, writing, reading, and sports earlier in his life because he derived a sense of challenge and excitement from them. Indeed, some financially compulsive individuals may have begun their careers with more realistic goals of earning a decent income or buying a house.

- Have there been moments in your life when you felt rested, relaxed, and satisfied?
- If this makes you lazy and complacent, then why did you go back to work?

The belief that satisfaction or even complacency will last forever—or will lead down a slippery slope of lassitude—is a common belief among these individuals. Patients may be asked why this state of relaxation did not become a permanent stupor. Comparisons with hunger drive and curiosity may be helpful—you can satisfy your hunger or curiosity, enjoy this for a while, sit back and relax—and, later, go back to work.

- Are you looking at satisfaction in all-or-nothing terms? Can you have various degrees of satisfaction?

A common cognitive distortion underlying dissatisfaction is the belief that satisfaction exists in dichotomous terms. One can imagine various degrees of satisfaction—slightly satisfied, somewhat satisfied, completely satisfied. Moreover, these degrees of satisfaction change over time. What would happen if one were "somewhat satisfied"? For example, the financially compulsive individual, focused on his portfolio, may say, "I'm not really satisfied with this." What would happen if he became "somewhat satisfied"? What would the costs and benefits be?

- Imagine yourself "satisfied" for the next four hours with things in your life. Do you really believe that you will never work hard again?

Again, the underlying belief is that satisfaction may lead to complacency in losing one's edge. For example, the patient with an eating disorder may fear that if she allows herself to feel satisfied with her body for an hour, then she will lose control over her eating. The therapist may ask, "Are there times during the day when you are not thinking about your body and about eating? Why didn't you lose control then?" This question highlights the fact that preoccupation with control—and with maintaining dissatisfaction—results in a sense of less control.

Examine Beliefs About "Perceived Opportunities"

Dissatisfied individuals often misperceive opportunities to gain satisfaction. For example, the compulsive investor may believe that checking his computer screen or obtaining even more information may result in satisfaction. The patient with an eating disorder believes that exercising for another hour will lead to satisfaction. The therapist can ask the patient, "When you feel uncomfortable or anxious, how do you handle it? What do you typically do?" Opportunities to reduce frustration are identified in the following examples: "Check the stock quotes," "Check my body in the mirror," "Exercise," or, "Examine my portfolio." For investors, dissatisfaction can often result in the pursuit of trading opportunities—"Look for a trade"—often to make up for what is perceived as a loss.

The individual's misperception of opportunities often maintains the compulsivity and increases higher risk behavior. For example, the belief that checking the screen for stock quotes increases opportunities for trades can be tested against the belief that it increases the chances of foolish and unnecessary trading. For example, many investors realize that they would have been better off had they not gone to work that day—since they made foolish and unnecessary trades. The search for trades is increased by exposure to information about investments, often leading to overvaluing the investment to be made (Shiller, 2000). It is useful to have the investor identify his *à priori* model of investment. For example, for one investor the model was "identify stocks of companies with a comparative advantage within their industry, establish a realistic buy and sell price, and stick with your plan." Spontaneous trading, because opportunities are seen because they are salient and immediate, changes the prudent investor into a day-trading gambler. Opportunities, then, are distinguished from emotionally risky behavior—very much like the over-eater in a pastry shop.

Evaluate Attentional Narrowing

As the individual becomes more concerned about dissatisfaction in one area, his attention is narrowed onto this. Attentional narrowing is a key component in the anxiety and mood disorders (Teasdale et al., 2000; Wells & Matthews, 1994). As attention is deployed toward the dissatisfaction, and the perceived opportunities available to end the dissatisfaction, there is less attention available for other behaviors. Thus, there is a greater likelihood of carrying forward the dissatisfaction cycle. The therapist should ask, "When you feel dissatisfied, are there other things that you no longer pay attention to?" These other things may include awareness of alternative behaviors available or positives that are present. Attentional narrowing also enhances the importance or salience of the dissatisfaction—further increasing the accessibility of negative thoughts about the self and one's emotions.

Distraction toward other stimuli may be helpful. For example, the patient, noticing his dissatisfaction, may be asked to deploy attention to objects in the room, such as furniture or the colors of books and magazines in the room. Attention may be deployed to positive memories or to positive aspects of the self. Many patients find it helpful to have a menu of images or thoughts that they can focus on to counter their attentional narrowing.

Utilize Mindfulness Training to Enhance Awareness

The role of attentional narrowing can also be addressed by the use of mindfulness exercises. Teasdale and his colleagues (Segal, Williams, & Teasdale, 2002; Teasdale, Segal, & Williams, 1995; Teasdale et al., 2000) have developed a meditative program to enhance one's focus on experiencing the present moment, be they sensory, cognitive, or affective experiences. According to Teasdale, individuals who think in abstract and general terms—especially about the past or future—are more prone to depression and anxiety. Mindfulness refers to the ability to focus one's attention and experience on the present sensations, sensory input, or environment without forming judgments, generalizations, or predictions (Kabat-Zinn, 1990). Dissatisfied individuals might be trained in mindfulness to enhance their ability to become more aware in the present moment. These techniques include becoming more mindful of one's breathing, focusing on the process of breathing in and out. Ideas or images or emotions that occur may be observed in a mindful detachment that allows the individual to experience the thoughts and feelings at a distance—without evaluation. These exercises may be helpful in modifying the attentional narrowing and in assisting the patient in affective regulation.

Modify Emotional Dysregulation

Although the foregoing interventions for attentional redeployment and mindfulness training may be helpful with regulating emotions, other interventions can also be utilized. The patient can consider the difference between the overly rational mind, the emotional mind, and the *wise mind* (Linehan, 1993; Segal et al., 2002). The wise mind is able to learn from both the rational and emotional mind, but can understand that neither is complete in itself. Beliefs about the nature of intense emotions may be helpful. For example, individuals who are prone to greater anxiety believe that their emotions do not make sense, they are not under control, they will last a long time, and others do not share the same feelings (Leahy, 2002, in press). The therapist can assist the patient in making sense of his emotions:

- "You feel anxious because your expectations are so demanding—perhaps impossible to meet".

- "What is the evidence that your emotions go up and down—so that they never last forever and never go completely out of control?"
- "Do you think that other people don't have feelings of anxiety? Or concerns about their appearance? Aren't some concerns somewhat normal—but, in your case, you have taken them further than others typically do?"

One factor that increases emotional dysregulation is the belief that one should ruminate on one's bad feelings in order to find a solution (Nolen-Hoeksema, 2000; Papageorgiou & Wells, 2001). The excessive self-focus, of course, further drives the dissatisfaction and the attentional narrowing, mentioned earlier. Alternatives such as attentional redeployment, mindfulness, and distracting activities may be utilized to decrease the rumination. It is helpful for patients to have a preset rule for what to do when they begin to ruminate—for example, "If ruminating, take a walk."

Examine How Reinforcement Works for the Individual

There are three ways that reinforcement may function for these individuals: (1) by providing pleasure (e.g., "I felt good when I saw that my stock went up"), (2) by reducing pain (e.g., "I did what I was supposed to do—I worked on it"), or (3) through distraction (e.g., "I was so busy looking at the screen, I didn't think about the research that I needed to do. I hate doing research"). The nature of a contingency trap is that the individual responds to short-term reinforcements while discounting longer-term costs. For example, the individual who spends money on credit today (at high interest rates) may forgo larger rewards later—such as the benefits of having money to live on. The myopic response to short-term gratification may take various forms: achieving pleasure (e.g., spending money), reducing pain (e.g., relieving anxiety by work-absorption), or distraction (e.g., focusing on something innocuous while avoiding more difficult tasks that are more important). These short-term benefits are often purchased at longer-term costs of much greater magnitude.

The patient may be asked to focus on how long the gratification or reinforcement lasts. "You thought you would reduce your anxiety by screen-watching, but how long did that work? What happened to your anxiety the next day when you realized you hadn't done the research on the company?" These rewards are ephemeral because they do not satisfy the underlying "cognitive and emotional problems"—that is, the underlying perfectionistic and compulsive beliefs and the intolerance of frustration are maintained.

These reinforcements are habituated rapidly—that is, their effect wears off very quickly. The consequence is that a feeling of deprivation ensues, further leading to more behavior that is compulsive. One reason for this, mentioned in the previous chapter, is that the individual may be using his feelings as a criterion of satisfaction. "I just felt like I couldn't do more," or, "I thought I had exhausted all the possible worries." The therapist may ask, "What will be the consequence if you use your emotions as the guide to your decision that you have done enough?" "Imagine that you planned to walk ten blocks to get to a store, but rather than stopping at ten blocks, you kept walking because you still had energy and time. Would you be able to shop in the store?" Many compulsive and anxious individuals use exhausting effort as a criterion for stopping rather than the criterion of reaching an established goal. For example, the therapist asked an investor, "How much money do you need to make to feel comfortable?" The man responded with bewilderment, realizing that his goal was to "make as much as I can." The consequence, of course, is that by defining a satisfying outcome in terms of unlimited possibility, he could never be satisfied.

Examine the Nature of Rewards

As indicated in the previous chapter, many rewards have symbolic value. "Making a lot of money symbolizes my success as a person," or, "Being thinner means that I am a better person—more in control." A problem with symbolic rewards is that they are elusive. How well does money reflect how worthwhile someone is? Since the underlying symbolism often is associated with ill-defined or meaningless ideas, the individual is insatiable. Thus, purchasing an expensive car ultimately leads to trading up for a more expensive car—especially when the car symbolizes manliness or success. There is no finite endpoint. The goal here is to remove the symbolic aspects of rewards and reframe them into specific behavioral or material goals. For example, rather than say, "If I accumulate X, then I am worthwhile," the question can be reframed behaviorally: "What are some behaviors that you want to engage in? How can you make that happen?" For example, if the individual wants to attract women, what are some behaviors that he can engage in to make that happen? If an individual wants to have a nice place to live in, how is that described or defined?

Another factor that contributes to persistence of ultimately unsatisfying behavior is the fact that much of this behavior is intermittently reinforced. Thus, the individual may not realize that a lot of his compulsive behavior is irrelevant. For example, the compulsive screen-watcher will intermittently make a good decision. If he attributes this to his screen-watching (rather than to a random walk down Wall Street), then he will continue in his compulsive behavior. Other rewards are repeated over and over, contributing to what Nevin (1993) calls behavioral momentum. For example, screen watching may repeatedly distract the investor from other more tedious and anxiety provoking behaviors, such as doing research. The repeated short-term gratification of distraction contributes both to dissatisfaction (since larger goals are not achieved) and to resistance to extinction (through behavioral momentum). Prior commitments of not watching the screen for long periods are necessary to break the reinforcing consequences of this distraction. The patient may be asked, "When you are not watching the screen, are terrible things happening to your stocks?"

Still another factor contributing to dissatisfaction is that many of the rewards that are imagined in the long-term are so delayed that they are never achieved. The idea that "I will eventually feel like I am more successful than everyone" will never be achieved. Delaying these perfectionistic rewards adds further to frustration, ironically fueling the compulsive behavior. The therapist can ask the patient to examine some immediate rewards, unrelated to the perfectionistic fantasy, which can be experienced. For example, one compulsive investor was asked to imagine some things that he could do with his family that were free—such as expressing affection, sharing stories, playing, eating food, and walking on the beach. By refocusing to immediate, obtainable, controllable rewards, the attraction of the delayed rewards was diminished.

Related to the delay of reward is the fact that "saving" the reward—e.g., building up a mass of wealth—may render much of this behavior resistant to extinction. Even though the individual is frustrated pursuing his compulsive behaviors, he is maintained by the cognitive mediation of his image of the longer-term consequences of saving. Again, focus can be shifted to behaviors that are currently, or in the short-term, rewarding. "You seem to be working hard to save up for a later day. That's a valuable thing to do, but are there some things that you can do now—or next week—that you can derive pleasure from?" This concept of diversifying the source of rewards available is similar to the diversified life portfolio that I discuss in a later chapter.

Change the Receding Referent

A key element in the contingency trap of compulsive trading is the fact that the goal keeps changing once it is achieved. This is referred to as a receding referent, which captures the idea that the bar is changed and never completely realized. The patient's attention should be drawn to the fact that when more is achieved, still more is desired. This is because the rewards are all short-term gratification with ephemeral value, thus resulting in rapid habituation. They don't last.

Precommitment strategies are helpful in addressing the receding referent problem. For example, the patient who claims that his goal is to achieve X, can be asked *before* the behavior takes place—"What are the advantages and disadvantages of quitting at X?" Of course, this question raises all of the resistant beliefs about the need to maintain an edge of motivation by remaining dissatisfied. In treating a dentist with compulsive demands on himself for more work, we examined the costs and benefits of limiting his practice to a certain number of hours. We examined the opportunity costs of not having time for exercise, friends, family, or his music (he was an accomplished pianist). His resistant receding-referent thought was, "There are referral sources that I don't want to turn down," followed by the belief that "If I turn them down, they'll stop referring and my practice will dry up." Thus, he felt compelled to move forward lest he fall back.

These beliefs were tested out for the costs and benefits—the costs being that he was exhausted, stressed at work, and began to resent his staff and his referral sources. We examined examples of other dentists who occasionally were too booked to take on new patients. He was encouraged to discuss this with a referral source who indicated to him, "Just tell me when you are able to take on patients and I'll refer some to you." He examined the possibility of hiring an associate to take on the extra work. We also worked on directing his attention toward other behaviors in his immediate environment—for example, scheduling going to the health club, seeing his friends, leaving the office earlier and scheduling lunch. To his satisfaction, his practice continued to be successful and he recognized that he could balance his life.

Use Awareness and Appreciation Exercises

The overfocus on the behavior that contributes to compulsive dissatisfaction can be offset by the use of awareness and appreciation exercises. In the following chapter, I describe the use of these interventions. Briefly, the patient is asked to imagine that he no longer has anything—no senses, body, memory, possessions, relationships, nothing. He is now faced with the problem of having to convince a "higher power" that he could value these things if they were returned to him one by one. In this game, he does not know how many of these items he will be granted—it all depends on how much he can show his appreciation for them. I have found this exercise to be a powerful, existential awareness intervention to focus the individual's attention on the everyday things that he takes for granted. For example, one patient, who complained that he had lost money in his portfolio and was falling behind in his ambitious race against others, was focused on appreciation. First, he asked for the return of his senses, justifying this by virtue of the fact that he needed to be aware of things to appreciate them. We then began to examine his capacity for awareness: how did he appreciate his sight, ability to hear, smell, and so forth.This served as a kind of existential mindfulness, making him stop and appreciate the sounds and smells that he had taken for granted. He then asked for his young child. The therapist asked him how he would use his senses and feelings to appreciate this child. What were those experiences like? As he went through a variety of things and senses that he wanted back, the therapist interrupted him: "I thought your investments were important to you. Why didn't you ask for them first?" This helped put his compulsive greed into perspective.

CONCLUSIONS

In this chapter, we have examined a number of interventions that may address insatiability. The goal here is not only to make life simpler, but also to make it better. This is accomplished by helping the individual understand the cycle of dissatisfaction by sharing a case conceptualization built on the model explicated in the previous chapter. Each point in the schematic of dissatisfaction is a possible point for intervention. We can modify the underlying beliefs that drive the cycle—beliefs about defectiveness or superior status—and we can modify the positive beliefs about dissatisfaction that motivates one to do better. The goal, of course, is to try to experience a better life, not simply accumulate more. This model of insatiability draws on operant conditioning processes and cognitive mediation providing us with psychological model of unlimited demand. From an economic and psychological view, one advantage of stabilizing individual demand for one product is that there will be sufficient resources to meet other needs. It is in the satisfaction of these other needs—relationships, leisure, or personal growth—that the individual will be able to balance his personal-life portfolio.

CHAPTER 10

Cognitive Therapy on Wall Street: Schemas and Scripts of Invulnerability

In this chapter, I focus on a cognitive analysis of the schemas and scripts of invulnerability of a number of my Wall Street clients. All of these clients initially appear extraordinarily successful in conventional terms: They are wealthy, respected, admired, attractive, charming, and popular with the opposite sex. In fact, because of their success, they are often bewildered as to their anxiety and depression, since they "have it all." It is not my purpose to characterize Wall-Streeters as narcissistic. However, in the present chapter I have chosen to focus on this quality of their personality.

First, I describe the development of narcissistic schemas and scripts of invulnerability. Next, I identify the themes of ambition, greed, and insatiability. Third, I discuss narcissistic impairment in investment styles. Fourth, I describe the narcissist's market value of the self. Fifth, I identify some techniques for modifying narcissistic assumptions. I conclude by outlining a case study that highlights this approach.

Development of Self-Other Cognition

According to Bowlby (1968; 1970), failure to develop and maintain affectional bonds during early childhood results in disturbances in object representations of secondary attachment figures. Although Bowlby gives essential importance to infant-parent attachments, in the present approach I argue for the importance of parent-child attachment throughout infancy and childhood. These object representations and self-representations may be disturbed by either actual or threatened abandonment, resulting in ambivalent or hostile attachment to secondary figures. As Guidano and Liotti (1983) and Leahy (1985; 1991) have indicated, the self may seek protection from further loss or punishment through the protective belt of avoidant and compensatory strategies. In the present sample of narcissistic patients, avoidance is indicated by the failure to develop intimacy (and its consequent vulnerability), thereby minimizing the presumed negative consequences of abandonment. In other cases, compensation for helplessness and the fear of dependency is gained by strategies of seeking invulnerability and achievement or through domination of others.

Considerable evidence now indicates that childhood experience has a substantial impact on both real and ideal self-image. Adolescents and young adults whose parents were nurturant, nonauthoritarian, and used inductive discipline, rather than physical punishment, had higher real self-images, lower self-image disparities, were less likely to be depressed and less likely to exhibit a depressive attributional style. Further, adults whose parents separated or died were more likely to be depressed (Leahy 1981 1989). These data on the quality of parenting and the experience of parental separation support Beck (1979) and Bowlby's (1976) contentions that negative schemas of the self are determined by earlier socialization experiences.

Development of Schemas and Scripts

Schemas refer to concepts that might be analyzed through multidimensional scaling techniques to yield concept spaces. Examples of these content areas in person perception are strong / weak, bright / dull, and extroverted / introverted. In schematic processing, the perceiver selectively attends to and recalls information consistent with the schema, thus reinforcing the schema. In developmental analysis in cognitive therapy (Guidano & Liotti, 1983; 1985; Leahy, 1985; 1991), early schemas of abandonment, evaluation, and punishment are examined and challenged with the intention of demonstrating persistent distortions in the selection and evaluation of information.

The script analysis guiding the present chapter has been proposed in an earlier article (Leahy, 1991). Specifically, scripts are mutually held expectations of social conduct through which player and audience receive mutual benefit and assure predictability and continuity. Examples of scripts are buyer-seller, victim-persecutor, patient-therapist, and narcissist-dependent. In *lifescripts,* individuals select other players who provide opportunities for continued performance of the script: Thus, life-scripts are conservative. These choices of specific players to the exclusion of others are referred to as the *interactive reality*.

The narcissists described here have selected other players with whom they play the game of invulnerability and acquisitiveness. For example, the compulsively unfaithful generally prefer partners who are also unfaithful (or illicit), thereby normalizing a cynical view of marriage. They choose other materialistic narcissists who will appreciate and be impressed with their achievements and who will not challenge their values. They will select emotionally and financially dependent partners and friends to avoid placing themselves in a position of dependency and consequent threat of abandonment.

Examples of the foregoing are the wife who chose married men for her affairs and chose friends who were similarly unfaithful. Similarly, an investor preferred sex with prostitutes ("a release"). Another venture capitalist surrounded himself with business associates who parasitically fed off his success: Because he knew the limitations of trusting them, he was never disappointed. When he became less committed to their values (and, consequently, less anxious and depressed), they belittled him. In another case, the same individual described a series of relationships with women who relied on him for financial and emotional support but from whom he got no support. He indicated that, when he thought of being dependent, he became extremely anxious and fantasized about physically assaulting the therapist. In each of the cases mentioned, one of the parents had threatened separation, divorced, or committed suicide. By selecting partners with whom one would not become dependent, further abandonment was averted.

Narcissistic Themes of Ambition, Greed and Insatiability

These narcissistic patients believe that their behavior has great visibility in the public domain of their lives. If they make a mistake, other investors will know and judge them poorly. Worse still is that word will spread and their reputation will be ruined. The exaggerated degree to which they believe that they are the focus of other's evaluation is similar to Elkind's (1966) description of adolescent egocentrism—"Everyone will be looking at me." Because of the emphasis on the public domain (and consequent visibility), these individuals are continually anxious about disclosures of their fears, vulnerabilities, and perceived inadequacies. Because of their imagined visibility, their private lives of trust, disclosure, and sharing are undeveloped: "You are the only one who really knows me."

These individuals believe that they have special talents, responsibilities, and destiny. Several mentioned that they came from a family "where more is expected of me," describing their destiny and potential. This is reflected in statements about training: "I graduated from Harvard Business School" ; or family traditions: "This is what my family expects of me." One industrialist claimed "God put me on the face of the earth for two reasons—to build factories and develop progeny." I refer to this as the *messianic illusion.*

Because of their sense of unique destiny, the messianic illusion is expressed in the belief in omnipotence in specific areas of their lives. For example, there are expansionary and omnipotent fantasies of wealth, special talents, and potential to develop great wealth and fame. One patient made a point of emphasizing his considerable talents in foreseeing market trends despite the evidence of also having lost considerable wealth in the market. This was apparent when he lost almost $400,000 in a single week during the Iraqi Crisis. Similarly, he even implied that (legally) he could manipulate the price of stocks by buying and selling to himself, thereby artificially driving up and down the book value of Fortune 500 companies. This claim was made despite the fact that he lost money on investments and that his share of the holdings of a company were a minor percentage of the trades of that stock.

In pursuit of the idealized view of the omnipotent self is the need to make perfect decisions. This, of course, conflicted with their associated need to make a big killing on their investments. (Investors are paid for risk: The bigger the risk, the greater the potential gain.) Rather than looking at decisions as learning experiences, hypothesis testing, or reasonable risks, each decision has the potential of being the final and complete test of their value as a person: "I bought those oil stocks a few years ago and lost millions. That shows how stupid I am"—in spite of the fact that he also made over 400% on his other investments over that period resulting in a net gain of $25 million. The need for perfect decisions also results in avoidance of decisions and obsessive fact gathering. One industrialist compulsively gathered data on different businesses, but could not decide which one to buy, since there were advantages and disadvantages for the various alternatives. His idea of a perfect decision was one in which there was no risk, but that there was a tremendous upside potential. Further, these individuals often expect that others will demand that they make perfect decisions, even though other investors (e.g., in a mutual fund) will usually expect some risk.

Not only do these messianic types believe that they should be perfect, but they also believe in an imperialistic obligation, that they should take care of everyone else. Thus, they believe that they should always deliver big payoffs for their investors (even if the market turns down). In their personal lives, they often protect and take care of other people. Several of the men would place large sums of money in bank accounts for girlfriends. One female broker was afraid of confronting her husband (whom she eventually divorced) because of her guilt that she was also responsible for taking care of his entire family. Because of these expanding and insatiable obligations, there is even greater pressure to accumulate more wealth. Ironically, a very common experience for these people is to spend incredible wealth pleasing others but t spend very little pleasing themselves. For example, one investor was thinking of buying a $2 million apartment for his ex-wife (to whom he had no legal or ethical obligation), while he lived in a one-bedroom apartment (which he rented): "She feels she needs it."

Most of these patients describe an inability to commit to an intimate relationship. One investor described his ex-wife as the only woman who "kept my interest"—as if he were describing a movie. They often pursue infidelity because they are bored or frustrated and are unable to accept the limitations of themselves and their partners. They seldom express guilt over these liaisons. Their developmental history is often marked by parental infidelity, threats or actual separations, and threats of homicide.

Compensation for Inferiority and Abandonment

The narcissistic idealization of the self in the messianic complex is often related to earlier experiences of abandonment, rejection, or inferior status. In some cases, the messianic complex is the result of parental overindulgence and treating the child as special and superior. In either case, a personal fable of the self as having unique potential, privilege, and obligation arises either as a compensation for or as a continuity of earlier experiences (see Millon, 1981).

A surprisingly high percentage of these narcissists had parents who either separated or threatened separation. For example, one father committed suicide after a divorce; others had divorced parents; one man was separated from his parents at a German concentration camp and was chased by Nazis and lived alone in the woods for four years; another person's parents divorced and remarried, while another (whose parents eventually divorced) threatened suicide with a pistol numerous times.

Compensation for earlier feelings of inferiority are also common: One investor, who took considerable pride in his martial arts capabilities, acknowledged that as a child he was considered smaller and more puny than other children. Another patient indicated that he was dyslexic as a child and struggled to be better than all the other children. In a number of these cases, the patient's parents emphasized that they and the family were special or unique. One patient brought a photograph to session of the family estate. Another patient described the family dynasty, while another described the intellectual superiority of his family and his need to continue the tradition.

Inability to be Satisfied

Acquisitive narcissists find themselves trapped in a double-bind: If they do not acquire more, then they believe that they have failed, but if they do acquire more it is never enough. Paradoxically, the underlying fear is the fear of being satisfied. Being *satisfied*—feeling that "This is *enough*"— is a condition to be avoided, since to the narcissist it represents giving up on the ideal self-image of unlimited potential and represents defeat of the omnipotent self and its sense of uniqueness. A young industrialist who had acquired a considerable degree of wealth responded to the idea of learning to be satisfied as equivalent to defeat, surrender, emptiness, meaninglessness, and failure. "I feel very anxious when you talk about being satisfied. I'm afraid that I would just give up and lose everything. All my assets would be bled away." He noted, "If I became satisfied and content, I would not fulfill my destiny." This inability to be satisfied is maintained by a *receding referent*—that is, whenever a specific goal is achieved, a new more distant goal is proposed. "Now that I've taken my company public, I'm no longer interested in that. I have more interesting work to do. We're talking about big numbers." Thus, a goal to which almost all other priorities have been subordinated becomes meaningless and empty once it is achieved. The receding referent serves the purpose of assuring helplessness—if we define helplessness as the inability to achieve goals. Since the goal is discounted once it is achieved, it no longer can be viewed as an achievement. This accounts for the paradoxical nature of the self-concept of these patients in which apparent fantasies of omnipotence alternate with anxious feelings of helplessness and frustration.

Investment Styles

Because failure in investments is equated with being a failure as a person, the depressed narcissist is overly concerned with exposure to risk. These individuals suffer from *hindsight bias* (Hastie, 1990) in that they view the outcome of their decisions as perfectly predictable by the information available prior to the decision. This hindsight bias results in a regret orientation such that the goal in making decisions is to always avoid bad outcomes because they will be regretted: "I should have known not to invest in those oil stocks." Further, negative outcomes are exaggerated in degree and positive outcomes are discounted. One investor observed, "The reason I have money problems today is that I lost money on those stocks," even though he had made a substantial gain on those very stocks. By comparing it to the highest historical price of the stocks during that period, he was able to call it a loss. I reminded him of Joseph Kennedy's famous dictum, "Only a sucker waits for the highest price." Further, these positive outcomes are attributed to external factors such as luck or advice. "Yeah, sure I made money, but I was lucky in some investments and I had good advice from my associates."

Contributing to the risk aversiveness is the focus on immediate outcomes. Thus, one investor who had secured a large position in a public company, predicted financial doom since the stock dropped during the first six months (even though the cash holdings of the company were roughly equivalent to the price of the stock). Since earnings on stocks are highly dependent on the length that they are held, the initial purchase may require years to yield profits. As the famous investor, John Templeton, remarked about the ideal time to hold a stock—"forever" (Lynch, 1989).

Protection of assets is a worry that accumulates with success. Since they have achieved financial assets on which they and their family rely, they find themselves (now) more reluctant to make risky investments (similar to the conservative strategies of retirees). However, they still believe they should be able to obtain the same high payoffs of earlier years without the associated risk. For example, an investor who owned several small companies was self-critical because he believed that he should be able to make substantial gains on investments while simultaneously guaranteeing protection of his capital. This resulted in an obsessive collection of data on investments with the inability to make a decision.

Once they accumulate wealth, they express a need to display it by spending it. This emphasis on conspicuous consumption of relatively useless, but *prestigious objects* (Veblen, 1928) (e.g., jewelry, antiques, art) results in several competing issues. First, there is increasing pressure to acquire even more wealth to support purchases. Second, competition with others who spend more results in an escalation of more conspicuous spending. Third, assets are "bled" in that wealth is not secured—that is, it is continually spent. For example, homes, property, jets, cars, boats, jewelry, and clothing are purchased, running down capital, and leaving these wealthy individuals with continued anxiety that they will not be able to earn enough. These self-imposed demands are further reinforced by spouses and partners. As one young investor remarked about his girl-friend: "I'd need a million a year to support her." Then he reflected, proudly, "I can do it."

A continual distortion is the *inability to recognize the randomness or unpredictability of market trends.* Like the pseudoscientific economic forecasts reported weekly in *Barrons',* investors believe that there are secrets or information that, if learned, will guarantee successful out-comes. Thus, when investments decrease, they blame themselves. The depressed narcissist externalizes success as due to luck. The nondepressed narcissist, on the other hand, may exaggerate his or her ability when profits are gained. One investor predicted several stocks would rise (and predicted the amount and the timing), indicating that one needed to be following investments 16 hours per day. As the stocks rose, he took great pride (although the market was rising). However, when these stocks fell, he was self-critical, claiming, "He should have seen it coming."

An interesting corollary to the above is the master of the universe syndrome which is based on the belief that "Since I'm making so much money, then I must be a genius," and "Things will get better and better." Underlying this is the belief that "I'm entitled to this money." For exam-ple, one young broker was resentful that he was making "only" $150,000 while other people were making $400,000. He failed to realize that he made $150,000 because he was lucky enough to be on Wall Street during a raging bull market. When he was fired (like thousands of others), he could not comprehend why he could not find work with equivalent com-pensation. He simply did not recognize that there was no market for his skills.

Tunnel Vision and Market Variability

Financial markets are largely unpredictable. The most successful inves-tors have a consistent edge of about 5% over a random investment in the Dow Jones industrial average. However, acquisitors on Wall Street may experience their fortunes and value as people fluctuating in enormous waves with each rise and fall in stock prices. The heuristic that is em-ployed is to give greater weight to information that is recent, salient, and frequent (Tversky & Kahneman, 1974). For example, any information about the financial markets (interest rates) that is recent, that is on the front page (and therefore salient), and that is repeated frequently is seen as predictive. Similarly, there is considerable emphasis placed on irrelevant information, simply because that information is available. The quality of the source, the availability of information about historic trends, the fundamentals of the company's financial structure, market share, and past profitability (all very boring and abstract data) are given less weight than recent, salient, and frequent data.

For example, one director of an investment fund predicted gloom and failure because the market was doing poorly recently, even though his past performance over 10 years had yielded consistently higher than market returns. The assumption guiding his analysis of recent data was that there was an inevitable linearity of trends: positive direction meant unlimited success, while negative direction meant bankruptcy. Two factors underlie these cognitive distortions in heuristics: first, the narcissist attempts to render the investment world predictable and controllable; second, he or she cannot accept limitations to acquisitiveness. Unpredictability is equated with helplessness and disaster, and limitation is equated with failure.

Envy and the Market Value of the Self

In the competitive world of these individuals, envy stands out as an important determinant of feelings of inadequacy. Envy is based on several interdependent assumptions: (a) people differ in their value as humans, (b) individuals may be ordered along a hierarchy, (c) individual achievement, wealth, power and prestige determine your value, (d) if someone is doing better than I, then they are more valuable, (e) if I am of less value, then I am of no value, (f) the achievements of others imply that the self is devalued, and (g) if I am of less value, then life is not worth living.

This *competitive devaluation of the self* reflects a market valuation of individual worth: Individuals are viewed as commodities whose market value depends on the valuation of other commodities (persons) in what is commonly known as a zero-sum game. For example, as my car ages, other newer models become more valuable making my car less valuable. In competitive envy, individuals are also valued in a market place of social exchange and comparative achievement. When a peer achieves a desired goal, the self is devalued since the assumption is that the other (as a commodity) has become more valuable, thereby devaluing the self. Thus, social mobility (of self and others) implies the possible devaluation of self.

The fundamental assumption is that there is a scarcity of respect, love, and valuation in the world, just as there is a scarcity of money in the economy. Consequently, once respect is spent on the other, there is little or none left for the self. The implication of such a system of evaluation is that individuals do not have intrinsic worth and, by implication, intrinsic rights. The default option for personal value is that the self is basically worthless but earns credits by achievement. In fact, as the self becomes less productive, the self becomes obsolete. The self has no place, no home to which it belongs (Lasch, 1977; 1984). There is no communitas, no place to which to return, no safe base of attachment and solace.

Note how this ethos of envy differs from other views of the self's value and place. I contrast this narcissistic emptiness and meaninglessness of self with other views of the self—specifically, the classic, tragic, romantic, religious and intimate (Arnold, 1983; Barzun, 1975; Buber, 1970; Eliot, 1949; Fromm, 1976; Sewall, 1959). Briefly, the classic view places the self within institutional and traditional cultural continuity: The self has value in its deference and continuation of cultural traditions. In contrast, the narcissist defers to nothing and traditions are viewed in utilitarian terms, usually implying that they have no value.

In the tragic view, the self expresses value by the agony of choice ("guilt and necessity"), reaffirming both the values of the tradition and the importance of the individual. In contrast, the narcissist, respecting no value except the market place, makes petty choices (as one would make purchases). There is no agony of right and wrong. In the romantic view, the self's values derive from the intensity, truth and sense of uniqueness of individual experience and expression. Although the narcissist does value his or her experience, it is not individual intensity and experience that are sought, but rather prestige, control, and power over others. In the religious view, the self has value in its relation to God as exemplified by adherence to proscription in everyday life. Similar to the traditional, the religious self is subordinated to the rules of religion. In contrast, the narcissistic self idealizes the self and the secular and, if religion is at all relevant, it is only in ceremony or as a testimony to the grandeur and prestige of the self (for example, contributions to churches and synagogues). In the intimate mode of existence, the self finds meaning through disclosing, sharing, bonding, and trust with another who is respected and valued as an equal. Closeness, loyalty, and honesty are the significant values. In contrast, for the narcissist, the other is viewed as a satisfier of needs and is subordinated to that task. Again, in utilitarian terms, once the other fails to meet these needs or, as costs in maintaining the relationship increase, the other is discarded. Rather than the object of intimacy and loyalty, the narcissist views the other as an opportunity.

In treatment with narcissists, I attempt to help them recover or gain empathy, respect, loyalty, and value of others as a means whereby they can come to value themselves. For example, a stockbroker who envied other men who had more hair, made more money, and had better-looking girlfriends believed that he was falling behind in the race toward success. Since there was no specific standard, goal or lasting value that he aimed for, every achievement was ipso facto obsolete once achieved: The goal, in fact, was ephemeral—that is, to stay ahead of the competition. We played out a feared fantasy in which he had lost all his hair, was making less than any of his classmates from school, and had the least attractive girlfriend. I, as therapist, played the obnoxious classmate at a reunion who bragged about all of my achievements. He found this ludicrous and said that he would think that such a classmate was not worth respecting. We examined what he wanted to be remembered for—achiever, playboy, friend, or loving family member. He chose the latter two. He was challenged with the idea that developing a friendship with someone who is weak, frail, who has no prestige and nothing to offer would be his greatest challenge. He subsequently became a Big Brother to a young, fatherless boy and began to value himself more because he was valuing someone else. A year after his termination, one of his Wall Street friends (a new patient of mine), commented on the remarkable change in him: "He is more at peace with himself."

CHALLENGING NARCISSISTIC ASSUMPTIONS

Elimination of Life Assets

One patient who had changed jobs and consequently thought that he had made a mistake which implied that he was stupid and would never get as far as he wanted in his career was asked to list the various parts of his body, the names of all close family members and friends, memory of positive experiences in his life, different abilities that had, job and specific financial assets. He was then told to ask the therapist which things he would want back and in which order. Because his family and his physical and mental status were considerably more important than were his financial assets or his job, he was able to see that he already had the most important things in his life: Acquiring more would simply be adding more of the less important assets.

Deserted Island

A patient who believed that competing successfully against others was the only way of measuring his success and value as a person was asked the following: "Imagine that you are to be placed on a deserted island, knowing that you will never again have contact with other people. Now, on this island, if you choose you will be allowed to bring several people, four books (or collection of books), some music, some clothes, your favorite cuisine (which will be magically prepared for you exactly the way you want it), some learning tools (like a computer), and four adult toys. What would you bring?" As the patient made out his list, he asked if he could also bring his parents (along with his wife), and he was told that he could have them visit as often as he wanted. He commented that his daily routine would be filled with outdoor activities, reading, and doing things he never had the time to do. Would he envy his colleagues back on Wall Street, working long hours and making lots of money? His comment was that he would pity them. "Don't you already have the ingredients for your deserted island—family, friends, culture, and play?" This was a novel perspective for him—that he already had enough.

Attending Your Own Funeral

A patient who devoted almost every waking moment to figuring out how he could amass more wealth, was asked what he wanted people to say about him the morning of his burial. I presented the options:

1. He always worked late in the office—a dedicated worker. He took pride in a job well-done
2. He was the richest man I knew.
3. He was never taken advantage of.
4. He was a loving and generous person—fun to be with."

Patients generally choose "loving and generous." Therapist: "Well, if that's your goal, how are you doing? Are you investing too much time in other goals?"

Feared Fantasy

The apprehension of ordinariness that the narcissist experiences may be treated as a phobia using imaginal or behavioral exposure. In imaginal exposure, the patient is asked to imagine experiencing being evaluated by respected individuals as average. For example, one young executive, a recent MBA, feared that he would not measure up to his parents' expectations of success. In a role-play, I played his father rejecting him because he had not become extremely successful, exaggerating my role by claiming, "Mom and I are moving to a different city and changing our names because we were so ashamed of him." He not only defused his anger by laughing at the absurdity of this image, but he was encouraged to confront his parents with this fear. This led to a revealing family dialogue in which his parents not only assured him that they loved him regardless of how much he achieved, but also comments by his mother to his father (a physician) that he (Dad) was so preoccupied with success that she did not have enough quality time with him.

CASE STUDY

Judy entered therapy wondering if she should leave her husband to whom she had been married for several years. She described him as "weak, a wimp" because he "had no self-control" as evidenced by his use of cigarettes and marijuana. She claimed that she could control anything about herself—she had given up chocolates and smoking. She complained of depression and anxiety and, although she denied the import of it, she had a long history of substance abuse, including marijuana, cocaine, amphetamines, and heroin. She was currently an alcohol abuser, suffering from blackouts, loss of memory, and frequent verbal abuse of her husband while she was drinking. She had a long history of bulimia, although she was currently not bulimic.

Her parents often argued, with her father threatening divorce and separation and, indeed, he did divorce, only to return the next year to remarry Judy's mother. Judy's father frequently threatened suicide during family arguments and attempted to overdose three times. Her brother also attempted suicide when he was an adolescent. Judy reported feeling guilty because she often witnessed her father physically abusing her brother. Her mother, who was chronically overweight, introduced Judy to purging by vomiting and solicited Judy to purchase amphetamines for her dieting.

As a young adolescent, Judy felt unattractive, but when her breasts developed and she switched from glasses to contact lenses, she found that boys were interested in her. She began a long period of acting out with drugs, alcohol, and sex, culminating in her college years when she supported herself and her boyfriend by being an erotic dancer. She claimed she enjoyed being an erotic dancer because she had control over men and attributed their sexual interest in her as a sign of their weakness. While on a date with a man, she was covertly sedated, taken back to his apartment, and submitted to multiple rapes by him and his companions. She never reported this to the police. Subsequently, while engaged in a strip performance at a club, a customer grabbed her and she attacked him and beat him severely. Two years later, after several relationships ended, she began a lesbian relationship, which she found somewhat satisfying. This ended and she subsequently returned to heterosexual relationships.

She complained that her husband was inferior to her because he made less money, was less educated, and had less self-control. However, she took pride in the idea that she occupied the traditional male role of provider and decision maker. She disliked physical affection (equating it with weakness) and said that she preferred straight intercourse with a minimum of foreplay. She often frequented bars, flirted with men, and had a series of extramarital affairs, claiming that she preferred married men because it was less complicated. She reported no guilt about this, claiming that men did this all the time as evidenced by the men she met in the bars.

She also alternated between pride and resentment about supporting her parents financially and claimed that, while they needed her support, she believed that they were demanding and parasitic. Her current income was around $70,000 (incidentally, the median income on Wall Street despite what media representations may portray), but she believed that she could earn one million dollars per year because of her extraordinary talents.

The transference relationship proved to be a revealing avenue to elicit her more private, vulnerable self-image. Initially quite friendly toward the therapist, she expressed considerable anger when confronted with his claims that she was an alcoholic. "You have a hang-up about this!" She was challenged with her view that she had self-control by asking her if she could go four weeks without a drink. She took up the challenge and reported nausea, dizziness and lethargy in the next session. In one session, she came in wearing glasses rather than her contact lenses and had difficulty maintaining eye contact with the therapist. Her automatic thoughts were that she was ugly and that I and other men would think less of her. She was asked what information she had that men found her ugly when she wore glasses and what qualities in addition to her looks that men and women liked about her. In still another session, she leaned forward provocatively and, apparently out of nowhere, asked me why men would allow women to perform oral sex on them since it gave the woman so much power. She was asked for other examples of how she manifested power over men and why she wanted to have power over them.

This de-eroticization of her transference led to a major change in her relationship to therapy: Knowing that she could not seduce the therapist, she now felt that she could trust him with her private feelings of helplessness: "If I don't have power over them, then they have power over me. They could destroy me—I mean, they could *kill* me."

We then examined the development of her script of controlling men and bolstering her self-importance by adapting obligations. She began to recognize that she always chose men who were inferior in some way, that she enjoyed erotic dancing because she not only was worshipped for physical beauty (which she harbored doubts about) but she also felt in control of the men who desired her. Her idea of being in obligation to her family was interpreted as her own construction of reality, which served the purpose of deflecting her attention from her own problems to the problems of others. Further, her friends were also people who formed dependent relationships on her, which she encouraged by portraying herself to them as an invulnerable, sophisticated Wall Streeter. She indicated that she had to be strong for them, which was interpreted as her compensation for her deeper schema, "I have to appear strong because I cannot tolerate my own weakness."

Her ideal self-image was invulnerability, total self-control over others, competence, and beauty. Her real or private self-image was that of weakness, chaos, hidden vices, and ugliness. Her private self-image was treated as an existential phobia—that is, she feared herself and her weakness. The therapist asked her to attempt to *stream* (repeat over 10 times), " I really feel weak and out of control." She resisted this and said, at first, "This is not what I feel," but was willing to try the challenge. While streaming, she began to cry (which was unusual for her) and acknowledged that she was weak and could not control her drinking. With my encouragement, she entered AA and began to find other people with whom she could share her problems.

She later decided to divorce her husband. At first, she wanted to criticize him for being weak. When it was pointed out to her that she had chosen him because he was weak, she decided to be more task-oriented and pursue a legal settlement fair to both of them. She later began a mature, equal relationship with a man with whom she felt comfortable acknowledging her vulnerabilities. When she expressed her fear that if she spoke up at AA meetings that she would start crying and that others would think that she was weak, I encouraged her to share that precise thought. In that way, she could practice being weak in front of others and learn that the greatest safety is in not having to be strong all the time. This proved to be a remarkable release for her and led to her stronger commitment to AA. Before leaving therapy (which was due to financial constraints, but which was not premature), she claimed that realizing that she could be weak and be accepted and loved by people saved her life. She indicated that she was thinking of leaving Wall Street because it seemed so meaningless and that she might pursue more rewarding work in business or banking.

PART IV

Development of Conceptions of Inequality

CHAPTER 11

The Development of Concepts of Economic and Social Inequality

Although social class and other categories of stratification (such as race, gender, age, and intelligence) have often been used as independent variables in the classification of subjects, relatively little research had been done until recently on how children and adolescents come to view stratification. Certainly, Clark and Clark's (1947) landmark work on racial differences in the perception of dolls was a noted exception to this tendency to view stratification as an independent variable in psychological research.

The study of how children come to understand, explain, justify, and challenge stratification may be viewed as a central and necessary component of our understanding of the socialization process. One might argue that the essential purpose of socialization is precisely this in a society—that is, to assure allegiance and consensus in the perception of stratification (Menon, 1957; Parsons, 1960). Failure to provide consensus and allegiance results in disruptive and competing interests among different groups.

I have been interested in how children and adolescents construct a variety of social stratification systems. My colleagues and I have studied the development of concepts of economic inequality (Leahy, 1981, 1983a, 1983b), sex roles (Leahy & Shirk, 1984), intelligence (Leahy & Hunt, 1983), and age maturity (Leahy & Bresler, 1982). In these investigations, we were generally guided by a cognitive-developmental model to the study of social cognition. In this chapter, I summarize our findings on the development of concepts of economic inequality and suggest some cognitive-developmental trends in the construction of other aspects of social inequality. Further, I propose that there are costs of social-cognitive development resulting in increasing tendencies to blame those (including the self) who fall below the average in different status hierarchies (Leahy, 1983c, 1985).

Theoretical Models of Stratification

The study of the development of concepts of social inequality must begin with an epistemology of what these concepts might be in their final, developed form—specifically, what is the individual developing into—and how we would characterize the child's knowledge in relation to the adult's knowledge of inequality. There are three models of relevance here—conflict, functional, and cognitive-developmental.

The conflict model emphasizes the view that perception of the stratification system will depend on the different strata occupied by individuals (Marx, 1966; Weber, 1946). For example, merchants and blue-collar industrial workers would view work, the products of labor, and class relations in a considerably different manner from one another. Those experiencing displacement, conflict, or exploitation within the stratification system would be most likely to achieve an understanding of class interests and historical factors, according to this model. This model of stratification concepts describes a rather pessimistic view of the endpoint of development and sheds little light on the developmental process. In regard to the study of the development of these concepts, however, we should expect from this model that different groups (classes, races, genders) would have disparate and conflicting views of the stratification process and that increasing age, marked by supposed increased understanding of class consciousness, should result in increased challenge to the stratification system.

In contrast to the conflict model, the functional model of socialization proposes that stratification concepts are widely shared and serve to justify and stabilize the stratification system (Merton, 1957; Parsons, 1960). An implication of functionalism is that socialization is viewed as the increasing allegiance to the stratification hierarchy. Thus, one might expect from this model that consensus, justification, and views of stabilized stratification should be reflected in the stratification concepts of children and that these qualities should be more widely established with increasing age.

The cognitive-developmental model I propose (termed structural-developmental) draws on the work of Piaget (1970) and Kohlberg (1969).

Specifically, I propose that stratification concepts undergo (a) qualitative change with age reflecting (b) a natural ordering of concepts that reflect (c) cognitive level. Further, these stratification concepts are marked by consistency across different themes—that is, concepts of intelligence, economic class, sex differences, deviance, and personality share similar structural properties. I refer to this as *organizational unity*. Finally, cognitive or stage transitions are viewed as a consequence of cognitive disequilibrium such that individuals experiencing greater conflict will more rapidly attain higher levels in that domain of conflict. This proposition suggests that greater class-consciousness (which is a higher level of conceptualizing economic stratification) should be manifested by more economically deprived individuals. This latter proposal is consistent with the conflict theory described above. Unlike conflict theory, however, cognitive-developmental theory offers no clear prediction regarding increasing justification, challenge, or stabilization with increased age. We shall now examine several implications of the cognitive-developmental approach in more detail.

Natural Ordering of Concepts

In contrast to a strict associationist or social learning theory model of social-cognitive development, the structural-developmental model proposes that there is a natural ordering of social concepts such that simple concepts are necessary but not sufficient precursors of higher-order concepts. Three general levels of stratification concepts are specified-peripheral, psychological, and systemic. Causal concepts of each of these phenomena are also ordered sequentially.

Peripheral concepts of persons refer to the external, observable, tangible qualities of individuals, such as their clothing, their physical attributes, and their simple behavior. Psychological concepts of persons refer to inferred, internal states of individuals, such as motivations, thoughts, feelings, and dispositions. Evidence of the sequentiality of these descriptions is found in studies of how children describe others and themselves, showing that increased age is associated with decreased reference to peripheral and increased reference to central (here, psychological) concepts of persons (Livesley & Bromley, 1973). Similarly, in studies of concepts of deviance (Coie & Pennington, 1976; Paget, 1983), intelligence (Leahy & Hunt, 1983), and sex roles (Williams, Bennett, & Best, 1975), peripheral or behavioral dimensions are the first dimensions identified by younger children, with psychological dimensions becoming increasingly more important with increasing age.

These studies, as well as the results of the class-concepts study that will be described in more detail, point to developmental regularities regarding peripheral and psychological concepts suggesting organizational unity. Why are psychological concepts more highly developed concepts? First, peripheral concepts are simply descriptions of behavior, whereas psychological concepts are generalizations about behavior—that is, they are classifications of behavior. Second, psychological concepts are inferences about unobservables and, therefore, are more abstract than peripheral concepts. Finally, psychological concepts are attempts to explain behavior by reference to thoughts or dispositions, whereas behavioral descriptions may simply be seen as descriptions without explanations. In other words, at the psychological concept level the individual is attempting to answer why someone did something.

A further step in the hierarchy of concepts of stratification is systemic thinking. By systemic thinking I mean the ability to recognize that the individual belongs to social groups that may affect the way he or she thinks and behaves and that the individual's behavior affects other people, who respond to this behavior—that is, systemic thinking is interactive.

Probably very few adults think systemically with any regularity. Evidence related to the development of systemic thinking has been presented by Selman (1980) in his studies of role-taking development. Selman found that preadolescents had considerable difficulty taking the third-person perspective on interaction—that is, the ability to see the self and others in mutual interaction from the perspective of another observer. This may be a rudimentary level of systemic thinking that involves at higher levels the ability to recognize how one produces behavior in others and how others produce behavior in oneself, thereby maintaining the stability of social interaction systems (Leahy, 1991). For example, the ability to understand Patterson's coercion cycle is an example of the ability to engage in this higher level of systemic thinking.

Applied specifically to the development of stratification concepts, systemic thinking entails what I have called sociocentric thinking. This involves the ability to understand that an individual's membership in a group (such as an economic class) has implications for life-quality opportunities (legal rights, employment, education, health)—which I refer to as life chances (see Weber, 1946). In addition, sociocentric conceptions refer to awareness that class membership affects how people view the stratification system or how they are viewed by others occupying different classes. I refer to this as class-consciousness (Marx, 1966).

Cognitive-Development and Stratification Concepts

The structural-developmental model proposes that nonsocial and social-cognitive developments are marked by structural isomorphism. This does not imply that one domain (for example, the nonsocial) is attained before the other as Kohlberg (1969) has argued. Rather, the structural model proposed here suggests that social and nonsocial cognition show similar sequences in development such that development in one domain affects development in another domain. Thus, we would expect positive correlations of performances on structurally similar social and nonsocial stimuli as well as positive correlations within a single domain. We may refer to this as the organizational unity principle.

According to the cognitive-developmental model, *decentration* is an ability that is attained primarily through social interaction rather than through the manipulation or experimentation with the nonsocial world (Feffer, 1970). Decentration refers to the ability to coordinate different perspectives within a system—for example, to be able to reconstruct the perspectives of different people in a spatial plane. Social interaction, which provides the opportunity for exposure to conflicting opinions and the opportunity to construct rules with peers, facilitates decentration. In fact, this emphasis on social interaction as a source of development of cognition was Piaget's earlier position (1926, 1965), which gave way to more formal structuralist descriptions of operative intelligence in his later writings (for example, Piaget, 1970). For the present discussion, I see decentration as a result of both social and nonsocial factors. Unlike Piaget, however, I view decentration as a life-span process of development such that there is an ongoing process (or possibility) of decentering from one's own thought to view that thought within a system. This system may be dyadic (for example, a couple interacting), familial, role-specified, (for example, sex roles), class-stratified, or racial.

We should be mindful that Piaget, who first advanced the idea of decentration, emphasized the coordination of elements within a system. Although his original discussion focused on spatial reasoning, the principle is applicable to all systems as Piaget (1970) emphasized in his volume on structuralism.

At the concrete operational level (by the age of 8), decentration is reflected in the ability to refocus on two dimensions and to coordinate these dimensions—for example, the ability to recognize that a decrease in height may be compensated by a decrease in width to conserve volume (Feffer, 1970). Younger, preoperational children tend to be centered on the physical stimuli and cannot anticipate correctly their possible transformations. This ability underlies role taking, not only in coordinating perspectives but also in being able to infer the psychological qualities of persons such as thoughts and dispositions. Further, decentration is involved in the ability to find causes of psychological processes—such as deviance—with increased decentering implied by recognizing that ultimate causes may be more important than immediate causes in explaining another's behavior (Coie & Pennington, 1976; Paget, 1983). More advanced decentration is essential in the ability to understand individuals within social systems—specifically, sociocentric thinking or class consciousness. As Elkind (1967) has indicated, the ability to decenter—to stand outside the self and view the self from another's perspective—continues beyond concrete operations into the formal operational period.

One may view any stratification system as a set of rules that maintain conventions of distributive justice—that is, rules that guide and justify unequal treatment of individuals within a group or society. *Postconventional* thinking involves the ability to stand apart from these conventions and question either their utility or justice. This is the difference between Kohlberg's (1969) conventional and postconventional levels of moral judgment, but postconventional thinking may be more general than moral judgments and may be viewed as any thinking that challenges a set of rules (see Turiel, 1978). The sequential model of cognitive development suggests that three stages should be discernible: (1) the absence of knowledge of conventions, (2) knowledge of conventions accompanied by the belief that these conventions are immutable, and (3) recognition that conventions may change.

In our study of stratification concepts, we have found some evidence of these 3 stages. In conceptions of sex roles, younger children (4 years old) lack knowledge of sex-stereotyped behavior, followed by rigid classification at age 6, and ending at age 8 with the recognition that sex-typed behavior may be manifested by either gender (Leahy & Shirk, 1984). Similarly, in our study of class concepts there was increasing justification of inequality with increasing age, but this tendency decreased for some adolescents who challenged inequality (Leahy, 1983b).

A second cognitive attainment with reference to stratification concepts is classificatory skill. Very young children (age 4) engage in configurative sorting such that they arrange objects into a design rather than distinct classes. This is followed by exhaustive sorting-the classification of objects by a single dimension that all class members share (such as color). Later, this gives way to multiple classifications such that classes, once formed, can be resorted into other categories. Once a class of red objects is formed, for example, they may be resorted into other classes of triangles and circles (Inhelder & Piaget, 1958). As already mentioned, we have found (Leahy & Shirk, 1984) that sex-role stereotypes developed in the expected age sequence and that the ability to classify social and nonsocial stimuli was positively correlated. This supported the organizational unity principle.

Finally, conceptions of distributive justice develop with age. Piaget (1965) proposed that between the ages of 6 and 11 there is a change from authority-based to equality-based to equity-based conceptions of justice. For example, the younger child (age 6) gives precedence to the authority of elders; this unilateral respect results in the view that what elders have decided must be right. At about 7 or 8, the child shifts to a belief in the equal distribution of rewards without considering individual differences in performance or needs. In contrast, older children (age 11) use an equity principle allocating greater reward based on merit. Several studies have yielded mixed findings as to whether equity gains precedence over equality in reward allocation as the child develops (Hook, 1982, 1983; Lane & Coon, 1972; Lerner, 1974; Leventhal & Lane, 1970). As a formalistic or structural model, equity is a more complex distributive model since it involves comparisons of relative inputs of different performers, while equality is a simple equal distribution. In our study of class concepts, we examined whether equity concepts gain precedence over equality distributions.

The Construction of Economic Inequality

One of the most significant tasks involved in socialization is the acquisition of an understanding of economic transactions and relationships. Between childhood and late adolescence, the child must learn the meaning of money, monetary transactions, an understanding of profit, savings and interest, credit, and conceptions of inequalities in the economic distribution system.

Four theoretical models are advanced here to account for developmental changes in economic conceptions. First, a Piagetian-constructivist model proposes that conceptions of economics reflect qualitative changes in nonsocial cognitive operations. Thus, the transition from preoperational to concrete operational to formal operational thinking will be manifested in conceptions of economic exchange and conceptions of inequalities among economic classes. Second, conceptions of economic roles (for example, consumer) will reflect role-transfers, or generalizations from one's social roles in other contexts (for example, child vs. parent). From this role-transfer model, we might expect that the dependent role of the child in the family would generalize to conceptions of economic transactions as altruistic and directed toward a caregiving function. Thus, sellers, manufacturers, and service providers would be perceived by the dependent child as motivated by desires to take care of the child rather than to obtain profits. A third theoretical model that is advanced is the functionalist model that stresses the likelihood of any socialization system to help the child internalize the rules and ethical principles of the dominant society or group. Thus, from this functionalist approach increasing exposure to socialization would lead to increased justification of the status quo in the economic system. Finally, a conflict model, or cognitive disequilibrium model, would suggest that experiences of conflict within the economic system would result in an increased awareness of contradictions or inequities that become increasingly challenged. Thus, from the conflict model, economic socialization might result in greater differences, with increased age, between individuals from different economic groups. In this chapter, we examine the evidence from a variety of sources on the development of economic thinking concerning these four theoretical positions.

Compensation for Work

There are large disparities in income within our population in North America—a factor that is an important social phenomenon in economic socialization. How do children learn about this and how do they make sense of it? In a study by Burris (1983) of children in 3 age groups ranging from 4 to 12, 3 levels of understanding of unequal income were identified. The first level emphasized the effort expended—people who work harder are paid more. The second level reflected the belief that the utility of the work to others determined the amount paid, while the third level reflected the importance of skill and training. Interestingly, these levels do not reflect the importance of demand and scarcity of a skill—that is, the market forces that determine differential pay. Nor do these levels reflect the value of competitive bargaining.

These conceptions of compensation reflect variations on just world (Lerner, 1974) beliefs—that is, at each level one can argue that there is equity in the compensation system—people who work harder, do more useful work, or who have achieved a level of skill are compensated more highly. Supply-demand concepts of labor value appear to be missing in these conceptions, although one might argue that payment for skill could imply such a concept of scarcity of a skill. However, one can be an expert violinist but be unable to make a living, simply because the demand for the skill is low.

Concepts of Profit

The idea that the seller will obtain more money from the buyer than the cost of the goods is not entirely acceptable to young children. Jahoda's (1979) study of children's ideas of profit indicates that it is not until age 11 that there is comprehension of profit. Furth (1980) examined how children of various ages conceptualized transactions of buying and selling at a shop. Initially, the young child (age 5) views the transaction as simply a handing-off of money for goods, with little idea of the differential value of various goods or monetary units and little understanding of the idea of profit. During later childhood and early adolescence, there emerges an understanding of the different relationships—buyer, seller, manufacturer—and the transactions entailed. The young child is not able to coordinate these other relationships—for example, the seller must obtain the goods from the manufacturer, raise capital, and hold the goods before they are sold.

Piagetian and role-transfer models are relevant here. At the earlier stages of concepts of profit, the child views a transaction as a one-to-one correspondence. "I give you a dollar for this item," with no awareness of other transformations, or "players" in the system. These other transformations—or determinants of cost—include the cost to the seller of the goods, the necessity to tie up capital, the cost of holding the goods, and the need for a profit motive to provide an incentive. With the acquisition of concrete operational thinking—and the ability to understand unobservable transformations or factors—such as the factors determining profit—there is increased awareness of the role of profit within economic transactions. One can view the manufacturer (M), shopkeeper (S), and buyer (B) relationship as one of "transitivity"—that is, $M > S > B$. These transitive relationships entail greater cost to the individual further to the right of the transaction.

Although the awareness of profit is attained by many children at age 11, there is further development in the awareness of what determines the price that is charged for a commodity. In a study by Leiser (1983), younger children (age 7) were far less likely than adolescents to understand the importance of market factors in determining the price of a good. The ability to understand that increases in the money supply (inflation) or changes in productivity and supply of goods (i.e., shortages or cost of manufacturing) can affect prices is not achieved until late adolescence—and, even then, this ability is not achieved by some adolescents. I have referred to such concepts as sociocentric in that they reflect an understanding of factors that transcend individuals or dyadic relationships (Leahy, 1981; 1983).

At the earlier stages, role-transfer is relevant since the young child views the seller as functioning like a benevolent parent who provides the goods the child needs or wants, rather than as an independent agent motivated by his own desire for profit.

Overview of Class-Concepts Study

There were 720 subjects drawn from 4 age groups (6, 11, 14, and 17), 2 racial groups (African-American and Caucasian), and 4 social classes (lower to upper middle), in three cities (New York, Boston, and Washington, D.C.). All subjects, except 67 Caucasian adolescents who responded to questions in written format, were individually interviewed between 1976 and 1978. Subjects from predominantly African-American schools were interviewed by two African-American graduate students, while the other subjects were interviewed by Caucasian graduate students. Each subject was asked the following questions:

   1. Describe rich people. What are they like?
   2. Describe poor people. What are they like?
   3. How are rich people different from poor people?
   4. How are rich people the same as poor people? What do they have in common?
5-6. Why are some people rich (poor) while others are poor (rich)?
7-8. Should some people be rich (poor) while others are poor (rich)?
   9. How could a poor person get rich some day?
 10. What would have to happen so that there would be no poor people?
 11. How could you get rich some day?

Answers to these questions were tape-recorded and scored into content categories developed based on the person perception and moral development literature and on sociological models of economic stratification. Categories were mutually exclusive, resulting in scorable responses for most subjects. Interjudge reliability was satisfactory (see Leahy, 1981 and 1983a, for more details).

Descriptions of Rich and Poor People

Categories of responses that showed significant age trends are shown in Table 11.1. References to the possessions of the rich and poor decreased with age—especially between ages 6 and 11. References to the appear-

Table 11.1 Categories Showing Significant Age Trends

Question / Category	6	11	14	17	Total	Age Effect
1. Rich						
Possessions	40.9	23.9	21.0	22.6	27.1	16.76**
Appearances	2.6	10.9	5.5	4.5	5.9	11.28**
Residence	3.8	11.9	7.0	4.5	6.8	9.09**
Traits	5.0	10.3	12.1	11.7	9.8	4.65*
Thoughts	2.0	4.6	7.6	10.0	6.0	10.32**
Class consciousness	1.8	8.5	11.5	12.1	8.5	10.93**
2. Poor						
Possessions	35.0	18.6	17.9	12.9	21.1	16.89**
Appearances	6.4	11.8	7.1	3.1	7.1	10.04**
Residence	5.8	11.7	8.7	4.3	7.6	7.19**
Thoughts	4.3	6.1	7.3	13.4	7.8	10.46**
3. Different						
Possessions	41.8	28.9	26.9	23.5	30.3	9.69**
Appearances	5.0	8.7	4.1	2.3	5.0	5.02**
Thoughts	8.3	4.8	7.1	13.5	8.4	5.42*
4. Same						
Behaviors	2.5	11.0	4.2	2.3	5.0	3.97*
Both people	3.4	23.0	22.4	17.8	16.7	15.43**
Thoughts	4.9	7.4	17.7	26.6	14.1	22.23**
Deny similarity	17.5	10.3	8.2	6.3	10.6	4.06*

Note. Only categories comprising more than 5% of responses are shown.
*$p < .01$, **$p < .001$.

ances of the rich and poor increased between six and eleven and decreased thereafter. Descriptions of the rich and poor in terms of their thoughts, traits, and class consciousness all increased with age. To focus our attention on the pattern of age trends, I have provided a summary of levels of social class concepts derived from the data of this study (see Appendix 1). Table 11.1 shows that many of the expected developmental trends were supported. However, we shall examine in more detail the individual trends as well as the interesting class and race qualifications to the developmental sequence.

There were substantial decreases with age in references to the peripheral characteristics of rich and poor people and comparisons of how they were different from each other. There was increasing emphasis on the psychological qualities of people, such as their thoughts and traits. Thus, younger children described classes in terms of their possessions (or lack of possessions) and by reference to appearance or behavior. Older children and adolescents were more likely to refer to thoughts, abilities, and personality ("smart," "lazy," "don't want to work"). The youngest children were more likely than older children to deny that rich and poor people had anything in common. This finding is consistent with the view that younger children have difficulty recategorizing classes—that is, once individuals are classified into one group (e.g., "poor"), there is difficulty in recategorizing them into another group (e.g., both have thoughts).

Older lower-class subjects were more likely than others to refer to the thoughts of the poor—a finding consistent with conflict theory. In contrast, upper-middle-class subjects more often described poor people in terms of traits. This finding is consistent with the view that poor children are better at taking the perspective of the poor, thus seeing the world from the perspective the thoughts of the poor, rather than simply labeling the poor as "different kinds of people." This is similar to the actor-observer bias in person perception, such that observers are more likely to attribute personality traits to others than they are to themselves.

There was an increase in adolescence in describing the class-consciousness of the rich consistent with cognitive-developmental theory. Inconsistent with conflict theory, however, these descriptions were more common in describing rich than poor people and there were no class or race differences in descriptions of class consciousness.

Younger children often found no basis of similarity between the rich and poor; 10-year-olds claimed that they were both people or had similar behavior; adolescents were more likely than others to claim they had similar thoughts. Apparently, the first criterion of similarity is peripheral qualities, while during adolescence psychological and sociocentric qualities (for example, both are citizens) become more salient. The findings for these analyses were predominantly age effects with few interactions or main effects associated with race or class.

These findings are consistent with other data on concepts of intelligence. In a study by Leahy and Hunt (1983), younger children had difficulty finding any basis of similarity between intelligent and unintelligent people. Similarly, in our study of sex-role stereotyping (Leahy and Shirk, 1984) we found that young children (age 6) had difficulty anticipating that males and females could both engage in opposite-sex-typed behavior. The class-concepts data, as well as data on other aspects of stratification concepts, suggest four levels of stereotyping: (1) failure to engage in stereotyping, (2) rigid classification with denial of similarities, (3) stereotyping but recognition of peripheral similarities, and (4) stereotyping but recognition of psychological and systemic (sociocentric) similarities. One conclusion that summarizes this pattern of results is that once stereotypes are formed they become less stereotypic with increased age.

Explanations of Economic Inequality

Clear cognitive-developmental age trends in explanations of economic inequality emerged in our study. These findings are shown in Table 11.2,

Table 11.2 Percentage of Responses for Explanations of Wealth and Poverty

Question / Category	Age (years)				Total	Age Effect
	6	11	14	17		
Why are people rich?[b]						
Definition	19.6[a]	4.5[b]	3.2	1.8	7.3	16.45**
Work	10.7[a]	27.2[b]	19.4	11.2[c]	17.1	9.56**
Effort	8.3[a]	7.4	11.5	18.8[b]	11.5	8.90**
Luck	7.7	10.7	7.6	7.8	8.5	.49
Education	.7[a]	4.0	9.9[b]	5.5	5.0	7.22*
Violate law	6.5	2.0	3.7	4.5	4.2	2.64
Inherit	21.2	21.0	21.6	27.2	22.8	1.29
Intelligence	.7[a]	2.5	4.4	6.6[b]	3.6	8.68**
Use of money	.0	.1	1.3	.8	.6	2.54
Demographic	2.1	.1	.3	7.1	2.4	1.86
Don't know	14.1[a]	3.2[b]	.0	.0	4.3	10.76**
Why are people poor?[c]						
Definition	25.3[a]	4.7[b]	2.9	1.3	8.6	24.42**
Work	7.5[a]	32.6[b]	21.9[c]	9.2[d]	17.8	20.79**
Effort	10.1	7.4	14.1	20.3	13.0	2.54
Luck	5.6	7.7	8.4	5.2	6.7	.57
Education	1.0[a]	5.1	12.4[b]	18.3	9.2	20.21**
Violate law	.0	4.7	5.2	.0	2.5	1.87
(Do not) inherit	10.0	9.0	11.5	12.9	10.9	.41
Intelligence	.6[a]	2.5[b]	6.3	6.7	4.0	4.59*
Use of money	13.6	13.3	10.8	4.4	10.5	3.19
Demographic	8.1	2.4	2.5	5.6	4.6	1.11
Don't know	8.1[a]	2.8[b]	1.3	.0	3.9	9.73**

Note. Only categories exceeding 6% of responses for either question at any age are shown here. Subscripts denote differences between means ($p < .01$) for Scheffé comparisons for adjacent comparisons.
[a]Age effects refer to *F* ratios for Age (4) x Class (4) ANOVAs for questions about poverty. Questions about wealth refer to Age (4) x Class (4) x Gender (2) ANOVAs. [b]$n = 699$. [c]$n = 510$.
*$p < .01$, **$p < .001$.

Table 11.3 Percentage of Responses for Justifications of or Challenges to Economic Inequality

Question / Category	Age (years)				Total	Age Effect
	6	11	14	17		
Should people be rich?[b]						
Definition	14.6[a]	4.2[b]	2.8	2.2	6.0	12.66**
Consequences to poor	25.4	28.3	19.8	18.0	22.9	1.86
Behavior-contingent	5.4	9.8[a]	28.5[b]	26.9	17.6	17.61**
Fatalistic	1.2	4.0	8.7[a]	18.2[b]	8.0	12.20**
Rich should help	7.5[a]	17.9[b]	10.6	8.1	11.0	4.72*
Equality	9.0[a]	16.7[b]	19.2	11.2[c]	14.0	2.19
Don't know	14.5[a]	1.4[b]	2.7	1.9	5.1	12.87*
Should people be poor?[c]						
Definition	3.7	1.3	1.0	.5	1.6	1.24
Consequences to poor	33.8	43.0	32.3	38.0	36.8	.93
Behavior-contingent	4.8[a]	18.6[b]	23.3	19.7	16.6	4.86*
Fatalistic	1.4	3.1	1.3[a]	11.2[b]	4.2	5.75**
Rich should help	8.1	5.1	1.6	5.2	5.0	2.47
Equality	2.3[a]	5.6	16.7[b]	5.3[c]	7.5	5.08*
Don't know	20.8[a]	2.5[b]	.0	1.0	6.1	23.69**

Note. Only categories exceeding 6% of responses for either question at any age are shown here. Subscripts denote differences between means ($p < .01$) for Scheffé comparisons for adjacent comparisons.

[a]Age effects refer to F ratios for Age (4) x Class (4) ANOVAs for questions about poverty. Questions about wealth refer to Age (4) x Class (4) x Gender (2) ANOVAs. [b]$n = 714$. [c]$n = 491$.

*$p < .01$, **$p < .001$.

and the data for justifications and challenges to inequality are shown in Table 11.3.

Younger children explained wealth and poverty primarily in terms of differences in possessions, inheritance, or the use of money—all peripheral descriptions. Psychological causes of inequality gained salience at ages 11 and 14-emphasizing work, effort, education, and intelligence. Thus increasing age was associated with explaining inequality by claiming that the rich and poor are different kinds of people, a finding consistent with their descriptions and comparisons. Examples of explanations by younger children are that poor people "can't buy a job," "they have no money," "they got no food," or "they spend their money on dumb things." Older children and adolescents explained inequality by claiming, "Rich people have better education," "they're smarter," "they have better jobs," or "they work harder." Contrary to conflict theory, there were very few references to sociocentric conceptions even during adolescence. There were generally similar age trends for both African-Americans and Caucasians; inequality became increasingly legitimated by reference to individual differences rather than social-structural or political factors. In fact, contrary to conflict theory, it was the 17-year-old lower-class males who were most likely to view wealth in terms of intelligence. These data are in clear support of the functionalist model of socialization.

Consistent with the concrete focus of young children, the 6-year-olds justified inequality by reference to the definitional differences between the classes—that is, rich people should be rich because they have money. Equality challenges to poverty (but not wealth) increased at age 14 but decreased at seventeen. The idea that the rich should help the poor increased at age 11 but decreased after. This curvilinear age trend for equality norms was due to 2 developments in justifying inequality during adolescence: First, there was an increase in behavior contingent justifications ("If you work hard, you should be rich"); second, there was an increase in fatalistic justifications ("There's always going to be poor people—that's human nature").

Two reasons are postulated to account for this curvilinear age trend for equality and equity concepts. The first cause-social-cognitive development-refers to the fact that older children and adolescents have greater capacity to identify individual psychological differences and greater ability to engage in social comparison and seriation of individual talent. These individual differences then become the basis for equity judgments. A second cause-functionalist socialization-refers to the shift from the mutuality and equality of the child's peer group to the meritocracy of the school culture that places greater emphasis on stratification in later school grades.

There was minor support for the conflict model: Caucasians were more likely than African-Americans to use fatalistic justifications, and lower-class subjects were more likely to show concern for the poor. However, the functionalist model received greater support than the conflict model. There was increasing justification of inequality with increasing age-for all classes and for both African-Americans and Caucasians. In fact, the belief that inequality is fated would appear to conflict with a Piagetian view that formal operations during adolescence facilitate counterfactual thinking. One might argue that the functionalist socialization to perceive inequality as legitimate is so strong as to override formal operational thinking. Conflict theory emphasizes sociocentrism (class concepts, life chances, class conflict, class resistance to economic change);

see Marx (1966) and Weber (1946). There were almost no challenges (less than 6%) of inequality referring to sociocentric factors. Class consciousness is not a major factor in the thinking of American youth.

Social Change and Individual Mobility

The data on concepts of social change offer strong support to a functionalist model. These data are shown in Tables 11.4 and 11.5. One response of special relevance to functionalist theory because it appears to be the hallmark of the functionalist view that societal complexity necessitates stratification (Parsons, 1960)—is the view held by many adolescents that economic inequality is a necessary or fated quality of society. The fatalism of inequality is not based on a view that classes would actively resist change; rather, it reflects a view that human nature and complex society require stratification. Further, socialization to the legitimacy of inequality is reflected in the fact that equity concepts of change (that is, "Poor people could work harder") increased substantially by age 11. The view that inequality could be ended by others (that is, the rich) giving to the poor increased between ages 6 and 11 and decreased substantially thereafter. Thus legitimization of economic inequality took the form of fatalistic and equity concepts and the decrease of equalization concepts during adolescence.

Table 11.4 Percentage of Responses for Conceptions of Social Change

Question / Category	Age (years)				Total	Age Effect
	6	11	14	17		
No more poor						
Get rid of people	7.7[a]	.3[b]	1.2	2.9	2.8	7.28*
Others give	25.4[a]	35.4[b]	20.3[c]	8.3[d]	22.4	16.30*
Equity	11.4[a]	23.5	28.7[b]	23.0	21.7	8.15*
Deny possible	3.3[a]	2.9	7.5	14.8[b]	7.2	9.37*
Resistance to change	.8	.8[a]	.5	4.7[b]	1.7	14.71*
Social structure	3.9[a]	20.5[b]	25.4	29.3	19.8	19.09*
Don't know	17.3[a]	1.7[b]	.3	.3	4.9	25.74*

Note. Resistance to change was included as a category because of the substantial emphasis by older Class 4 subjects on this category. Subscripts denote differences between means ($p < .01$) for Scheffé comparisons for adjacent comparisons. $N = 701$.
[a]Age effects refer to F ratios for Age (4) x Class (4) x Gender (2) ANOVAS.
*$p < .001$.

Table 11.5 Percentage of Responses for Conceptions of Individual Mobility

Question / Category	Age (years)				Total	Age Effect
	6	11	14	17		
Poor become rich[b]						
Ask others	27.4[a]	7.1[b]	1.7	1.4	9.4	36.68*
Work	23.0[a]	37.2[b]	30.2	21.1[c]	28.1	5.63*
Education	2.1	5.6[a]	28.9b	17.5	13.5	10.60*
Effort	3.3[a]	11.4[b]	10.8	18.1	10.9	7.60*
Invest/spend	8.9[a]	19.6[b]	19.2	9.2[c]	14.3	7.68*
Violate law	7.5	1.5	3.6	8.3	5.2	2.34
Luck	6.5	6.3	3.4	5.5	5.4	.90
Get right connections	.5	3.2	2.0[a]	7.0[b]	3.2	8.48*
Don't know	10.1[a]	1.7[b]	1.7	.5	3.5	10.04*
Self become rich[c]						
Ask others	32.4[a]	1.1[b]	.6	2.8	9.2	38.95*
Work	23.2[a]	41.1[b]	28.2[c]	28.8	30.3	8.91*
Education	5.4[a]	10.5	20.0[b]	19.9	14.0	18.60*
Effort	7.2	12.9	14.1	13.8	12.0	2.80
Invest/spend	12.6	19.0	16.3	12.4	15.1	.62
Don't want to be	3.4	2.6[a]	2.5	9.1[b]	4.4	5.88*
Violate law	6.1	1.7	2.1	1.2	2.8	3.58
Luck	2.1	3.5	2.0	3.9	2.9	.75
Get right connections	.3	2.7	4.2	3.7	2.8	2.43
Don't know	8.3[a]	.5[b]	2.0	.9	2.9	6.72*

Note. Only categories exceeding 6% of responses for either question at any age are shown here. Subscripts denote differences between means ($p < .01$) for Scheffé comparisons for adjacent comparisons.
[a]Age effects refer to F ratios for Age (4) x Class (4) x Gender (2) ANOVAS. [b]$n = 697$. [c]$n = 706$.
*$p < .001$.

There was also support for conflict theory regarding social change concepts. African-Americans were more likely than Caucasians to emphasize changing the social structure, and upper-middle-class subjects were more likely than others to claim that changing values could end poverty. The present data do not provide a basis for determining the children's views concerning whose or what values should change and what new values could be attained. However, the impression one gains from the interviews is that individual attitudes toward work (that is, equity values) are the most commonly mentioned or implied values. Middle-class Caucasians were more likely than other groups to deny the possibility of change. Resistance to change was found with frequency only among lower-class adolescents, especially males.

Cognitive-developmental theory gains support in that sociocentric concepts increased during adolescence. This age trend was demonstrated for all classes and both races but was qualified by the interaction effects mentioned above.

Concepts of individual change showed strong developmental trends. Young children personified their own mobility by claiming that they or a poor person could become rich by asking others for money ("You can go to the bank and ask them for money" or "The waiter could give me money.") Equity conceptions increased with age—for example, references to education or effort. Again, for all classes and both races there were similar age trends for most of these analyses. There were only two notable exceptions to this pattern: lower-class adolescents were more likely to say that they did not want to be rich, and references to work as a source of mobility were more common for lower-class subjects than for other classes.

CONCLUSIONS

Most of the analyses indicated that significant effects were largely age related. Given the large number of analyses conducted, it may appear surprising that so few class or race effects emerged. Two conclusions may be tentatively warranted: First, class concepts are largely determined by cognitive level; second, functionalist influences toward greater legitimization of social inequality are relatively stronger than the influence of class consciousness.

There are some data in support of conflict theory—for example, greater concern by African-Americans or lower-class subjects for the consequences to the poor and greater willingness to challenge the economic structure. However, one must also note that for almost all analyses, there were similar age trends and that most of these age trends were in favor of greater legitimization of inequality.

The increasing emphasis on equity concepts in explaining and justifying inequality is consistent with other studies of person perception (Livesley & Bromley, 1973) and the development of concepts of intelligence (Leahy & Hunt, 1983). By the age of 10, the child has come to view different strata not only in terms of the different possessions or behavior of those in that strata but also in terms of their being different people. Of course, once the child views them as different people it becomes easier for him or her to justify a distributive justice system for extremes of wealth and poverty.

In our study of concepts of intellectual difference (Leahy & Hunt, 1983), we found that three levels of conception could be distinguished (see Appendix 2). We refer to these levels as peripheral-obedient, psychological, and social interaction conceptions. As Appendix 2 indicates, there is a shift from emphasis on concrete, peripheral behavior to recognition of inferred psychological qualities to recognition of the importance of the social context of intelligence. These trends are similar to those described in Appendix 1, in which levels of class concepts are shown. Concepts of social inequality undergo considerable qualitative change with age resulting in the view that different strata are occupied by different kinds of people, not simply people with different possessions or different behavior. I have proposed that cognitive development often carries costs, such that increasing development is associated with increasing capacity to engage in self-criticism and inequitable social comparison (Leahy, 1983c, 1985). The data on conceptions of social inequality—and the similar age trends irrespective of class or race— suggest that along with the stabilizing social effects of consensus, development also results in more stable dimensions (such as personality and worthiness) on which to judge the sell or others. These equity explanations of inequality have the consequence of assuring a belief in a just world where the losers are viewed as obtaining their just due. Thus, the unemployed—or in the extreme, the homeless—who have been displaced would be viewed as failing to make it in a just world rather than being viewed as the innocent victims of market and labor policies.

APPENDIX A

CONCEPTIONS OF CLASS

Level 1: Peripheral-Dependent Conceptions (Ages 6–11)

Here the focus in descriptions is on the observable, external qualities of class, such as possessions and appearances. Explanations of class differences lack causal reasoning and focus on the definitional or peripheral aspects of wealth and poverty. Although there is concern for consequences to the poor, class differences may be justified because the rich and poor meet the definitional criteria of class. Mobility and social change are viewed largely in terms of either the rich or others helping people by giving them money. The child views the economy as functioning out of benevolence for the poor or for the child's own interests.

Level II: Psychological Conceptions (Ages 11–14)

At this level, classes are described in terms of their inferred psychological qualities, such as traits, thoughts, and motivations. Classes are seen as being similar primarily because they share peripheral commonalities (for example, "Both are people"). Inequality is explained in terms of differences in work, education, effort, and intelligence. Class differences are challenged by equality principles or justified by equity considerations. Mobility is seen largely in terms of education, effort, work, and investment. Social change is viewed in terms of either the rich sharing their wealth or the poor gaining education, working hard, and getting jobs. The economy is seen as rewarding merit reflected by individual differences in inputs.

Level III: Sociocentric Conceptions (Ages 14–17)

Here the descriptions focus on differences in life chances and class consciousness. Classes are viewed as similar because they share psychological commonalities. Explanations still focus on equity. There is an increasing emphasis on the difficulty of changing the social system and claims that social change would meet with resistance by the rich. Changing the social structure is viewed as one way to change poverty. The economy is seen as being functionally based on equity principles, although there is a recognition of competing class interests. The economy is viewed in impersonal terms such that its functioning is seen as a reflection of the invisible hand of earned merit or as the expression of the interests of the wealthy. Emphasis is on conflict (for example, class consciousness) or the futility of conflict (for example, fatalism).

APPENDIX B

CONCEPTIONS OF INDIVIDUAL DIFFERENCES IN INTELLIGENCE

Level I: Peripheral-Obedient Conceptions

Intelligence is defined by actions, reading, knowledge of specific acts, and obedience to adult authority. Causes and changes in intelligence are conceptualized by passive obedience to adult authority or attendance at school. The view at this level is that the school should punish children who are not smart. Children deny the similarity of intelligent and unintelligent people.

Level II: Psychological Conceptions

Intelligence is defined by performance on tests, with an increased awareness that the intelligent and unintelligent groups are similar in that both are people and both can learn. Differences are attributed to motivation, studying, and training. Moral evaluations emerge, focusing on the lack of motivation presumed to characterize the unintelligent. Emphasis is on special tutoring and classes for the unintelligent.

Level III: Social Interaction Conceptions

There is emphasis on specific intellectual abilities associated with different kinds of intelligence. Intelligence is viewed as involving social competence, with groups of intelligent and unintelligent people seen as differing in personality traits. Differences in intelligence are attributed to social conformity and self-direction. Changes in intelligence are seen as resulting from psychological or motivational support and association with others.

Conclusions

What do we know now that we did not know before? The research and model of the construction of economic inequality indicates that young children think like little Marxists but later develop a belief in economic inequality. The younger child thinks of the economic system as an extension of his or her role within a family. Shopkeepers, bus drivers, and merchants are there to meet the needs of the individual patron. The idea of profit seems anathema. Rich and poor are simply people with different possessions—one group having more than the other.

However, by late childhood and early adolescence there are new ideas of wealth and poverty—ideas that are consistent with cognitive-developmental theory and functionalist theory. These older children view the rich and poor as different kinds of people whose inequality is justified by equity concepts of effort and ability. Moreover, the idea of changing inequality becomes, for many, increasingly impossible to imagine, further lending a sense of justification to the distribution system.

A second line of work reported here describes the elaboration of the modern portfolio model as applied to mundane decision making, depression, mania, and personality disorders. Economists have become accustomed in recent years to the use of cognitive psychology to inform their understanding of investment anomalies. The area of behavioral finance has relied on the importance of heuristics in understanding consistencies in irrational behavior. The current use of the modern portfolio model is in the tradition of the work of Becker and others who view everyday decisions as reminiscent of economic principles of tradeoffs in utilities. In the extension of modern portfolio theory in the current book, we are able to see how depression may affect mundane decision-making and how a pessimistic portfolio model may maintain depression.

As complicated as the computational model may appear to be, there is considerable support in the study described here that depression is related to portfolio concerns. The model is also extended to the understanding of manic risk-preference, suggesting that much of the risky behavior of those with symptoms of mania reflects underlying portfolio assumptions of unlimited current and future resources, intuitive grasp of information, high predictability, and an exaggerated ability to recover from loss. Indeed, what seems like risk to the rest of us during our sober-minded moments may, to a person with manic disorder, appear to be a sure thing. Risk may be in the jaundiced eye of the beholder.

When I have presented these ideas to psychologists at conventions, I have often been asked about how this could be applied to the stock market. My speculation is as follows. First, the market is not rational, as Schiller's (2001) brilliant book *Irrational Exuberance* illustrates. Second, my reading of the literature suggests that no single investment model (e.g., fundamentals, trends, efficient market) works consistently enough to keep a steady return better than a chance investment. Third, it may be an unnecessary truism to comment that investment decisions are made by human beings who are often beset by their own irrationalities.

Having said this, I would ask the reader to consider the following hypothesis. "The equities market is a bipolar illness." I mean by this that the equities market can be viewed as a cyclical mood disorder with occasional euthymic phases of normalcy. During the depressed phase of the market, individuals will require considerable information to make decisions, will try to hedge and diversify, will hold onto cash in order to avoid the risk of exposure, and will stop out quickly as they are hyper-vigilant for any sign of loss or negative movement. In contrast, the manic phase of the market—as we saw in part of the 1990s in the high-tech sector and the "concept" stocks that seemed too sexy to avoid—the investor was focused on pursuing every opportunity that presented itself. Exposure was desired—compulsively sought by some through high leveraging. Risk was discounted as the concern of the old economy that had long outlived its usefulness and was viewed as an annoying reminder of the generations past that did not understand the brilliance of the *new new new thing*.

As the manic investor in the manic market continued to put his money on the table for each new bet on a promise of future performance, sugarplum fantasies of magnificent lifestyles danced in their heads. A leading financial magazine called me and asked me about the latest trend of buying someone else's house with everything in it—buying a life with a history and a sense of panache, presumably because the purchaser was too busy with his next big deal to spend the time shopping. Others observed the manic investor charging forward in the manic market with what I would call portfolio envy—after all, we didn't invest in those high-fliers that were orbiting above and beyond the gravity of this humble earth.

As many have observed, what goes up must come down. The manic risk-loving investment style turned into a bubble that burst and left many holding options in businesses that would no longer exist. The market was marked by a flight from risk into more conservative investments, such as cash. Cycling into a depressive phase, like a manic-depressive, the market seemed to be saying, "Get out while you still can."

Perhaps there is no single model of the market because there are many phases of markets. When I talk to a patient in a manic phase, I believe that I may sound like the depressed person in the room. I offer caution and point out all the bad things that could happen. I suggest how one can regret terrible things and how positive predictions are illusions. In contrast, when I talk with depressed patients I am the beacon of hope, searching for any sign of a positive outcome, encouraging what to the patient seems like risky behavior.

Markets have cycles. They can't be cured by lithium. In fact, they may not be curable and the cycles may offer some opportunities for those who take the longer view. Looking at how the investor looks at the market— and the collective mind of the market at any given time—may be a guide to how to make a move. The question, as in many things in life, is one of timing and the horizon of investment.

Turning to the issue of self-limitation and sunk costs, I have found that many of my patients have been helped by being guided in conceptualizing their hedging strategies as attempts to avoid further loss and in understanding that they often get trapped by sunk costs in decisions that have already proven to be a failure. Let's take self-limitation as a risk-management strategy. I have outlined numerous signs of self-limitation, including perfectionistic procrastination, hedging, straddling, and self-handicapping. The smaller failures that are involved in these self-limitation moves are more acceptable to the risks that one faces in moving forward too rapidly. Getting unstuck from these sunk costs and hidden agendas is a key problem for many people whose investment strategy is to prevent greater unexpected losses later.

Finally, I have offered a multidimensional model of insatiability. I can say, with tongue in cheek, that this will not be completely satisfying to some. Perhaps some processes have been overlooked or emphasized too much. Yet, I do believe that the economic and social problems of the overworked and overspent American can be understood in terms of these issues of insatiability. As much as we define ourselves as a society of greater opportunity, the cost of these increased options may be the inability to be satisfied. This dissatisfaction is not limited to the economic sphere. Indeed, as children get older, they become more and more dissatisfied with their appearance.

The book was sometimes fun to write. Fun, because it stretched me in new directions on what may be thin ice for a psychologist playing in the pantheon of the ideas of the economist. This intellectual journey has led me to greater respect for the intriguing models of economics and for the need for an understanding of the bounded rationality of the emotional and irrational economic man. The classic view may have been of economic man as a rational, hedonic calculator. I hope that I have added to the understanding that we as humans are beset by our assumptions, past decisions, need for a belief in a just world, and a desire for optimism that may not always be justified by the facts that we seldom grasp.

References

Abramson, L. Y., Seligman, M. E. P., & Teasdale, J. (1978). Learned helplessness in humans: Critique and reformulation. *Journal of Abnormal Psychology, 87,* 49–74.

Abramson, L., Metalsky, G. I., & Alloy, L. (1989). Hopelessness depression: A theory-based subtype of depression. *Psychological Review, 96,* 358–372.

Abramson, L. Y., Seligman, M. E. P., & Teasdale, J. D. (1978). Learned helplessness in humans: Critique and reformulation. *Journal of Abnormal Psychology, 87,* 102–109.

Adler, A. (1926/1964). *Social interest: A challenge to mankind.* New York: Capricorn Books.

Alford, B. A., & Beck, A. T. (1994). Cognitive therapy of delusional beliefs. *Behaviour Research and Therapy, 32,* 369–380.

Alloy, L. B., Abramson, L. Y., Metalsky, G. I., & Hartledge, S. (1988). The hopelessness theory of depression. *British Journal of Clinical Psychology, 27,* 5–12.

Alloy, L. B., Reilly-Harrington, N., Fresco, D. M., Whitehouse, W. G., & Zechmeister, J. S. (1999). Cognitive styles and life events in subsyndromal unipolar and bipolar disorders: Stability and prospective prediction of depressive and hypomanic mood swings. *Journal of Cognitive Psychotherapy: An International Quarterly, 13,* 21–40.

Arkes, H. R. (1991). The costs and benefits of judgment errors: Implications for debiasing. *Psychological Bulletin, 110,* 486–498.

Arkes, H. R. (1996). The psychology of waste. *Journal of Behavioral Decision Making, 9,* 213–224.

Arkes, H. R., & Ayton, P. (1999) The sunk cost and concorde effects: Are humans less rational than lower animals? *Psychological Bulletin, 125,* 591–600.

Arkes, H. R., & Blumer, C. (1985). The psychology of sunk cost. *Organizational Behavior and Human Decision Processes, 35,* 124–140.

Arkin, R. M., & Oleson, K. C. (1998). Self-handicapping. In J. M. Darley and J. Cooper (Eds.), *Attribution in social interaction: The legacy of Edward E. Jones* (pp. 313–347). Washington, DC: American Psychological Association Press.

Arnold, M. (1983). *The nostalgia of classicism.* New York: Chelsea House.

Atkinson, J. W. (1957). Motivational determinants of risk-taking behavior. *Psychological Review, 64,* 359–372.

Atkinson, J. W. (1983). Old and new conceptions of how expected consequences influence actions. In N. T. Feather (Ed.), *Expectations and actions: Expectancy—value models in psychology* (pp. 17–52). Hillsdale, NJ: Erlbaum.

Atkinson, J. W., & Raynor, J. O. (1978). *Personality, motivation, and achievement.* Washington, DC: Hemisphere.

Baron, J. (1994). *Thinking and deciding.* New York: Cambridge University Press.

Baron, J. (1994). *Thinking and deciding (2nd ed.).* Cambridge, UK: Cambridge University Press.

Barzun, J. (1975). *Classic, Romantic, and Modern.* Chicago, IL: University of Chicago Press.

Basco, M. R. & Rush, A. J. (1996). *Cognitive-behavioral therapy for bipolar disorder.* New York: Guilford.

Beck, A. T. (1967). *Depression: Causes and treatment.* Philadelphia, PA: University of Pennsylvania Press.

Beck, A. T. (1970). *Depression.* Philadelphia: University of Pennsylvania Press.

Beck, A. T. (1976). *Cognitive therapy and the emotional disorders.* New York: International Universities Press.

Beck, A. T. (1987). Cognitive models of depression. *Journal of Cognitive Psychotherapy, 1,* 5–37.

Beck, J. S. (1995). *Cognitive therapy: Basics and beyond.* New York: Guilford.

Beck, A. T., Emery, G, & Greenberg, R. L. (1985). *Anxiety disorders and phobias: A cognitive perspective.* New York: Basic Books.

Beck, A. T., & Freeman, A. M. (1990). *Cognitive therapy of personality disorders.* New York: Guilford Press.

Beck, A. T., & Steer, R. A. (1987). *Manual for the Revised Beck Depression Inventory.* San Antonio, TX: Psychological Corporation.

Beck, A. T., & Steer, R. A. (1990). *Beck Anxiety Inventory manual.* San Antonio, TX: Psychological Corporation.

Beck, A. T., Rush, A. J., Shaw, B. F., & Emery, G. (1979). *Cognitive therapy of depression.* New York: Guilford.

Becker, G. S. (1976). *The economic approach to human behavior.* Chicago: University of Chicago Press.

Becker, G. S. (1991). *A treatise on the family.* Cambridge, MA: Harvard University Press.

Becker, G. S., Grossman, M., & Murphy, K. M. (1991). Rational addiction and the effect of price on consumption. *American Economic Review, 81,* 237–241.

Becker, G. S., & Murphy, K. M. (1988). A theory of rational addition. *Journal of Political Economy, 96,* 675–700.

Bell, D., Raiffa, H., & Tversky, A. (1988). Descriptive, normative and prescriptive interactions in decision making. In D. Bell, H. Raiffa, & A. Tversky (Eds.), *Decision making: Descriptive, normative and prescriptive interactions* (pp. 9–32). New York: Cambridge University Press.

Berglas, S. & Jones, E. E. (1978). Drug choice as a self-handicapping strategy in response to noncontingent success. *Journal of Personality and Social Psychology, 36,* 405–417.

Bodie, Z., Kane, A., & Marcus, A. J. (1996). *Investments.* Chicago: Irwin Publishing.

Bornstein, B. H., & Chapman, G. B. (1995). Learning lessons from sunk costs. *Journal of Experimental Psychology: Applied, 1,* 251–269.

Bowlby, J. (1968). *Attachment and loss: I. Attachment.* London: Hogarth.

Bowlby, J. (1969). *Attachment and loss: Vol. I. Attachment.* New York: Basic Books.

Bowlby, J. (1973). *Attachment and loss: Vol. II. Separation: Anxiety and anger.* New York: Basic Books.

Bowlby, J. (1980). *Attachment and loss: Vol. III. Loss: Sadness and depression.* London: Hogarth Press.

Brown, G. W., & Harris, T. (1978). *The social origins of depression.* London: Tavistock.

Buber, M. (1970). *I and Thou.* (trans. by W. Kaufmann). New York: Scribners.

Carver, C. S., & Scheier, M. F. (1990). Origins and functions of positive and negative affect: A control-process view. *Psychological Review, 97,* 19–35.

Clark, K. B., & Clark, M. P. (1947). Racial identification and preference in Negro children. In T. M. Newcomb & E. L. Hartley (Eds.), *Readings in social psychology.* New York: Holt.

Case, K. E., & Fair, R. E. (1989). *Principles of microeconomics.* Englewood Clark, D. A., Beck, A. T., & Alford, B. A. (1999). *Scientific foundations of cognitive theory and therapy of depression.* Chichester, UK: Wiley.

Cliffs, NJ: Prentice-Hall.

Coie, J. D., Pennington, B. F. (1976). Children's perception of deviance and disorder. *Child Development, 47,* 407–413.

Davis, R. D., & Millon, T. (1999). Models of personality and its disorders. In T. Millon & P. H. Blaney (Eds.), *Oxford textbook of psychopathology* (pp. 485–522). New York: Oxford University Press.

Derogatis, L. R. (1977). *Symptom Check List-90 administration, scoring, and procedures manual I for the R(evised) version.* Baltimore, MD: John Hopkins University School of Medicine.

Deiner, E., Sandvik, E., Seidlitz, L., & Diener, M. (1993). The relationship between income and subjective well-being: Relative or absolute? *Social Indicators Research, 28,* 195–223.

Derogatis, L. R. (1977). *Symptom Check List-90 administration, scoring, and procedures manual I for the R (evised) version.* Baltimore, MD: John Hopkins University School of Medicine.

Dweck, C. S. (1975). The role of expectations and attributions in the alleviation of learned helplessness. *Journal of Personality and Social Psychology, 31,* 674–685.

Dweck, C. S., Davidson, W., Nelson, S., & Enna, B. (1978). Sex differences in learned helplessness: II. The contingencies of evaluative feedback in the classroom and III. An experimental analysis. *Developmental Psychology, 14,* 268–276.

Eliot, T. S. (1949). *Notes toward the definition of culture.* New York: Harcourt, Brace, & Co.

Elkind, D. (1967). Egocentrism in adolescence. *Child Development, 38,* 1025–1034.

Fairburn, C. G., Marcus, M. D., & Wilson, G. T. (1993). Cognitive-behavioral therapy for binge eating and bulimia nervosa: A comprehensive treatment manual. In C. G. Fairburn & G. T. Wilson (Eds.), *Binge eating: Nature, assessment, and treatment* (pp. 361–404). New York: Guilford.

Fairburn, C. G., & Wilson, G. T. (1993). Binge eating: Definition and classification. In C. G. Fairburn & G. T. Wilson (Eds.), *Binge eating: Nature, assessment, and treatment* (pp. 3–14). New York: Guilford.

Feffer, M. (1970). A developmental analysis of interpersonal behavior. *Psychological Review, 77,* 197–214.

Festinger, L. (1957). *A theory of cognitive dissonance.* Stanford, CA: Stanford University Press.

Festinger, L. (1961). The psychological effects of insufficient rewards. *American Psychologist, 16,* 1–11.

Fisher, R., & Ury, W. (1981). *Getting to yes: Negotiating agreement without giving in.* Boston: Houghton-Mifflin.

Freud, S. (1917). Mourning and melancholia (J. Strachey, Trans.). In J. Strachey (Ed.), *Complete Psychological Works* (Standard ed., Vol. 14). London: Hogarth Press.

Fromm, E. (1976). *To have or to be?* New York: Harper & Row.

Furby, L. (1980). The origins and development of early possessive behavior. *Political Psychology, 1,* 3–23.

Furby, L. (1991). Understanding the psychology of possessions and ownership: A personal memoir and an appraisal of our progress. *Journal of Social Behavior and Personality, 6,* 457–463.

Furnham, A., & Argyle, M. (1998). *The psychology of money.* Florence, KY: Taylor and Francis/Routledge.

Gardner, R. (1982). Mechanisms in manic-depressive disorder: An evolutionary model. *Archives of General Psychiatry, 39,* 1436–1441.

Gardner, R. M. (2001). *Predictors of eating disorder scores in children.* Paper presented at the British Association of Behavioural and Cognitive Psychotherapies, Glasgow, Scotland, UK.

Garland, H. (1990). Throwing good money after bad: The effect of sunk costs on the decision to escalate commitment to an ongoing project. *Journal of Applied Psychology, 75,* 728–731.

Garland, H., & Newport, S. (1991). Effects of absolute and relative sunk costs on the decision to persist with a course of action. *Organizational Behavior and Human Decision Processes, 48,* 55–69.

Geer, J. H., Davison, G. C., & Gatchel, R. I. (1970). Reduction of stress in humans through nonveridical perceived control of aversive stimulation. *Journal of Personality and Social Psychology, 16,* 731–738.

Geer, J. H., & Maisel, E. (1972). Evaluating the effects of the prediction-control confound. *Journal of Personality and Social Psychology, 23,* 314–319.

Gilovich, T., Medvec, V. H., & Chen, S. (1995). Commission, omission, and dissonance reduction: Coping with regret in the 'Monty Hall' problem. *Personality and Social Psychology Bulletin, 21,* 182–189.

Guidano, V. (1988). *The complexity of the self.* New York: Guilford.

Guidano, V. F., & Liotti, G. (1983). *Cognitive processes and the emotional disorders.* New York: Guilford.

Haddock, G., Tarrier, N., Spaulding, W., Yusupoff, L., Kinney, C., & McCarthy, E. (1998). Individual cognitive-behavior therapy in the treatment of hallucinations and delusions: A review. *Clinical Psychology Review, 18*(7), 821–838.

Hayes, S. C., Jacobson, N. S., & Follette, V. M. (Eds.). (1994). *Acceptance and Change: Content and Context in Psychotherapy.* Reno, NV: Context Press.

Hook, J. G. (1982). The development of equity and altruism in judgments of positive and negative justice. *Developmental Psychology, 18,* 825–834.

Hook, J. G. (1983). The development of children's equity judgments. In R. L. Leahy (Ed.), *The child's construction of social inequality.* (pp. 207–222). New York: Academic Press.

Ingram, R. E., Miranda, J., & Segal, Z. V. (1997). *Cognitive vulnerability to depression.* New York: Guilford.

Inhelder, B., & Piaget, J. (1958). *The growth of logical thinking from childhood to adolescence.* New York: Basic Books.

Janis, I. L., & Mann, L. (1977). *Decision making: A psychological analysis of conflict, choice and commitment.* New York: Free Press.

Johnson, S. L., & Roberts, J. (1995). Life events and bipolar disorder: Implications from biological theories. *Psychological Bulletin, 117,* 434–449.

Jones, E. E., & Davis, K.E. (1965). From acts to dispositions: The attribution process in person perception. In L. Berkowitz (Ed.), *Advances in Experimental Social Psychology* (vol.2, pp. 219–266). New York: Academic Press.

Jones, E. E., & Rhodewalt, F. (1982). *The Self-Handicapping Scale.* Available from F. Rhodewalt, Department of Psychology, University of Utah.

Kabat-Zinn, J. (1990). *Full catastrophe living: Using the wisdom of your body and mind to face stress, pain, and illness.* New York: Delacorte Press.

Kahneman, D. (1995). Functions of counterfactual thinking. In N. J. Roese & J. M. Olson (Eds.), *What might have been: The social psychology of counterfactual thinking* (pp. 169–198). Mahwah, NJ: Lawrence Erlebaum.

Kahneman, D. (1995). Varieties of counterfactual thinking. In N. J. Roese & J. J. Olson (Eds.), *What might have been: The social psychology of counterfactual thinking.* (pp. 375–396). Mahwah, NJ: Lawrence Erlbaum Associates, Inc.

Kahneman, D., & Tversky, A. (1972). Subjective probability: A judgment of representativeness. *Cognitive Psychology, 3,* 430–454.

Kahneman, D., & Tversky, A. (1979). Prospect theory: An analysis of decision under risk. *Econometrica, 47,* 263–291.

Kelley, H. H. (1971). *Attribution in social interaction.* Morristown, NJ: General Learning Press.

Kernberg, O., & Senia, G. (1995). Narcissistic personality disorders. *Journal of European Psychoanalysis, 1,* 7–18.

Kernberg, O. F. (1974). Further contributions to the treatment of narcissistic personalities. *International Journal of Psycho-Analysis, 55,* 255–267.

Kernberg, O. F. (1975). *Borderline conditions and pathological narcissism.* New York: Jason Aronson.

Kernberg, O. F. (1998a). Narcissistic personality disorders. *Journal of European Psychoanalysis, 7,* 7–18.

Kernberg, O. F. (1998b). Pathological narcissism and narcissistic personality disorder: Theoretical background and diagnostic classification. In E. F. Ronningstam (Ed.), *Disorders of narcissism: Diagnostic, clinical, and empirical implications* (pp. 29–51). Washington, DC: American Psychiatric Press.

Kiesler, C. A. (1969). *The psychology of commitment.* New York: Academic Press.

Kohlberg, L. (1969). Stage and sequence: The cognitive-developmental approach to socialization. In D. A. Goslin (Ed.), *Handbook of socialization: Theory and research.* Skokie, IL: Rand McNally.

Lane, I., & Coon, R. (1972). Reward allocation in preschool children. *Child Development, 43,* 1382–1389.

Lasch C. (1979). *Haven in a heartless world.* New York: Basic Books.

Lasch, C. (1984). *The minimal self: Psychic survival in troubled times.* New York: Norton.

Leahy, R. L. (1981). Parental practices and the development of moral judgment and self-image disparity during adolescence. *Developmental Psychology, 18,* 580–594.

Leahy, R. L. (1981). The development of the conception of economic inequality: I. Descriptions and comparisons of rich and poor people. *Child Development, 52,* 523–532.

Leahy, R. L. (1983a). The development of the conception of economic inequality: II. Explanations, justifications, and conceptions of social mobility and social change. *Developmental Psychology, 19,* 111–125.

Leahy, R. L. (1983b). The development of the conception of economic class. In R. L. Leahy (Ed.), *The child's construction of social inequality.*(pp. 79–108). New York: Academic Press.

Leahy, R. L. (1983c). Development of self and the problems of social cognition: Identity formation and depression. In L. Wheeler & P. Shaver (Eds.), *Review of personality and social psychology.* (pp. 206–236). Newbury Park, CA: Sage.

Leahy, R. L. (1985). The costs of development: Clinical implications. In R. L. Leahy (Ed.), *The development of the self* (pp. 267–294). New York: Academic Press.

Leahy, R. L. (1989). Effects of child-rearing practices on depression and attributional style. Paper presented at World Congress of Cognitive Therapy, Oxford, U.K.

Leahy, R. L. (1991). Scripts in cognitive therapy: The systemic perspective. *Journal of Cognitive Psychotherapy, 5,* 291–304.

Leahy, R. L. (1992). Cognitive therapy on Wall Street: Schemas and scripts of invulnerability. *Journal of Cognitive Psychotherapy: An International Quarterly, 6,* 1–14.

Leahy, R. L. (1995). Cognitive development and cognitive therapy. *Journal of Cognitive Psychotherapy, 9,* 173–184.

Leahy, R. L. (1996). *Cognitive therapy: Basic principles and applications.* Northvale, NJ: Jason Aronson.

Leahy, R. L. (1996, November). *An investment model of resistance.* Paper presented at meetings of the Association for the Advancement of Behavior Therapy, New York.

Leahy, R. L. (1997a). An investment model of depressive resistance. *Journal of Cognitive Psychotherapy: An International Quarterly, 11,* 3–19.

Leahy, R. L. (1997b). Depression and resistance: An investment model of decision-making. *The Behavior Therapist,* 3–6.

Leahy, R. L. (1997c). Resistance and self-limitation. In R. L. Leahy (ed.), *Practicing cognitive therapy: A guide to interventions.* Northvale, NJ: Jason Aronson.

Leahy, R. L. (1998). Resistance and self-limitation. In R. L. Leahy (Ed.), *Practicing cognitive Therapy: A guide to interventions.* (pp. 61–84). New York: Jason Aronson.

Leahy, R. L. (1999). Depressive decision-making. *Journal of Cognitive Psychothera-py: An International Quarterly, 13,* 1–25.

Leahy, R. L. (1999). Strategic self-limitation. *Journal of Cognitive Psychotherapy: An International Quarterly, 13,* 275–293.

Leahy, R. L. (1999). Decision making and mania. *Journal of Cognitive Psychotherapy, 13,* 83–105.

Leahy, R. L. (2000). Mood and decisions: Implications for bipolar disorder. *Behavior Therapist,* 62–63.

Leahy, R. L. (2001). Depressive decision making: Validation of the portfolio theory model. *Journal of Cognitive Psychotherapy, 15,* 341–362.

Leahy, R. L. (2001). *Overcoming resistance in cognitive therapy.* New York: Guilford.

Leahy, R. L. (2002 in press). A model of emotional schemas. *Cognitive and Behavioral Practice.*

Leahy, R. L., & Beck, A. T. (1988). Cognitive therapy of depression and mania. In R. Cancro & A. Georgotas (Eds.), *Depression and Mania* (pp. 517–537). New York: Elsevier.

Leahy, R. L., & Bresler, J. (1982). *Judgments of sex-role traits: Masculinity-femininity or age maturity?* Paper presented at meetings of the Eastern Psychological Association, Baltimore, MD.

Leahy, R. L, & Hunt, T. (1983). A cognitive-developmental approach to the development of conceptions of intelligence. In R. L. Leahy (Ed.), *The child's construction of social inequality.* (pp. 135–160). New York: Academic Press.

Leahy, R. L, & Shirk, S. (1984). The development of classificatory skills and sex trait stereotypes. *Sex Roles, 10,* 281–292.

Lerner, M. (1974). The justice motive: 'Equity' and 'Parity' among children. *Journal of Personality and Social Personality, 29,* 539–550.

Leventhal, G., & Lane, D. (1970). Sex, age and equity behavior. *Journal of Personality and Social Personality, 15,* 312–316.

Lewinsohn, P. M., & Gotlib, I. H. (1995). Behavioral theory and treatment of depression. In E. E. Beckham & W. R. Leber (Eds.), *Handbook of depression* (2nd ed., pp. 352–375). New York: Guilford.

Lindquist, A. (1981). A note on determinants of household saving behaviour. *Journal of Economic Psychology, 1,* 39–57.

Linehan, M. M. (1993). *Cognitive-behavioral treatment of borderline personality disorder.* New York: Guilford.

Livesley, W. J. (1998). Suggestions for a framework for an empirically based classification of personality disorder. *Canadian Journal of Psychiatry, 43,* 137–147.

Livesley, W., & Bromley, D. (1973). *Person perception in childhood and adolescence.* New York: Wiley.

Livesley, W. J., Schroeder, M. L., Jackson, D. N., & Jang, K. L. (1994). Categorical distinctions in the study of personality disorder: Implications for classification. *Journal of Abnormal Psychology, 103,* 6–17.

Locke, H. J., & Wallace, K. M. (1959). Short marital adjustment and prediction tests: Their reliability and validity. *Marriage and Family Living, 21,* 251–255.

Lynch, P. (1989). *One up on Wall Street.* New York: Penguin Books.

Markowitz, H. (1952). Portfolio selection. *Journal of Finance, 7,* 77–91.

Marks, I. M. (1987). *Fears, phobias, and rituals: Panic, anxiety, and their disorders.* New York: Oxford University Press.

Marx, K. (1966). Economic and philosophical manuscripts. In E. Fromm (Ed.), *Marx's concept of man.* New York: Ungar. (Originally published 1844.)

Menzies, R. G. (1995). The etiology of phobias: A non-associative account. *Clinical Psychology Review, 15,* 23–48.

Merton, R. (1957). *Social theory and social structure.* New York: Free Press.

Miklowitz, D. J., & Goldstein, M. J. (1997). *Bipolar disorder: A family–focused treatment approach.* New York: Guilford.

Millon, T., Davis, R., Millon, C., Escovar, L., & Meagher, S. (2000). *Personality disorders in modern life.* New York: Wiley.

Myers, D. G. (2000). *The American paradox: Spiritual hunger in an age of plenty.* New Haven, CT: Yale University Press.

Myers, D. G., & Diener, E. (1996, May). The pursuit of happiness. *Scientific American, 54–56.*

Needleman, L. D. (1999). *Cognitive case conceptualization: A guidebook for practitioners.* Mahwah, NJ: Lawrence Erlbaum.

Nevin, J. A. (1988). Behavioral momentum and the partial reinforcement effect. *Psychological Bulletin, 103,* 44–56.

Nevin, J. A. (1993). Behavioural momentum: Implications for clinical practice. *Behaviour Change, 10,* 162–168.

Newman, C., Leahy, R. L., Beck, A. T., Gyulai, L., & Reilly-Harrington, N. (2001). *Bipolar disorder: A cognitive therapy approach.* Washington, DC: American Psychological Association Press.

Nolen-Hoeksema, S. (1987). Sex differences in unipolar depression: Evidence and theory. *Psychological Bulletin, 101,* 259–282.

Nolen-Hoeksema, S. (2000). The role of rumination in depressive disorders and mixed anxiety/depressive symptoms. *Journal of Abnormal Psychology, 3,* 504–511.

Orford, J. (2001). *Excessive appetites: A psychological view of addictions.* Chichester, UK: Wiley.

Packard, V. (1959). *The status seekers.* New York: McKay.

Paget, K. F. (1983). Conceptions of deviance and disorder. In R. L. Leahy (Ed.), *The child's construction of social inequality.* (pp. 223. New York: Academic Press.

Papageorgiou, C., & Wells, A. (2001). Metacognitive beliefs about rumination in major depression. *Cognitive and Behavioral Practice, 8,* 160–163.

Papageorgiou, C., & Wells, A. (2001). Positive beliefs about depressive rumination: Development and preliminary validation of a self-report scale. *Behavior Therapy, 32*(1), 13–26.

Parsons, T. (1960). *The social system.* New York: Free Press.

Persons, J. B. (1993). Case conceptualization in cognitive-behavior therapy. In K. T. Kuehlwein & H. Rosen (Eds.), *Cognitive therapies in action: Evolving innovative practice* (pp. 33–53). San Francisco, CA: Jossey-Bass.

Persons, J. B., Davidson, J., & Tompkins, M. A. (2001). *Essential components of cognitive-behavior therapy for depression.* Washington, DC: American Psychological Association.

Piaget, J. (1926). *The language and thought of the child.* New York: Norton.

Piaget, J. (1965). *The moral judgment of the child.* New York: Free Press. (Originally published 1932.)

Piaget, J. (1970a). *Genetic epistemology.* New York: Columbia University Press.

Piaget, J. (1970b). *Structuralism.* New York: Basic Books.

Plous, S. (1993). *The psychology of judgment and decision making.* New York: McGraw-Hill.

Rehm, L. P. (1990). Cognitive and behavioral theories. In B. B. Wolman & G. Stricker (Eds.), *Depressive disorders: Facts, theories, and treatment methods* (pp. 64–91). Oxford, England: John Wiley.

Riskind, J. H. (1997). Looming vulnerability to threat: A cognitive paradigm for anxiety. *Behaviour Research and Therapy, 35,* 685–702.

Riskind, J. H., Long, D. G., Williams, N. L., & White, J. C. (2000). Desperate acts for desperate times: Looming vulnerability and suicide. In T.E. Joiner, & M.D. Rudd, (Eds.). *Suicide science: Expanding the boundaries,* (p. 105–115). Norwell, MA: Kluwer Academic Publishers.

Salkovskis, P. (1996). The cognitive approach to anxiety: Threat beliefs, safety-seeking behavior, and the special case of health anxiety and obsessions. In P. Salkovksis (Ed.), *Frontiers of Cognitive Therapy* (pp. 48–74). New York: Guilford.

Schor, J. B. (1991). *The overworked American: The unexpected decline of leisure.* New York: Basic Books.

Schor, J. B. (1998). *The overspent American: Upscaling, downshifting, and the new consumer.* New York: Basic Books.

Schwartz, B. (1978). *Psychology of learning and behavior.* New York: W. W. Norton.

Segal, Z. V., Williams, M. J. G., & Teasdale, J. D. (2002). *Mindfulness-based cognitive therapy for depression: A new approach to preventing relapse.* New York: Guilford.

Seligman, M. E. P. (1975). *Helplessness: On depression, development, and death.* New York: W. H. Freeman.

Selman, R. L. (1980). *The growth of interpersonal understanding.* New York.: Academic Press.

Sewall, R. B. (1959). *The vision of tragedy.* New Haven: Yale University Press.

Shafran, R. (2001). *Advances in the understanding and treatment of body image disturbance.* Paper presented at the British Association of Behavioural and Cognitive Psychotherapies, Glasgow, Scotland, UK.

Shiller, R. J. (2000). *Irrational exuberance.* Princeton, NJ: Princeton University Press.

Simon, H. A. (1956). Rational choice and the structure of the environment. *Psychological Review, 63,* 129–138.

Simon, H. A. (1979). Rational decision making in business organizations. *American Economic Review, 79,* 293–304.

Simon, H. A. (1992). *Economics, bounded rationality, and the cognitive revolution.* Aldershot, UK: Elgar.

Simonson, I., & Nye, P. (1992). The effect of accountability on susceptibility to decision errors. *Organizational Behavior and Human Decision Processes, 51,* 416–446.

Sloman, L., & Price, J. S. (1987). Losing behavior (yielding subrontine) and human depression: Proximate and selective mechanisms. *Ethology and Sociobiology, 8,* 99–109.

Snyder, C. R., Higgins, R. L., & Stucky, R. J. (1983). *Excuses: Masquerades in search of grace.* New York: Wiley.

Spitzer, R. L., Williams, J. B. W., Gibbon, M., & First, M. B. (1990). *User's guide for the Structured Clinical Interview for DSM-III-R (SCID).* Washington, DC: American Psychiatric Press.

Staw, B. M. (1976). Knee-deep in the Big Muddy: A study of escalating commitment to a chosen course of action. *Organizational Behavior and Human Performance, 16,* 27–44.

Staw, B. M. (1981). The escalation of commitment to a course of action. *Academy of Management Review, 6,* 577–587.

Staw, B. M., Barsade, S. G., & Koput, K. W. (1997). Escalation at the credit window: A longitudinal study of bank executives' recognition and write-off of problem loans. *Journal of Applied Psychology, 82,* 130–142.

Staw, B. M., & Fox, F. V. (1977). Escalation: The determinants of commitment to a chosen course of action. *Human Relations, 30,* 431–450.

Staw, B. M., & Ross, J. (1978). Commitment to a policy decision: A multi-theoretical perspective. *Administrative Science Quarterly, 23,* 40–64.

Staw, B. M., & Ross, J. (1987). Behavior in escalation situations: Antecedents, prototypes, and solutions. In L. L. Cummings & B. M. Staw (Eds.), *Research in organizational behavior* (Vol. 9, pp. 39–78). Greenwich, CT: JAI Press.

Sullivan, T. A., Warren, E., & Westbrook, J. L. (2000). *The fragile middle class: Americans in debt.* New Haven, CT: Yale University Press.

Taylor, J. (1989). *Circus of ambition: The culture of wealth and power in the eighties.* New York: Warner Books.

Taylor, S. E. (1989). *Positive illusions: Creative self-deception and the healthy mind.* New York: Basic Books.

Teasdale, J. D. (1999). Metacognition, mindfulness and the modification of mood disorders. *Clinical Psychology and Psychotherapy, 6,* 146–155.

Teasdale, J. D., Segal, Z., & Williams, J. M. G. (1995). How does cognitive therapy prevent depressive relapse and why should attentional control (mindfulness) training help? *Behaviour Research and Therapy, 33,* 25–39.

Teasdale, J. D., Segal, Z. V., Williams, M. J. G., Ridgeway, V. A., Soulsby, J. M., & Lau, M. A. (2000). Prevention of relapse/recurrence in major depression by mindfulness-based cognitive therapy. *Journal of Consulting and Clinical Psychology, 68,* 615–623.

Thaler, R. (1980). Toward a positive theory of consumer choice. *Journal of Economic Behavior and Organization, 1,* 39–60.

Thaler, R. (1985). Mental accounting and consumer choice. *Marketing Science, 4,* 199–214.

Thaler, R. H. (1992). *The winner's curse: Paradoxes and anomalies of economic life.* Princeton, NJ: Princeton University Press.

Thaler, R., & Shifrin, H. M. (1981). An economic theory of self-control. *Journal of Political Economy, 89,* 392–406.

Tommasi, M., & Ierulli, K. (Eds.). (1995). *The new economics of human behavior.* New York: Cambridge University Press.

Tomassi, M., & Ierulli, K. (Eds.) (1995). *The New Economics of Human Behavior.* Cambridge, UK: Cambridge University Press.

Turiel, E. (1978). Social regulations and domains of social concepts. In W. Damon (Ed.), *Moral development. New directions for child development, No.2.* San Francisco: Jossey-Bass.

Tversky, A., & Kahneman, D. (1972). Availability: A heuristic for judging frequency and probability. *Cognitive Psychology, 4,* 207–232.

Tversky, A., & Kahneman, D. (1974). Judgment under uncertainty: Heuristics and biases. *Science, 185,* 1124–1131.

Tversky, A., & Kahneman, D. (1981). The framing of decisions and the psychology of choice. *Science, 211,* 453–458.

Veblen, T. (1899/1979). *Theory of the leisure class.* New York: Mentor.

Veblen, T. (1928). *The theory of the leisure class.* New York: Vanguard Press.

Weber, M. (1946). *Essays in sociology.* (H. Gerth & W. Mills, trans.). Oxford, UK: Oxford University Press.

Weiner, B. (1974). Achievement motivation as conceptualized by an attribution theorist. In B. Weiner (Ed.), *Achievement motivation and attribution theory.* Morristown, NJ: General Learning Press.

Weiner, B. (1985). An attributional theory of achievement motivation and emotion. *Psychological Review, 92,* 548–573.

Wells, A. (1995). Meta-cognition and worry: A cognitive model of generalized anxiety disorder. *Behavioural and Cognitive Psychotherapy, 23,* 301–320.

Wells, A. (1997). *Cognitive therapy of anxiety disorders: A practice manual and conceptual guide.* Chichester, UK: Wiley.

Wells, A. (2000). *Emotional disorders and metacognition: Innovative cognitive therapy.* New York: Wiley.

Wells, A., & Carter, K. (2001). Further tests of a cognitive model of generalized anxiety disorder: Metacognitions and worry in GAD, panic disorder, social phobia, depression and nonpatients. *Behavior Therapy, 32,* 85–102.

Wells, A., & Matthews, G. (1994). *Attention and emotion: A clinical perspective.* Hillsdale, NJ: Lawrence Erlbaum.

Wenegrat, B. (1990). *Sociobiological psychiatry: Normal behavior and psychopathology.* Lexington, MA: Lexington Books/D. C. Heath and Company.

Whyte, G. (1993). Escalating commitment in individual and group decision-making: A prospect theory approach. *Organizational Behavior and Human Decision Processes, 54,* 430–455.

Williams, J., Bennett, S., & Best, D. (1975). Awareness and expression of sex stereotypes in young children. *Developmental Psychology, 11,* 635–642.

Young, J. E. (1990). *Cognitive therapy for personality disorders: A schema-focused approach.* Sarasota, FL: Professional Resource Exchange.

Young, J., & Flanagan, C. (1998). Schema-focused therapy for narcissistic patients. In E. F. Ronningstam (Ed.), *Disorders of narcissism: Diagnostic, clinical, and empirical implications* (pp. 239–262). Washington, DC: American Psychiatric Press.

Zigler, E., & Glick, M. (1984). Paranoid schizophrenia: An unorthodox view. *American Journal of Orthopsychiatry, 54,* 43–70.

Zigler, E., & Glick, M. (1988). Is paranoid schizophrenia really camouflaged depression? *American Psychologist, 43,* 1079–1080.

Index